Law In and As Culture

The Fairleigh Dickinson University Press
Series in Law, Culture, and the Humanities

The Fairleigh Dickinson University Press Series in Law, Culture, and the Humanities publishes scholarly works in which the field of Law intersects with, among others, Film, Criminology, Sociology, Communication, Critical/Cultural Studies, Literature, History, Philosophy, and the Humanities.

General Editor: Caroline Joan "Kay" S. Picart,
M.Phil. (Cantab), Ph.D., J.D., Esquire
Attorney at Law/Of Counsel, Tim Bower Rodriguez, P.A.

Publications

Caroline Joan "Kay" S. Picart, *Law In and As Culture: Intellectual Property, Minority Rights, and the Rights of Indigenous Peoples* (2016)

On the Web at http://www.fdu.edu/fdupress

Law In and As Culture

Intellectual Property, Minority Rights, and the Rights of Indigenous Peoples

Caroline Joan "Kay" S. Picart

FAIRLEIGH DICKINSON UNIVERSITY PRESS
Madison • Teaneck

Published by Fairleigh Dickinson University Press
Copublished by The Rowman & Littlefield Publishing Group, Inc.
4501 Forbes Boulevard, Suite 200, Lanham, Maryland 20706
www.rowman.com

Unit A, Whitacre Mews, 26-34 Stannary Street, London SE11 4AB

British Library Cataloguing in Publication Information Available

Library of Congress Cataloging-in-Publication Data

Names: Picart, Caroline Joan, 1966– , author.
Title: Law in and as culture : intellectual property, minority rights, and the rights of indigenous peoples / Caroline Joan "Kay" S. Picart.
Description: Madison, New Jersey : Fairleigh Dickinson University Press, 2016. | Includes bibliographical references and index.
Identifiers: LCCN 2015048248 (print) | LCCN 2015051469 (ebook) | ISBN 9781611477214 (cloth : alk. paper) | ISBN 9781611477221 (Electronic)
Subjects: LCSH: Indigenous peoples—Legal status, laws, etc. | Intellectual property.
Classification: LCC K1401.5 .P53 2016 (print) | LCC K1401.5 (ebook) | DDC 346.04/8089--dc23
LC record available at http://lccn.loc.gov/2015048248

∞™ The paper used in this publication meets the minimum requirements of American National Standard for Information Sciences—Permanence of Paper for Printed Library Materials, ANSI/NISO Z39.48-1992.

Printed in the United States of America

Contents

Acknowledgments

I dedicate this book to my loving husband, Jerry Rivera, and the Picart, Terrell, and Rivera families. Parts of this book have been adapted and updated from articles previously published as: Caroline Joan "Kay" S. Picart, "Cross Cultural Negotiations and International Intellectual Property Law: Attempts to Work Across Cultural Clashes Between Indigenous Peoples and Majoritarian Cultures," *Southern California Interdisciplinary Law Journal* 23, no. 1 (January 2014): 37–65; Caroline Joan "Kay" S. Picart and Marlowe Fox, "Beyond Unbridled Optimism and Fear: Indigenous Peoples, Intellectual Property, Human Rights and the Globalization of Traditional Knowledge and Expressions of Folklore (Part II)," *International Community Law* 16, no. 2 (March 2014): 3–37; Caroline Joan "Kay" S. Picart and Marlowe Fox, "Beyond Unbridled Optimism and Fear: Indigenous Peoples, Intellectual Property, Human Rights and the Globalization of Traditional Knowledge and Expressions of Folklore (Part I)," *International Community Law Review* 15, no. 3 (2013): 319–39; and Caroline Joan "Kay" S. Picart, "Rethinking Resistance: Reflections on the Cultural Lives of Property, Collective Identity, and Intellectual Property," *John Marshall Law Review* 47 (November 2014): 1349–69. I thank the *Southern California Interdisciplinary Law Journal*; the *International Community Law Review* and Brill; and *the John Marshall Law Review* for permission to adapt the articles for this monograph. This book has grown from initially separate projects, which, across time and upon deeper reflection, have sprung from intersecting questions regarding cultural clashes between majoritarian cultures and indigenous peoples and minority groups in relation to issues of intellectual property and property rights. I also thank Marlowe Fox for his assistance with the articles published with the *International Community Law Review*, and Berta Hernandez, Danaya Wright, Stephen Powell, and Iris Burke for their comments on prior versions of parts of this book. Finally, I owe a debt of gratitude to John Edgar Browning, for his kind and patient assistance with finding appropriate camera-ready images in the public domain and formatting an extremely complex bibliography; Margaret Petty, for her conscientious and thorough assistance with preparing this monograph and the index in its final form; and to the director, editor, and editorial staff of the Fairleigh Dickinson University Press and Rowman & Littlefield, especially Harry Keyishian, Brooke Bures, Zachary Nychum, and Hannah Fisher and the production staff for their professionalism and patience with bringing this process to completion.

1

Between Mirroring Master Narratives of Fear and Optimism

PRELIMINARY REMARKS

What inspires this book are several factors: (1) a growing interest in intersections binding culture and the law as evidenced by more books and articles being published on the topics of indigenous peoples and intellectual property;[1] and (2) a lack of a sustained critical examination of, in particular, cultural and legal interactions between colonial or majoritarian cultures, and colonized and indigenous peoples, and evolving understandings of what constitutes property and intellectual property. This book begins by characterizing the paradigmatic nature of cultures in relation to law, which itself has its own culture. After generally characterizing how culture operates, this book examines culture in, and as, intellectual property by analyzing descriptions of culture embedded in intellectual property law, as well as the assumptions built into Western intellectual property law.

From there, this book analyzes various cases of attempts to protect the intellectual property of indigenous peoples in relation to the three descriptions of "culture" implicit in intellectual property law. An aspect of this book's method is, to some extent, autoethnographic and as illustration, it deals with the particular culture clashes occurring between minorities or indigenous peoples and majoritarian cultures. Thus, Geert Hofstede, Gert Jan Hofstede, and Michael Minkov's cultural rubric of individualism versus communitarianism is employed to sketch the cultural conflicts embedded in, for example, the disagreement between the German band, Enigma, and the Ami tribal couple, the Duanas, over the ownership of an Ami traditional folk song. Additionally, as a supplementary theoretical tool, Hofstede, Hofstede, and Minkov's cultural schema of hierarchy versus egalitarianism is used to draw out key elements of the cultural conflict between the Chilean government and the Mapuche/Pehuenche tribe over control of the right to build a dam that would flood the tribe's ancestral lands.

This book then does a general survey of various instruments and strategies, potentially to protect the rights of minorities and indigenous peoples. From there, the book comparatively analyzes Josephine Baker's and Katherine Dunham's struggles to own both their identities and choreographic creations as women of color, against the backdrop of exotic stereotypes, which reflected less about colonized or marginalized cultures than the imagined assumptions of the colonial or majority culture, replete with projections and fears of a dominant culture. Though Baker's dance improvisations long predated federal copyright protection, the inquiry is useful as a precursor to understanding the legal development of intellectual property protection of choreographic works in the United States. Baker's and Dunham's struggles highlight, in contrastive ways, the success of George Balanchine's estate in commanding complete control of Balanchine's choreographies as protectable private property. Crucial to that thesis is a genealogy of the workings of whiteness as status property, functioning as cultural capital, and thus helping undergird what constitutes "authentic" artistic choreographic creation. This chapter also examines similarities between the situations Baker and Dunham faced in their attempts to gain respect and recognition for their artworks as women of color, to the challenges Australian Aboriginal artists faced in seeking intellectual property protection for their visual expressions of folklore.

Hence, this book examines genesral programs of action and specific legal strategies in potentially overcoming these cultural barriers in the encounter between majority and minority or indigenous cultures. Ultimately, it also recounts the elements that worked to establish Katherine Dunham's ownership of her choreographic works (as opposed to her predecessor, Josephine Baker) much of which is traceable but not utterly reducible to, Dunham's partial possession (compared to Baker) of whiteness as status property. Eventually, the book also outlines key principles and specific strategies and incentives for negotiation in attempting to overcome cultural clashes between indigenous cultures (such as the Kani tribe in India, the Ami tribe in Taiwan, and the Mapuche/Pehuenche tribe in Chile) and various majoritarian cultures. Crucial to this book is the notion that intellectual property creation is not a monopoly of metaphorical "northern" cultures, but that intellectual property is generated everywhere, as a function of the human cultural potential to generate forms of knowledge and artistic objects.

TOWARD A THEORY OF LAW IN AND AS CULTURE

Despite the plethora of books about indigenous peoples and the law, few critical manuscripts attempt to create a coherent theoretical framework concerning law as embedded in the social, and as itself constituting a culture. What sets *Law In and As Culture* apart from other monographs about this topic is its critical examination of connections binding law and culture especially in relation to (1) property and intellectual property law; (2) the explosion of studies concerning strategies of protecting indigenous peoples' rights, especially given the occasional dramatic clashes between majoritarian cultures and the cultures of first peoples; and (3) scholarship on colonial appropriations of minority groups' cultures and intellectual property rights, and these groups' attempts at resisting such appropriation, especially as glimpsed in the examples of Josephine Baker and Katherine Dunham. Moreover, each of these competing texts has different areas of focus that distinguish them from the current project.

Berta Hernandez-Truyol and Stephen J. Powell's *Just Trade*[2] focuses primarily upon intersections binding international human rights and trade, and the various instruments and institutions associated with the regulation and enforcement of both. Using a historical framework that examines the uneasy relationship between trade and human rights, Hernandez-Truyol and Powell's book is a comprehensive look at human rights for various marginalized and oppressed groups, such as victims of human trafficking; women, especially of marginalized groups; poor immigrant laborers; and children. Unlike this book, indigenous peoples are discussed in only one chapter, and there is little examination of connections binding indigenous peoples' property and intellectual property rights. The theoretical framework of Hernandez-Truyol and Powell's book is more deontological, focusing on how a human rights perspective can guide ethical imperatives for trade, as opposed to this book, which uses the framework of law as embedded in culture/s, and as itself functioning as a culture. So while Hernandez-Truyol and Powell's book is predominantly normative, this book is more analytic and deconstructive, with some suggestions for strategic reworking of persisting power differentials based on actual historical cases.

Along a parallel track, Jane E. Anderson's *Law, Knowledge, Culture*[3] similarly focuses on a social theory of law. Anderson's work focuses on an alternative epistemology of knowledge embedded in indigenous culture, especially those of tribes in Australia. However, while Anderson's book sketches a general framework of law as socially embedded, the theoretical framework this book deploys, as a heuristic, is much more specific, building upon the insights of Hofstede, Hofstede, and Minkov,[4] who are principally anthropologists and negotiators in business. Hofstede, Hofstede, and Minkov focus on various organizing principles of societies, such as identity (individualism versus collectivism), hierarchy (high power distance versus low power distance), gender (masculinity versus femininity), truth (uncertainty avoidance versus uncertainty tolerance), and virtue (long-term orientation versus short-term orientation). In addition, while Anderson's book focuses solely on the plight of indigenous peoples in Australia, this book uses a broader lens, and analyzes comparative case studies of indigenous peoples in, for example, Chile, India, and Taiwan, among others.

Similarly, Silke von Lewinski's *Indigenous Heritage and Intellectual Property*,[5] an edited collection, has eight contributors, all of whom argue, using different case studies, that the commercial exploitation of indigenous knowledge and resources occur amid a significant clash of cultures. All eight contributors explore ways in which intellectual property law potentially can expand to accommodate the interests of indigenous people as applied to the ownership and control of their traditional knowledge, genetic resources, indigenous names and designations, and folklore. Though there are some similarities between von Lewinski's anthology and this book, this project differs because of its attempt to forge the outlines of a coherent, overall framework, as applied to not only intellectual property rights but also property rights, in relation to not only indigenous peoples but also minorities, with a focus on the United States.

Along a parallel but more specialized track, Rosemary Coombe's *The Cultural Life of Intellectual Properties*[6] also examines a culturally based theory of intellectual property law, specializing in trademarks. Coombe includes a very broad characterization of what constitutes "cultural life," drawing from cultural studies, anthropology, postcolonial theory, and political theory to analyze practices of interpretation and appropriation in an increasingly privatized public sphere. Although influenced by Coombe, this book differs from Coombe's work through its focus on the nexus between property and intellectual property. Furthermore, this project is distinguishable in its emphasis on developing strategies of communication and possibly overcoming cultural clashes, through a rigorous analysis of selected case studies of both minorities and indigenous peoples, in the United States, as well as globally. Additionally, this book does not limit itself purely to the study of trademark law, but also examines how patent and copyright law operates in relation to property law, using specific case studies.

Offering a rigorous and multidisciplinary framework, Hofstede, Hofstede, and Minkov's *Cultures and Organizations*[7] provides part of the theoretical framework that this book develops and applies through concrete case studies. Hofstede, Hofstede, and Minkov's work is based on empirical research conducted in more than seventy countries over a forty-year span. Hofstede, Hofstede, and Minkov's collaboration examines the "moral circles" from which national societies are built, and the ingrained cultural rules through which people think, feel, and act. Among other things, Hofstede, Hofstede, and Minkov's research analyzes stereotyping and other intercultural dynamics. However, unlike this project, Hofstede, Hostede, and Minkov's framework is not specifically applied to an analysis of the cultural roots of property or intellectual property law, or to the social and legal conditions within which encounters between majoritarian cultures and minority groups or indigenous peoples occur. That is the terrain this book attempts to explore.

A TALE OF TWO MIRROR-IMAGING MASTER NARRATIVES[8]

This book is written in the vein of one of Friedrich Nietzsche's works, *Beyond Good and Evil,* where Nietzsche attempted to show that the binary between the moral "Good" and the immoral "Evil" is simplistic, tyrannical, and, ultimately, sterile.[9] Similarly, there appear to be two oppositional narratives in relation to telling the story of indigenous peoples in relation to globalization, with its attendant expansion and inter-linkage of world markets, and in particular, in relation to intellectual property rights, which is the focus of this book. The first, the narrative of Optimism, is a story of the triumphant opening of brave new worlds of commercial integration and cultural inclusion. The second, the narrative of Fear, is a story of endangerment, mourning, and loss. While the story of Optimism deploys a rhetoric of commercial mobilization and "innovation"—a celebration of the hybrid and nontraditional, born from the ashes of the "old" and "no longer relevant" or "useful"—the story of Fear emphasizes the rhetoric of preserving something "pure" and "traditional" that is "dying." Both narratives have compelling rhetorical force, and actually need each other, in order to move their opposing audiences into action. However, the realities behind these rhetorically framed political parables are more complex than a simple binary. Hence, the narrative this book explores is an account that attempts to move dialectically across an aspiration toward hope rather than unbounded Optimism, and the alertness of a precautionary perspective, rather than of Fear.

For example, as will be discussed more fully in chapters 2 and 3, the German band, Enigma, incorporated a sample of a song from the Ami, a Taiwanese indigenous population, into its composition, *Return to Innocence. Return to Innocence* was adopted as the theme of the 1996 Atlanta Olympic Games. That pirated and remixed musical excerpt, originally performed by two members of the Ami tribe, was traced to a 1978 recording initially done by visiting ethnographers; this same excerpt was later included in a compilation of Chinese folk music and an album released in France, whose exploitation did not commercially benefit the Ami.[10] The tale of the appropriation of the excerpt of the Ami folk song thus initially emerges as a cautionary tale. In contrast, the legend of Mulan was falling into oblivion in Chinese culture because it was a fixture of the Beijing Opera and more traditional art forms; however, Disney's cinematic appropriation and reinterpretation of the folk story re-enlivened the story of Mulan, and awakened youthful national pride in the legend.[11] The result in the case of the legend of Mulan thus contrasts sharply with the case of the appropriated Ami folk song. These case studies show that the issue of how best to address the issue of indigenous peoples' and minorities' intellectual property rights against a constantly changing landscape subject to numerous forces of negotiation is complex, at best.

Nevertheless, numerous stories that decry the abysmal failure of global international frameworks to protect the traditional knowledge (and consequently, the intellectual property rights) of indigenous peoples abound. Repeatedly, stories of the postcolonial conquest of traditional knowledge, in particular the biopiracy of various chemical compounds, especially when used in sacred rites by indigenous peoples, such as the case of Loren Miller's patenting of the ayahuasca vine's active ingredient,[12] are ubiquitous. Despite the prevalence and truthfulness of these narratives covering the biopiracy of genetic substances, this book focuses, as well, on another type of borrowing—on cultural piracy. Thus, the book explores, among other things, folklore, the metaphorical genetic code of a culture, whose phenotype becomes expressed in different artifacts, both tangible and intangible. Admittedly, the distinction between piracy and biopiracy—between culture and nature—is thin, especially in the case of chemical substances used for sacred rituals.

Nevertheless, this approach makes that distinction for analytic purposes. Although this book begins with cases dealing with the biopiracy of traditional knowledge (the more scientific cases), as that is where much case law lies, this book aims to analyze these cases in order to arrive at guiding principles that might be useful in examining how traditional cultural expressions (inclusive of folklore and its artifacts), could probably also be equitably protected. Hence, this book aspires to balance the thrust toward development with respect for the integrity of indigenous cultures.

This project chooses neither Fear nor Optimism but attempts to steer a nuanced path between two mirroring and competing master narratives. Additionally, arguably, this approach constitutes a more holistic approach because it locates biopiracy within the context of a larger notion of "piracy." Furthermore, this approach ultimately problematizes the assumption of equating "borrowing" with "stealing," given that cultures are porous and that the nature of creativity always entails some derivation from prior art—both in scientific and extra-scientific senses. This perspective is instrumental to exploring the conditions of possibility within which bridges, not grand Syntheses, may be built across the chasms separating the many prevailing binaries this study explores.

Organizationally, after establishing pragmatic working descriptions of who "indigenous peoples" are, and what folklore (or "traditional cultural expression") is, as compared with, but dialectically related to, "traditional knowledge," this book eventually aims to examine, briefly, why Western assumptions built into intellectual property law (inclusive of patent, copyright, and trademark systems) make this area of law a problematic tool, as a way of protecting traditional knowledge (TK) and expressions of folklore (EoF) or traditional cultural expressions (TCE) of indigenous peoples.

Eventually, as part of chapter 5, this book moves into creating a general sketch of human rights–related legal instruments that could be and have been harnessed, with varying degrees of success, in relation to the attempt to protect the intellectual property of indigenous peoples. Furthermore, later chapters also attempt to examine possible core principles, induced (rather than deduced) from actual practices already in place in the areas of patents, copyrights, and trademarks in relation to protecting TK and EoF. This is an important area of research as its discussion potentially could allow contemporary discussions regarding indigenous peoples' and minorities' property and intellectual property rights to become less adversarial and more dialectic.

As a final methodological note, this book starts with an inductive method beginning from particular and concrete practices, rather than beginning abstractly, from principles that have not been tested in the field. This is not to say that the approach this book adopts is devoid of any deduction. Rather, much as the scientific method is hypothetico-deductive, moving dialectically across inductive and deductive modes of reasoning, based on results, so does this book attempt to ground its explorations in concrete and lived collective experience.

The next section begins with attempting a pragmatic, working characterization of who indigenous peoples are, as one cannot begin discussing their intellectual property rights before first establishing who they are.

CHARACTERIZING INDIGENOUS PEOPLES, TRADITIONAL KNOWLEDGE, AND EXPRESSIONS OF FOLKLORE

Forming a Working Description of Indigenous Peoples

How does one find commonalities across the Kayapo tribe of Mato Grosso, Brazil; the Inuit people from Cape Dorset, Canada (figure 1.1);

Figure 1.1. Inuit Family Aboard Their Traditional Qamutik Sled, Cape Dorset, Canada. Photo taken by Ansgar Walk, April 1, 1999.

the Negrito tribe from the Philippines; the Tuareg nomads of southern Algeria; the San tribe from Namibia; the Navajo tribe in Monument valley, Arizona in the United States; the Ainu people from Hokkaido, Japan; the Nenet tribe from the Yamal Peninsula, Russia; the Huli tribe from the southern Highlands, Papua, New Guinea, among other "first peoples"?

A sufficient definition of who "indigenous peoples" are is difficult to fashion, due to the inherent diversity of the groups that would have to be contained within such a definition.[13] In acknowledgment of the sociopolitical complexity of the problem, the United Nations (U.N.) system body has not adopted an official definition; in its stead, the U.N. diplomatically provides a "modern understanding" based on the following:

- Self-identification as indigenous peoples at the individual level and accepted by the community as a member of their group;
- Historical continuity with precolonial or pre-settler societies;
- Strong link to territories and surrounding natural resources;
- Distinct social, economic, or political systems;
- Distinct language, culture, and beliefs;
- Form nondominant groups of society;
- Resolve to maintain and reproduce their ancestral environments and systems as distinctive peoples and communities.[14]

In addition, the U.N. provides generic terms that may be used in lieu of "indigenous" including: tribes, first peoples, aboriginals, ethnic groups, adivasi, and janajati.[15] The U.N. holds the view that the most productive approach is to "identify, rather than define indigenous people."[16] The issue of defining or identifying indigenous peoples is further complicated by the fact that the term "indigenous" often "has negative connotations."[17] Indigenous peoples may also be identified by their unique language, knowledge systems and beliefs, and sustainable practice of managing natural resources.[18] Alternatively, they may also be identified by the following: "[a] lack of political representation and participation, economic marginalization and poverty, [a] lack of access to social services and discrimination."[19]

A description of the concept of "indigenous" may be found in José R. Martínez Cobo's *Study of the Problem of Discrimination against Indigenous Populations*.[20] The definition is as follows:

> Indigenous communities, peoples and nations are those which, having a historical continuity[21] with pre-invasion and pre-colonial societies that developed on their territories, consider themselves distinct from other sectors of the societies now prevailing on those territories, or parts of them. They form at present non-dominant sectors of society and are determined to preserve, develop and transmit to future generations their ancestral territories, and their ethnic identity, as the basis of their continued existence as peoples, in accordance with their own cultural patterns, social institutions and legal system.[22]

Cobo's definition of "indigenous" also includes self-identification.[23] Similarly, Article 33 of the U.N. Declaration of the Rights of Indigenous People "underlines the importance of self-identification."[24] It states the following:

1. Indigenous peoples have the right to determine their own identity or membership in accordance with their customs and traditions. This does not impair the right of indigenous individuals to obtain citizenship of the States in which they live.
2. Indigenous peoples have the right to determine the structures and to select the membership of their institutions in accordance with their own procedures.[25]

Benedict Kingsbury, professor of law and director of the Institute for International Law and Justice at New York University, observes that there has not been "any general agreement to meaning [of the term "indigenous peoples" or] even an agreement on a process by which its meaning might be established."[26] Instead of giving up on any kind of heuristic scheme, Kingsbury identifies two approaches to describing the concept of indigenous peoples: positivist and constructionist.[27]

Generally characterized, the positivist approach demands an exact legal definition in order to "determine . . . exactly who does or does not have a particular status, enjoy a particular right, or assume a particular responsibility."[28] However, as with all rules, there are concerns about a formalist approach to a dynamic and ever-changing concept.[29] Thus, applying rules or definitions may lead to manifestly unjust or inequitable results.[30] Yet still, the positivist approach is a "concept of great normative power for many relatively powerless groups that have suffered grievous abuses."[31] Pragmatically speaking, the positivist approach serves "as a concept designating a locus of groups and issues . . . [and] has proved remarkably serviceable"; lastly, Kingsbury notes "there is no contending replacement."[32] Conversely, the constructivist approach "embod[ies] a continuous process" in which specific issues "are abstracted in the wider institutions of international society, then made specific again at the moment of application in . . . particular cases and societies."[33]

Nevertheless, given the binary pairing of positivism and constructivism, Kingsbury ultimately concludes that "[n]either approach suffices entirely on its own."[34] He argues the constructivist approach "better captures its functions and significance in global institutions and normative instruments."[35] However, such abstract principles are often unable sufficiently to address the "specific problems as to the meaning of 'indigenous peoples.'"[36] Kingsbury offers some of the following examples of such conundra: Who is the proper authority to represent an indigenous people in a land claim?[37] Are children of a marriage between a member and nonmember entitled to be full members?[38] Who benefits from royalties for a therapeutic drug derived from a plant used by several groups?[39] Kingsbury concludes that these questions "can only be resolved through specific contextual decisions . . . that are influenced by, and influence, the more abstract global concept."[40]

Thus, it is clear that the debate over whether or not to establish a definition for "indigenous peoples" is an epistemological one. Applying a formal definition would promote uniformity and predictability. Nevertheless, a formal definition's rigidity could result in inequitable or absurd results when applied to specific issues. Conversely, a dynamic concept malleable enough to adapt to various circumstances has the potential of leading to equitable results. However, such a contextual concept, in practice, could compromise uniformity in its collective application thereby making it difficult to administer whether socially, politically, or legally. Furthermore, administrative inefficiency, due to a lack of a pragmatic definition, could block access to legal solutions. In the end, it seems the debate on whether or not to define "indigenous peoples" engenders more nuanced, philosophical debates, such as, to name only a few possibilities, an epistemological debate between formalism and instrumentalism; a political debate between justice and efficiency; and a metaphysical debate between nominalism and realism. However, such debates do not help further or achieve the current project's aims.

Hence, this section has both a modest and pragmatic solution, as a working heuristic. This section offers the preliminary strategy of identifying characteristics of "indigenous peoples" as a pragmatic starting point, not an attempt to constrain the term to a formal definition. Such a heuristic values the usefulness of an objective starting point, while allowing room for more subjective or contextual nuancing.

One such starting point can be glimpsed in Hernandez-Truyol and Powell's characterization of who are "indigenous peoples," which grounds itself in article 1 of the International Labor Organization (ILO) Convention concerning Indigenous and Tribal Peoples in Independent Countries.[41] Hernandez-Truyol and Powell succinctly distill the following description: "those who inhabit a country or area within a country at the time of conquest, colonization, or establishment of the present state boundaries and who, irrespective of their legal status, retain some or all of their own social, economic, cultural and political institutions."[42] That description provides a practical working definition. Nevertheless, the term "indigenous" is difficult to precisely capture, and Operational Directive 4.20 of the World Bank cautions that "[b]ecause of the varied and changing contexts in which indigenous peoples are found, no single definition can capture their diversity."[43] Nevertheless, perhaps hardly surprisingly, the World Bank description of key characteristics of indigenous peoples focuses on their subsistence economy and their poverty, relative to the majority population.

Indigenous peoples are commonly among the poorest segments of a population. They engage in economic activities that range from shifting agriculture in or near forests to wage labor or even small-scale market-oriented activities. Indigenous peoples can be identified in particular geographical areas by the presence in varying degrees of the following characteristics:

a) a close attachment to ancestral territories and to the natural resources in these areas;
b) self-identification and identification by others as members of a distinct cultural group;
c) an indigenous language, often different from the national language;
d) presence of customary social and political institutions; and
e) primarily subsistence-oriented production.[44]

In comparison, the chairperson of the Working Group on Indigenous Populations, although acknowledging that a single definition cannot exhaust all facets, focuses on a set of factors that contribute to the self-identification, and recognition by the majority population, of the cultural uniqueness of indigenous populations. Thus, she outlines a few essential characteristics:

a) priority in time, with respect to occupation and use of a specific territory;
b) the voluntary perpetuation of cultural distinctiveness, which may include the aspects of language, social organization, religion and spiritual values, modes of production, laws, and institutions;
c) self-identification, as well as recognition by other groups, or by state authorities, as a distinct collectivity; and
d) an experience of subjugation, marginalization, dispossession, exclusion, or discrimination, whether or not these conditions persist.[45]

Thus, an overall working characterization takes note of two crucial principal identifying factors that set apart indigenous peoples from the majority: (1) their relative economic poverty; and (2) their significant cultural difference. Both of these characteristics make them vulnerable to discrimination and marginalization by the majority.

In summary, this section's characterization of indigenous peoples is principally pragmatic and geared as a preliminary heuristic, not an all-encompassing definition. In keeping with this book's autoethnographic dimension, this characterization is based on consequences (real-world observations) as opposed to antecedents (long-accepted axioms). Based on empirical evidence (rather than abstractly deduced principles), this section arrives at two principal factors that distinguish indigenous peoples compared to majoritarian groups: relative economic poverty and significant cultural difference.

Characterizing Traditional Knowledge and Expressions of Folklore

A similar definitional conundrum arises when attempting to pin down exactly what TK and EoF are. At a preliminary level, this would appear a less precarious endeavor, because, rather than attempt to describe a class of people, it merely attempts to characterize certain rights. Nevertheless, particularly given the cultural context of their production and reception as intellectual property, TK and EoF often take on a sacred value in many indigenous communities and the protection thereof has significant spiritual and cultural resonance within communities.

What is "traditional knowledge" (TK) and what makes it different from other types of "knowledge"? Does the fact that the knowledge has been cultivated by a tribe make it "traditional"? If so, why should it deserve protection and not be available for general public consumption, for the betterment of humankind?

The Secretariat of the Convention on Biological Diversity (CBD)[46] defines traditional knowledge in the following way:

> Traditional knowledge refers to the knowledge, innovations and practices of Indigenous and local communities around the world. Developed from experience gained over the centuries and adapted to the local culture and environment, traditional knowledge is transmitted orally from generation to generation. It tends to be collectively owned and takes the form of stories, songs, folklore, proverbs, cultural values, beliefs, rituals, community laws, local language, and agricultural practices, including the development of plant species and animal breeds. Traditional knowledge is mainly of a practical nature, particularly in such fields as agriculture, fisheries, health, horticulture, and forestry.[47]

Additionally, as Taubman and Leister point out, it is neither the type of knowledge, nor its ancient origins that makes TK what it is:

> Knowledge is not "traditional" because of its object, nor its subject matter nor content, nor its age or antiquity, nor its aesthetic qualities. What makes it traditional is the way it has been preserved and transmitted between generations within a community. . . . TK has a profoundly local quality. . . . It has an inherent normative and social component . . . alienation of components of a TK system from the original community—by its consent or otherwise—inevitably entails loss of legal, cultural and intellectual context.[48]

Thus, the crux of the battle waged over TK and intellectual property ownership is: "what kind of legal liability should continue to reach back to the source community when elements of a TK system are transferred and used by third parties beyond the community?"[49] In other words, how does one "compensate" a community for the exploitation of knowledge that is crucial to the very lifeblood and identity of that community, particularly when the idea of "compensation" is itself incommensurable with the paradigmatic foundations of that particular community? For example, as Posey points out, from the points of view of indigenous peoples, knowledge emanates from a spiritual base; all creation is sacred; and the sacred and the secular are inseparable.[50] Thus, for indigenous peoples, traditional knowledge is not merely "local" knowledge but knowledge of the universal, which is bound to a concomitant moral obligation of stewardship, not an entitlement of ownership, of this universal knowledge.[51]

In addition, contrary to stereotypical depictions of TK, TK is neither "dead," "inert," nor rigidly fixed. TK, rooted in fluctuating and evolving contexts, responds in turn by changing and adapting, through a communally negotiated process of incremental innovation and transmission to future generations. Thus, the recognition, promotion, and "valuation" of TK require a broader perspective than one fixed in categories of "raw" data access, storage, and dissemination. Such a project should, this chapter argues, also take into account the processes of innovation and transmission—processes that are just as creative and innovative, even if they are rooted in a communal entity, not an enlightened individual inventor.

The 2007 Annex to the World Intellectual Property Organization (WIPO), on the Protection of Traditional Knowledge, has described TK in the following manner:

> the content or substance of knowledge resulting from intellectual activity in a traditional context, and includes the know[-]how, skills, innovations, practices and learning that form part of traditional knowledge systems, and knowledge embodying traditional lifestyles of indigenous and local communities, or contained in codified knowledge systems passed between generations. It is not limited to any specific technical field, and may include agricultural, environmental and medicinal knowledge, and knowledge associated with genetic resources.[52]

As the descriptions above show, the line allegedly separating TK and "expressions of folklore" (EoF) and "traditional cultural expressions" (TCE) is porous. It does not mean that line is not a real one. But it does mean the same object can be viewed from multiple and intersecting perspectives, as both an object of TK and TCE/EoF, much as the same "object" can be simultaneously protected by both patent law and copyright law. In a manner analogous to many well-known visual illusions, characteristic of, for example, Escher's prints, an object, like seed, can be simultaneously viewed as a physical object, a botanical type, a particular genotype, as the physical embodiment of a particular form of TK, and as part of a particular cultural heritage, among others. Thus, there are corresponding legal protections that could be deployed, in keeping with the multifarious ways in which this same object can be "framed." As an example, Taubman creates a table (see table 1.1) to explore how a seed can be both an object of TK and TCE/EoF.[53]

Nevertheless, for analytic and strategic purposes relevant to this project, it is wise to parse apart TK from EoF/TCE. There appears to be some disagreement as to whether the term "EoF" or the term "TCE" is the better rhetorical instrument given the possible negative connotation of a "primitive" culture; there is even debate on whether the use of these terms "taints" the

Table 1.1. Ways of Framing Seed as Property and Possible Strategies of Legal Protection

Ways of Seeing/Framing	*Conceptions of Property/Possible Strategies of Legal Protection*
The seed as physical object	—ownership as personality (a distinct chattel) —associated with land ownership or real property —covered by conceptual constraints on use after access afforded (e.g., a material transfer agreement) —access constrained by controls on entry to land —access conditioned on a permit or regulation governing prospecting of genetic resources —national resource sovereignty more broadly —national sovereignty in determining the conditions of entry and exit to the country concerned —regulations on bioprospecting, biosafety, endangered species protection or quarantine (restricting or condition access to the seed and the right to remove it)
Botanical variety (phenotype)	—Plant variety right (if variety meets substantive criteria) —Plant patent (if variety meets substantive criteria)
Genetic makeup (genotype)	—Patent (e.g., if seed is of inventively transformed plant)
Embodiment of traditional knowledge or heritage of plantbreeding (TK)	—Traditional knowledge protection (where accorded) —Custodial responsibilities under customary law —Farmers' rights
Element of cultural heritage (TCE/EoF)	—Links to customary land use or other rights based on customary law and practice —Association with local agricultural products and associated branding and regional identity

effects.[54] Nevertheless, there is agreement that EoF/TCEs are intimately imbricated with a particular group's unique cultural character.

In summary, establishing a pragmatic starting point for a working characterization of TK is fraught with complexity. For example, legal concepts of "property," "ownership," and "compensation" are principally Western cultural constructs, which are absolutely alien to some indigenous communities, because in these indigenous communities, there are no such analogous concepts, but only a moral obligation of stewardship. Similarly, Western assumptions about individual property rights and invention have biased cultural perceptions that negatively value the protection of communally shared, creative endeavors and communally generated, innovative processes. Nevertheless, though the differences between TK and EoF or TCE are porous, one pragmatic advantage of different definitions is having multiple potential legal avenues to protect indigenous peoples' property interests. All the other chapters in this book flow from these introductory characterizations, conceived as a working heuristic.

A GENERAL SURVEY OF ATTEMPTS TO USE LEGAL INSTRUMENTS TO PROTECT INDIGENOUS PEOPLES' INTELLECTUAL PROPERTY RIGHTS

This section begins by providing a brief summary of human rights instruments related to the protection of TK and EoF, which have evolved across the years. Next, the section provides a descriptive analysis of the Nagoya Protocol and the changes the protocol has undergone. From there, the section then examines the Nagoya Protocol's conflict with the Agreement on Trade-Related Aspects of Intellectual Property Rights (TRIPS Agreement), and attempts both constructive criticism of this conflict, and an assessment of potentially promising developments in the light of that conflict. Additionally, the chapter explores the WIPO's comparatively more progressive approach to reconciling intellectual property law and indigenous communities' interests in protecting their TK and EoF.

Finally, this book returns to the Fear/Optimism binary, examined in depth in earlier sections of this chapter, and attempts to pose pragmatic solutions that go beyond the impasse provided by these two mirror-imaging Master Narratives. The book consistently employs a pragmatic approach by using empirical evidence, drawn from an intersectional, multidisciplinary perspective, and using induction to outline core principles from existing and evolving practices in the field. The project, in general, offers general and specific recommendations for strategies aimed at protecting TK and EoF, and in conclusion, aspires to establish a heuristic for exploring pragmatic solutions to these problems by teasing out convergences from the seemingly multiple incommensurable oppositions between indigenous communities and more mainstream populations.

A GENERAL SURVEY OF INTERNATIONAL HUMAN RIGHTS INSTRUMENTS RELATED TO THE PROTECTION OF TK AND EOF

To ground this project within the relevant legal literature, this section begins with a brief overview of various international human rights-related developments, both positive and negative, which have been deployed in the attempt to protect the intellectual property rights of indigenous peoples. Some of the most basic protections proscribe discrimination based on race, religion, language, social origin, or other status, such as the protections provided by Article 2 of the Universal Declaration of Human Rights (the Universal Declaration), the International Covenant on Civil and Political Rights (ICCPR), and the International Covenant on Economic, Social, and Cultural Rights (ICESR).[55] Similarly, Article 17 of the Universal Declaration protects a human right to own property that includes intellectual property.[56] Some human rights treaties merely adopt or recognize an article in another treaty; for example, Article 15(c) of the ICESR recognizes the human right contained in Article 27(2) of the U.N. Declaration: the human right of inventors.[57] However, the ICCPR affords more specific protections; for example, paraphrased, Article 27 recognizes the human right of minorities to preserve their linguistic and religious cultures "in community with others."[58] In effect, Article 27 of the ICCPR provides the missing language from Article 2 of the ICESR and the Universal Declaration.[59] In addition, Article 1 of both the ICCPR and the ICESR employ broad language to ensure individual autonomy.[60] Both of these instruments confirm the human right to self-determination, which includes the right freely to pursue economic, social, and cultural development.[61]

Ironically, the U.N. initially treated problems unique to indigenous populations as a subset of labor issues, and thus, relegated these issues to the International Labor Organization (ILO).[62] Indeed, the underlying assumption of the 1957 ILO treaty is that labor integration into the mainstream would be the panacea to all these problems.[63] However, over thirty years later, in an ironic 180-degree turn, the 1989 ILO Convention urged governments to respect and protect indigenous identities and cultures (a referent to the protection of TK and TCE/ EoF) and, as a corollary, to honor the collective relationships inherent in the social structure of these populations.[64] Finally, the Draft Declaration of the Rights of Indigenous Peoples, adopted in 2007, specifically Article 4, identifies the right of indigenous people to maintain their distinct political, social, and cultural characteristics, while retaining their right to participate fully, if they choose to, in the political life of the state.[65] Furthermore, Article 7 of the U.N. Declaration of the Rights of Indigenous Peoples (UNDRIP) also affords indigenous people the collective and individual right to not be subjected to "ethnocide and cultural genocide."[66] Lastly, Article 30 confirms the right to self-determination and requires free and informed consent in the "development of their lands, territory and other resources."[67]

Additionally, predating any discussions at the General Agreement on Tariffs and Trade (GATT) and subsequently, TRIPS, on the issue of ownership of biodiversity, such as the knowledge of the uses of medicinal plants and access to them, the Agreement on Copyright and Cultural Heritage of the African Intellectual Property Organization (OAPI),[68] which was established on March 2, 1977, at Bangui, had several provisions defending the intellectual property rights of indigenous peoples, especially in relation to folklore. For example, Annex VII of the Agreement, "Copyright and the Cultural Heritage" has Article 8, which states that "folklore belongs, in the first instance, to the cultural heritage."[69] Additionally, Article 45 declares that "ethnographic material, such as . . . products of pharmacopeia, traditional medicine and psychotherapy" should be seen as "belonging to the cultural heritage of the nation."[70] In like vein, Article 8(5) states that proceeds from royalties proceeding from the exploitation of these works "shall be used for cultural and social purposes. The conditions under which such royalties are shared shall be fixed in a rule to be promulgated by the competent national authority."[71] Furthermore, Article 50 criminalizes the unlawful denaturization, destruction, exportation, sale, alienation, or transference of "any of the constituent elements of the cultural heritage."[72] Finally, Article 74 states that anyone who willfully violated any of these provisions could be punished by imprisonment anywhere between a month to two years, including a fine, without a prejudice to damages.[73]

However, the existence of such a progressive agreement has not deterred various forms of biopioracy. As other chapters will illustrate as well, enforcement of these provisions is consistently a key issue. For example, as Russell Lawrence Barsh notes, there have been several high profile cases of flagrant violations of the OAPI Agreement, such as the "unauthorized over-harvesting of bark for *Prunus africana* in Cameroon for use in a European herbal medicine to treat benign prostatic hypertrophy (BPH)."[74] Because a French company possesses the commercial exploitation permit to collect and export the bark, from 1985–1991 alone, 11,537 tons of *Prunus africana* bark were harvested to produce an extract used to treat BPH.[75]

Ultimately, as discussed in greater depth in a later section, the Convention on Biological Diversity (CBD) declared government control of the intellectual property rights of indigenous peoples' TK.[76] Along a parallel track, Hernandez-Truyol and Powell point out that the CBD "requires prior informed consent before a corporation may have access to genetic resources. Prospective resource users, however, must seek this consent not from the indigenous population but from the signatory government."[77] However, Article 29 of the Draft Declaration of Indigenous Peoples' Rights reversed the CBD; it provided that indigenous peoples are entitled to the recognition of full ownership (and thus control and protection) of their cultural and intellectual property.[78] Further, the Draft Declaration of Indigenous Peoples' Rights recognized control and protection of cultural and intellectual property as a necessary correlative of the human right of self-determination, nondiscrimination, respect for cultural integrity, control over land and resources, social welfare and development of self-government.[79]

In contrast, the TRIPS Agreement exacerbated the struggle to make human rights enforceable through trade rules.[80] TRIPS made the protection of intellectual property (IP) uniform on a global level, and required members to take positive steps to enact and enforce laws to facilitate trade by protecting the rights of intellectual property owners by requiring adherence to the Berne Convention for copyright law, the Paris Convention for patent and trademark protection, and the Washington Treaty for protection of integrated circuits.[81] The TRIPS Agreement went much further than WIPO, by extending the scope of IP protection, largely for multinational corporations (MNCs),[82] by: (1) eliminating disputes in trademark (by presuming the same mark on the same type of good creates confusion);[83] (2) increasing patent terms to twenty years (patent terms were formerly upheld for seventeen years or less in the United States);[84] and (3) treating computer programs as literary works under the Berne Convention.[85]

Thus, one basic point of conflict between CBD and TRIPS has been ownership of TK. The CBD regards a product or process that has been integrated into a culture for a long time as essentially the property of the tribe. In contrast, TRIPS views such unpatented products or processes as part of the commons, and thus, is open to exploitation. Thus, it is hardly surprising that in November 2001, the declaration of the Fourth Ministerial Conference in Doha, Qatar, called for a review of TRIPS provisions, and a harmonization of CBD and TRIPS.[86] From January 1999 to October 2005, the TRIPS Council extensively reviewed: (1) the provisions of Article 27.3(b); (2) the relationship between the TRIPS Agreement and the CBD; and (3) the protection of traditional knowledge and folklore.[87] While there still persisted disagreement about whether or not the conflict between the CBD and TRIPS required an amendment of TRIPS provisions,[88] attempts were made to resolve the CBD's emphases on prior informed consent and benefit-sharing through two approaches: (1) a "national-based approach,"[89] which places the responsibility of ensuring that these principles are honored using state-based systems; and (2) a supplementary "disclosure" requirement as an addendum to national legislation and contracts.[90] While the review did appear to make CBD and TRIPS less at odds with each other at an initial glance, tensions remain, as the next sections will illustrate.

Thus, as illustrated above, the non-linear progression of intellectual property law has resulted in several developments, some advantageous, with others detrimental in terms of the protection of indigenous peoples' intellectual property rights. Nevertheless, the end result, as this book shows, remains, in some ways, the same: current intellectual property law shoehorns TK and EoF into incommensurable, Western-derived categories alien to the cultures that generated them.

GLOBALIZATION AND ATTEMPTS AT PROMOTING THE PROTECTION OF INDIGENOUS PEOPLES' TK AND EOF: REVIEWING THE CBD, THE NAGOYA PROTOCOL, TRIPS, AND WIPO

This section starts with an examination of the Nagoya Protocol and its relation to other international human rights-related developments, both progressive and regressive, in order to provide a comprehensive analysis of the regulations protecting the TK and EoF of indigenous peoples. The chapter then contrasts these progressive and regressive developments, identifying specific negative consequences of the TRIPS Agreement. Next, the chapter describes WIPO's fact-finding mission in its attempt to reform the TRIPS Agreement and ameliorate its negative consequences. This overview ends on a note of some hopefulness; the growing power of developing countries like India and Brazil may garner significant leverage to lobby effectively for some of the reforms needed.

The Nagoya Protocol

The Nagoya Protocol on Access to Genetic Resources and the Fair and Equitable Sharing of Benefits Arising from their Utilization to the Convention on Biological Diversity (the "Nagoya Protocol" or the "Protocol") is a supplement to the CBD.[91] The Nagoya Protocol aims to promote the policy of "contributing to the conservation and sustainable use of biodiversity."[92] In other words, it deals with "access and benefit sharing [in] countries or local communities when inventors use genetic materials and any associated traditional knowledge."[93] Thus, the protocol seems to signal a departure from Western assumptions about intellectual property rights (IPR) and instead focuses more on the importance of biodiversity and sustainability.

The CBD as a Backdrop to the Development of the Protocol

The Convention on Biological Diversity (CBD) aimed to promote sustainable development. It was signed by 150 government leaders at the 1992 Rio Earth Summit.[94] Its three main objectives were: (1) the conservation of biological diversity; (2) the sustainable use of the components of biological diversity; and (3) the fair and equitable sharing of the benefits arising out of the utilization of genetic resources.[95] Furthermore, the CBD was prompted by "the interest of establishing rules to ensure that scientific collecting activities 'give back' to the various communities involved in biodiversity conservation."[96] The CBD aspired to remedy the "inequitable nature of the intellectual property system . . . further strengthened by [the TRIPS Agreement]."[97]

Thus, Article 3 of the CBD allows parties to use resources so long as it is "pursuant to their own environmental policies."[98] Article 15(5) requires "prior informed consent" in order to access genetic resources.[99] Nevertheless, Article 15 requires further conditions for access to resources such as the requirements that such use is environmentally sound; that access is on mutually agreed terms; and that the benefits are shared in an equitable manner.[100]

Additionally, Article 8(j) declares that State Parties are required to:

> respect, preserve and maintain knowledge, innovations, and practices of indigenous and local communities embodying traditional lifestyles relevant for the conservation and sustainable use of biological diversity and promote the wider application with the approval and involvement of the holders of knowledge, innovations and practices and encourage the equitable sharing of the benefits arising from the utili[z]ation of such knowledge, innovations and practices.[101]

Nonetheless, the provision is subject to the following caveats: it is subject to national law and is required only as far as possible and appropriate.[102] The same conditions apply to the provisions requiring that the use of TK be with the "approval and involvement of [indigenous communities] as well as to encourage the equitable sharing of benefits."[103]

Despite all these safeguards theoretically in place, in practice, modern intellectual property rights have produced ambiguous results in the attempts to remedy the "inequitable outcomes for agricultural communities in the developing world."[104] Indeed, commentators disagree on the gains of the CBD. For instance, Simon West points out that the current approach is antithetical to traditional ways of "rewarding innovation in many rural . . . societies which tend to see knowledge as inherently non-excludable and non-alienable, emphasizing community contributions to knowledge developed over generations."[105] Hence, West reiterates the "long voiced" lament that the profit derived from genetic resources has come at the "expense of rural and indigenous communities."[106] In contrast, Surendra J. Patel views the CBD as "a big step forward in the recognition of the contributions of indigenous knowledge [b]ut it does not do anything to build a bridge between indigenous knowledge and IPR [intellectual property rights]."[107]

Despite some negative perceptions of it, the protocol does provide the legal framework for one of the three aforementioned objectives of the CBD: the fair and equitable sharing of the benefits arising from the utilization of genetic resources.[108] The protocol, signed on October 29, 2010 at Nagoya, Japan, is comprised of three elements: "access to genetic resources, benefit-sharing and compliance."[109] Thus, Paragraph I of Article 5 of the protocol deals with benefit-sharing and provides that "sharing [between the country of origin and the acquiring party] shall be on mutually agreeable terms."[110] However, Article 6 of the protocol provides for state rights over natural resources and guidance on prior informed consent.[111] Nevertheless, Article 8 of the protocol attempts to prompt research "that contributes to biodiversity and sustainable development."[112] Additionally, Article 17 of the protocol deals with the "monitoring [of] the utilization of genetic resources" and establishes "checkpoints."[113]

Hardly surprisingly, given these ambiguous points of comparison with the CBD, scholars debate the merits of the protocol. For example, Kabir Bavikatte and Daniel F. Robinson argue that "the rights that were gained by communities in the [protocol] may not be perfect, but they are undeniably a giant leap from the tame provisions . . . of the [CBD]."[114] In contrast, Veit Koester concludes that the protocol specifies better enforcement mechanisms than the CBD but is still comprised "more as general principles than operational rules."[115]

The Nagoya Protocol and its Conflict with the TRIPS Agreement

The relationship between the Nagoya Protocol and intellectual property rights has been an obstacle in establishing cohesion between the World Trade Organization (WTO) and the CBD.[116] During the March 1, 2011, WTO Council meeting handling intellectual property rights, tensions continued between the TRIPS Agreement and the Nagoya Protocol.[117] Additionally, the CBD Secretariat was not invited to brief the TRIPS Council on the Nagoya Protocol and, despite "repeated calls for a future briefing by the [CBD]" by countries like Brazil, South Africa and India,[118] there was still no consensus.[119] Finally, in 2005, WTO ministers mandated that consultations take place to explore the relationship between CBD and the TRIPS Agreement.[120]

One point of contention between the CBD and TRIPS is the disclosure requirement, which would "require patent applicants to disclose at least the source or origin of genetic resources used in inventions."[121] However, "a few Parties categorically [reject] any mention of disclosure obligation in patent applications and patent offices as checkpoints."[122] In contrast, other countries, including Brazil, India, China, Peru, South Africa, Columbia, and Turkey,[123] want to amend the TRIPS Agreement to require disclosure. More so, some countries prefer an amendment to the Nagoya Protocol and the CBD because disclosure is not yet mandatory.[124] Conversely, other countries, including Australia and Canada,[125] argue that the Nagoya Protocol was only recently agreed and should not be renegotiated; furthermore, they argue that the WTO's TRIPS Agreement is not the proper means to enforce it.[126] Likewise, they believe that the best means of regulating misappropriation and biopiracy remain in the form of "databases, contracts and other means."[127] Lastly, some developed countries, most notably the United States, argue that a disclosure requirement would be "unduly burdensome and stifle innovation."[128]

Other suggestions for a proposed TRIPS amendment include requiring "information on 'prior informed consent' and benefit sharing."[129] The Nagoya Protocol already requires checkpoints to establish "prior informed consent" and ensure compliance with its provisions.[130] However, these provisions "were left quite vague as to the appropriate checkpoints for collection of information including certificates of compliance."[131]

West argues that the protocol "reasserts the position of dominant forms of [IP] protected within [TRIPS]" and does not provide any "normative legal change."[132] Furthermore, he states that the Nagoya Protocol has "creat[ed] subservient obligations attached to conventional [intellectual property rights] that . . . positions [indigenous] communities in a state of legal dependency," and "institutionalizes [their] exclusion from legal rights to intellectual and genetic resources."[133] West premises this conclusion on the fact that developing States can "assert sovereign rights over genetic resources through the [CBD] at the same time as investing in industrial knowledge protection standards under [TRIPS]."[134] Despite the fact that the protocol is a continuation of "dominant [intellectual property rights] norms,"[135] the dialogue between the TRIPS Council and the CBD Conference of Parties has "reveal[ed intellectual property rights] as a contingent social construction."[136] West argues that "[intellectual property rights] do not exist externally to legal structures," though TRIPS allows them to operate as "supposed . . . 'natural' law."[137] He concludes that the "rapidly changing geo-political context" of international law is an appropriate setting for change,[138] but the protocol as "the sole institutionalized response" is an obstacle to "undo[ing TRIPS] . . . or provid[ing] equal rights to . . . indigenous peoples."[139]

In summary, international law is evolving in relation to the protection of the intellectual property rights of indigenous peoples. Patel concludes that the CBD was a progressive step forward from TRIPS in terms of the protection of indigenous peoples' intellectual property rights. Even more dramatically, Bavikatte and Robinson believe that the Nagoya Protocol was a "giant leap" from the CBD. However, Koester argues that while the principles of the protocol may be sound, it lacks a proper enforcement mechanism. Alternatively, West argues that the protocol reiterates dominant intellectual property rights norms. Nevertheless, West acknowledges the dialogue inspired by the protocol's negotiations has successfully revealed intellectual property rights as a "contingent social structure."

Globalization and Its Effects

Increased globalization only heightens the tensions between those in favor of the Nagoya Protocol and those who are convinced that Art.27.3(b) of TRIPS sufficiently allows for adequate protection of genetic resources and traditional knowledge.[140] For example, Kerry ten Kate and Sarah A. Laird have observed a parallel growth between science and technology and the patent system; "[it] has undergone a process of regulatory globalization and harmonization, and the scope of what is regarded as patentable has quietly expanded."[141] The growth of patentability may be most pronounced in the field of biotechnology as it has "coalesced [with globalization] to result in drug development in every potential environment."[142] Furthermore, Bryan A. Liang argues that despite TRIPS "provid[ing] clear guidelines for drug development by western, culturally acclimated players . . . [it] has also resulted in . . . biopiracy."[143]

Upon the Nagoya Protocol's inception, "developing countries had high expectations."[144] Some developing countries believed that patenting lifeforms violates the sacred beliefs of indigenous people, promotes capitalism, and perpetuates an economic hegemony.[145] In contrast, the TRIPS Agreement allows patents for "biological materials and plants (and often associated traditional knowledge) that have been bioprospected, researched, and are being commercialized."[146]

Some remain hopeful, observing that the protocol demonstrates that "the multilateral system could reach consensus on sensitive and important issues."[147] Still, despite wide international support for prior informed consent and equitable benefit sharing, disagreements regarding implementation have continued to create division.[148] Nevertheless, on a more optimistic note, "the Doha Ministerial Declaration mandated work on the relationship" between the TRIPS Agreement and the CBD; similarly, the WTO has a current mandate to "review the linkages" between CBD and TRIPS."[149] Thus, one may reasonably infer there is room for compromise.

Assuming an agreement can be reached regarding compliance with access and benefit sharing, pointed questions remain, such as how compliance can be managed, who bears the burden, and how said burden is allocated between the provider and the user of genetic resources.[150] However, according to Koester, "negotiations on disclosure requirements seem to be deadlocked."[151]

TRIPS: A Criticism and Illustration of Potential Promising Developments

As prior sections have shown, the TRIPS Agreement has been subject to a great deal of criticism. For example, Mitsuo Matsushita, Thomas J.

Schoenbaum, and Petros C. Mavroidis[152] outline five principal critiques of the TRIPS Agreement in relation to the issue of development. First, there is the view that the TRIPS Agreement only benefits developed countries. For example, as Hernandez-Truyol and Powell remark: "The [TRIPS] Agreement is a codification of Western international property norms and presents potential obstacles to sustainable development, or the rights of indigenous populations to continue to use their traditional resources."[153] Second, the TRIPS Agreement, in its current form, does not protect developing countries' property interests in their TK and EoF. Third, as prior sections have shown, the TRIPS Agreement probably conflicts with the U.N. CBD,[154] which affirms developing countries' access to their genetic resources. Fourth, food security in developing countries may be rendered vulnerable by the rising costs of seed and plant supplies. And fifth, the TRIPS Agreement endangers public health in developing countries because it impacts pharmaceutical cost and access.

Nevertheless, as we shall see in the later part of this section, in relation to core values and pragmatic solutions, potentially promising developments have occurred. For example, the TRIPS Council received a proposal from a cluster of developing countries (including WTO major players such as Brazil, India, and Thailand) that the TRIPS Agreement should be amended to "prevent biopiracy (illegal access and use) or ensure prior informed consent and fair and equitable sharing of benefits."[155] To achieve this end, the group proposed imposing certain conditions on acquiring patent rights, particularly in relation to biological materials or TK. For example, patent applicants for TK should disclose the source of the origin of the biological resource and its accompanying traditional knowledge, and should present evidence of prior informed consent and benefit-sharing.[156]

Protecting EoF: WIPO's More Progressive Approach

In terms of the protection of EoF, WIPO has presented a more progressive approach compared with the TRIPS Agreement. WIPO began work on trying to protect EoF at the end of the 1970s and the beginning of the 1980s, generally in conjunction with the United Nations Educational, Scientific, and Cultural Organization (UNESCO).[157] In 1982, an expert group convened by WIPO and UNESCO "developed a *sui generis* model for the [intellectual property]-type protection of EoF's: the [WIPO-UNESCO] Model Provisions."[158] These were widely used by WIPO member states for realizing *sui generis* protection of EoF, especially in the area of national law.[159] However, despite the general acknowledgment that protection in international law was also necessary, there was no consensus on a treaty in the 1980s.[160] In 1996, the UNESCO/WIPO World Forum on the Protection of Folklore occurred; the forum adopted a plan of action and recommended further consultations in order to build consensus on the international protection of EoF.[161] In addition, in December 1996, WIPO member states adopted the WIPO Performances and Phonograms Treaty (WPPT), which provides neighboring rights to a performer of folklore.[162]

Between the years of 1998 and 1999, WIPO conducted fact-finding missions in twenty-eight countries[163] "in order to study current approaches to, and future possibilities for, the protection of [TK], as well as the feasibility of establishing [TK] databases."[164] Within the context of these studies, TK included EoFs as a sub-set.[165] Among the three thousand subjects consulted regarding the need to protect TK and EoF were "indigenous and local communities, non-governmental organizations, governmental representatives, academics, researchers and private sector representatives."[166] WIPO released the results of its fact-finding missions in April 2001.[167] In addition, in 1998 and 1999 two roundtables on intellectual property and TK occurred; the roundtables were designed to facilitate an exchange of views among policy makers and indigenous peoples in relation to the protection of TK.[168] As a consequence of these inquiries into the needs and expectations of indigenous peoples and other TK holders, WIPO, as part of its mission, "provide[s] intellectual property training workshops for holders of [TK] and conducts case studies and pilot projects regarding the interfaces between intellectual property and [TK.]" Also in 1999, WIPO set up regional consultations regarding the protection of EoF with, for example, African countries (March 1999), Asian and Pacific countries (April 1999), Arab countries (May 1999), and Latin American and Caribbean countries (June 1999).[169] Resolutions or recommendations emerged from these consultations, which "unanimously specified that future work in these areas should include the development of an effective international regime for the protection of [EoF]."[170]

In 2000, at the WIPO General Assembly's 26th Session, WIPO member states established the Intergovernmental Committee on Intellectual Property and Genetic Resources, Traditional Knowledge and Folklore (the Committee), which convened eleven times up until 2007.[171] WIPO's own description of its methods heralds its approach as probably the better avenue, compared to the TRIPS approach. That description states:

> Under the guidance of the Committee, the Secretariat of [WIPO] has issued a detailed questionnaire on national experiences, and undertaken a series of comprehensive analytical studies based on the responses to the questionnaire and other consultations and research. The studies have formed the basis for ongoing international policy debate and assisted in the development of practical tools.[172]

The approach this book uses is very much influenced by WIPO's inductive and consultative framework, although it does not idealize the WIPO approach. However, historically, in terms of the actual enforcement of legal instruments, WIPO has not been as effective, unlike the TRIPS Agreement. If there were some way to use the results of the WIPO studies as an empirical basis for forming a schema for plotting a country's relative stage of development, and combining that schema with the TRIPS Agreement's comprehensive enforcement rules, allowing for exceptions for the special circumstances of developing markets (as in the EC Bananas case),[173] perhaps that would be the ideal combination. Unfortunately, given what we know of the political economies behind these two institutions, with WIPO being an arena friendly to developing countries and TRIPS being a forum that tends to privilege developed countries, there may be no pragmatic short-term mechanism to bridge the gulf between the two. But as the prior discussion has shown, developing countries such as India and Brazil have been gaining some leverage for at least discussions on better addressing the protection of TK in the face of rampant biopiracy. These may signal promising new developments in forming concrete bridges between WIPO and the TRIPS Agreement.

In summary, some of these legal developments seem regressive in terms of the protection of indigenous peoples' intellectual property rights. For example, the TRIPS Agreement systematically seems to favor developed countries, conflicts with the more progressive CBD, may adversely affect food security and negatively impacts pharmaceutical costs. Some developing countries have proposed amendments that would require: disclosure of the origin of biological resources, evidence of prior informed consent, and benefit sharing. In contrast, WIPO and UNESCO have proposed a *sui generis* approach to intellectual property-type protections. WIPO developed empirical evidence from twenty-eight countries and performed several regional consultations. Its findings seem to suggest that WIPO's approach is potentially more effective than TRIPS in achieving the aims of prior informed consent and benefit-sharing. However, despite the appeal of WIPO's intellectual approach, that is, inductive and consultative, it has been described as ineffectual, in terms of enforcement, compared with TRIPS. Lastly, it would seem most practical for the TRIPS regime to employ the empirical evidence garnered by WIPO to develop an equitable remedy. However, historically, WIPO has been seen as friendly to developing countries, whilst TRIPS tends to favor the privileged. On the other hand, the growing power of developing countries like India and Brazil are hopeful signs that this gap perhaps may soon be bridged. Nevertheless, on a cautious note, there may only be a select few countries able to meet the standards of the developed world while the disparity between developed and developing countries continues to grow. As Kenneth J. Armour and Peter S. Harrison note: "Overall . . . the balance of power may be changing—with the growing economic influence of China, India and Brazil the primacy of the 'developed' world in these negotiations can no longer be taken as rea[l]. That said, the collapse of the Doha round of WTO free-trade trade talks . . . highlights the delicate nature of these power plays."[174]

A GENERAL OVERVIEW

This book is divided into five chapters. Chapter 1, the introductory chapter, serves principally an explanation for the scope of the book (including a rationale for inclusions and exclusions), and the various methodologies it employs. It also establishes pragmatic working definitions for key terms such as "indigenous peoples," "traditional knowledge" (TK), and "expressions of folklore" (EoF). Furthermore, this chapter grounds this project within the context of a brief summary of legal instruments that have attempted to protect indigenous peoples' rights, and their ambiguous gains. Thus, chapter 1 provides an overall map of the trajectory of the project.

Chapter 2, "Law In and As Culture," sets forth a general framework. This chapter begins with the insight that culture is "paradigmatic" in the sense in which Thomas Kuhn originally used the word in 1966—well before its explosion into ubiquity in several disciplines.[175] Simply described, a paradigm is the cultural matrix that directs attention to certain questions and ignores others, and maps acceptable methods of attempting to solve these selected problems for a particular community at a particular point in time. Culture is the "collective programming of the mind,"[176] and entails sharing "particular symbols, meanings, images, rule structures, habits, values and information processing and transformational patterns."[177] Thus, chapter 2 starts from the conviction that there is no omniscient perspective from which one can record cultural interactions from a clinical distance. This does not mean there is no such thing as "objectivity," but that the notion of "objectivity" itself reflects a complex, historical and sociological unfolding in which participant-observers are always already implicated, even as, for instance, lawyers, who are trained to keep an objective distance.

Chapter 3 is titled the "Cultural Meanings of Intellectual Property," and begins with Rodolfo Stavenhagen's three underlying conceptions of culture, implied in the practice of international and intellectual property law. The first, of culture as "capital," conceives of culture as "the accumulated material heritage of humankind in its entirety, or of particular human groups, including monuments and artifacts."[178] This view, most compatible with free trade markets, views the "right to culture" as "equal access by individuals to . . . accumulated cultural capital"[179] and can be viewed as an extension of the right to development.

The second, of culture as "creativity," is the more traditional description of culture in intellectual property law: as the "process of artistic and scientific creation."[180] This view of what "culture" is, is infused with Eurocentric and colonial assumptions—assumptions that undergird distinctions made between "high" culture (which is deemed genuinely creative and therefore protectable) and "low" culture (which is deemed not truly "original" and therefore in the public domain).

Finally, the third description, of culture as a "total way of life," is more anthropological and therefore integrative. In this third meaning, culture is "the sum total of the material and spiritual activities and products of a given social group which distinguishes it from other similar groups."[181] This description is probably the one most useful in protecting indigenous peoples' ancestral lands, traditional knowledge and traditional cultural expressions as constitutive of as an indivisible whole—that is, as "a coherent self-contained system of values, and symbols as well as a set of practices that a specific cultural group reproduces over time and which provides individuals with the required signposts and meanings for behavior and social relationships in everyday life."[182] From there, the chapter examines the tensions that result between majoritarian cultures and minority groups or indigenous peoples as a result of these simultaneously existing embedded descriptions of culture in intellectual property law. Such descriptions of culture are also imbricated with larger circulating cultural understandings of "property" and "ownership."

Chapter 3 also focuses on attempting to negotiate differences in cultural clashes between majoritarian cultures and indigenous peoples. Cultural complexities are magnified even more when minorities, attempting to protect their own intellectual property rights, and indigenous populations, attempting to protect their traditional knowledge (TK), expressions of folklore (EoF), ancestral lands, and cultural identities, come in contact with either the culture of international globalization, or the majoritarian culture of their own country. As part of this chapter, two particular cultural clashes are analyzed, using Hofstede, Hofstede, and Minkov's framework of cultural programming, both in terms of general pragmatic strategies and a review of their actual resolutions, based on case studies.

Chapter 4 is titled "Colonial Appropriations of Marginalized Cultures and Possible Strategies of Resistance." Given law's embeddedness in culture, and functioning as a culture, possible avenues of resistance are multiple. One such avenue involves simply giving voice to those normally silenced, with their ambivalent alliances and their porous identities as members of several communities. Another avenue involves deconstructing front-stage myths of civic order and equality to reveal back-stage realities of prejudice and hegemony. A third alternative lies in adapting prevailing legal and cultural categories to give voice to, as well as recast, new legal expectations for justice and equality. Various strategies are deployed in relation to a critique of the evolution of American dance choreography in relation to a history of copyright protection, as illustrated briefly in the examples of Loïe Fuller, Josephine Baker, and Katherine Dunham.

Throughout the chapter, law will be analyzed as partaking of an evolving cultural life: that as legal meaning is circulated, such meaning is communicated in a nonlinear manner, and that the direction can be shifted, depending on who frames the narrative for specific audiences, and who receive and interpret these circulations of meaning, in different contexts. Re-evaluating the construction of categories of law in relation to differing collective identities and individual subjectivities has generated new and diverse ways of reflecting upon the law, legal processes, and legal power that reshape the multitude of legal engagements and interactions within various social contexts.

Attempting to leverage a system entails the insight that law generates and operates in lacunae in which hegemonic struggles occur, and signs and symbols are always contested, and always at risk. Legal strategies and legal institutions may lend weight to some interpretations while tending to deny such privileged status to others, often forming hegemonic binaries, which can be potentially leveraged. Similarly, the relationships binding authorship, agency, and alterity bear closer examination, with greater sensitivity to the politics of textuality, metaphorics, and materiality in various social circles. Law's constitutive or generative power, in addition to its prohibitive or punitive possibilities, must therefore always be kept in mind, if one is to attempt to continually re-engage what effective strategies of resistance are possible to enact, within multiple contexts.

Chapter 5, the concluding chapter, draws the prior chapters into a coherent flow, and suggests a way in which law can be negotiated and lived in and as culture. Based on current and ongoing attempts at collaboration between majoritarian groups and indigenous peoples, some core principles have been identified as a way of balancing the rights of indigenous peoples to protect their cultural identities, traditional resources and ancestral lands (technically, "first generation" human rights),[183] alongside the right, of developing countries, for example, to pursue development and scientific progress (technically, a "third generation" human right).[184] Among these are: prior informed consent, mutually agreed terms, and benefit-sharing.[185] The effectiveness of these principles as pragmatic guidelines to working across cultural differences is illustrated in the case of the production of a commercially viable form of Jeevani, an anti-fatigue agent established in consultation and cooperation with the Kani tribe in

India. This third case illustrates Stavenhagen's first description of culture: as "capital," and is one example of how the principles outlined above happened to work effectively, to produce an effective and materially lucrative outcome for both the indigenous tribe and a multinational corporation. Nevertheless, without idealizing this case, this chapter proposes that the Jeevani example is only one, among many ways, in which law in and as culture, can operate, finding a rapprochement, however contingent, between the imperative to protect indigenous peoples' property and intellectual property rights and a developing country's right to progress.

NOTES

1. Viewpoints regarding indigenous peoples' property and intellectual property rights tend to be highly polemical. For a range of viewpoints that are supportive of indigenous peoples' rights, see Kristen A. Carpenter, et. al., "In Defense of Property," *The Yale Law Journal* 118 (2009): 1022–1125; Anupam Chander and Madhavi Sunder, "Romance of the Public Domain," *California Law Review* 92 (2004): 1331–1374; Angela R. Riley, "'Straight Stealing': Towards an Indigenous System of Cultural Property Protection," *Washington Law Review* 80 (2005): 69; Rebecca Tsosie, "Reclaiming Native Stories: An Essay on Cultural Appropriation and Cultural Rights," *Arizona State Law Journal* 34 (2002): 299; Christine H. Farley, "Protecting Folklore of Indigenous Peoples: Is Intellectual Property the Answer?" *Connecticut Law Review* 30 (1997): 1. For a variety of perspectives that are more doubtful, see Barton Beebe, "Intellectual Property Law and the Sumptuary Code," *Harvard Law Review* 123 (2010): 809, 875–80; Naomi Mezey, "The Paradox of Cultural Property," *Columbia Law Reivew* 107 (2007): 2004; Stephen Munzer and Kal Raustiala, "The Uneasy Case for Intellectual Property Rights in Traditional Knowledge," *Cardozo Arts & Entertainment Law Journal* 27 (2009): 37; Sean A. Pager, "Folklore 2.0: Preservation Through Innovation," *Utah Law Review* (2012): 1835; Michael Brown, *Who Owns Native Culture?* (Cambridge, MA: Harvard University Press, 2004).

2. Berta Hernandez-Truyol and Stephen J. Powell, *Just Trade: A New Covenant Linking Trade and Human Rights* (New York: New York University Press, 2009).

3. Jane E. Anderson, *Law, Knowledge, Culture: The Production of Indigenous Knowledge in Intellectual Property Law* (Northampton, MA: Edward Elgar, 2009).

4. Geert Hofstede, Gert Jan Hofstede, and M. Minkov, eds. *Cultures and Organizations: Software of the Mind* (New York: McGraw-Hill, 2010).

5. Silke von Lewinski, ed. *Indigenous Heritage and Intellectual Property: Genetic Resources, Knowledge and Folklore* (The Netherlands: Kluwer Law International BV, 2008).

6. Rosemary Coombe, *The Cultural Life of Intellectual Properties: Authorship, Appropriation, and the Law* (Durham, NC: Duke University Press, 1998).

7. See generally, Hofstede, Hofstede, and Minkov, *Cultures and Organizations.*

8. A portion of this section previously appeared as part of a two part-article: Caroline Joan "Kay" S. Picart and Marlowe Fox, "Beyond Unbridled Optimism

and Fear: Indigenous Peoples, Intellectual Property, Human Rights and the Globalization of Traditional Knowledge and Expressions of Folklore (Part I), 15," in *International Community Law Review* 3 (2013), 319–39; and Caroline Joan "Kay" S. Picart and Marlowe Fox, "Beyond Unbridled Optimism and Fear: Indigenous Peoples, Intellectual Property, Human Rights and the Globalization of Traditional Knowledge and Expressions of Folklore (Part II), 16," in *International Community Law Review* 2 (March 2014), 3–37. I thank the *International Community Law Review* and Brill for permission to adapt the material for this book.

9. Friedrich Nietzsche, *Beyond Good and Evil: Prelude to a Philosophy of the Future* (Walter Kaufmann, trans., Vintage Books, 1989), 207–8, 221–22.

10. Chong Hui-yeung, "IPR draft law for Aborigines under attack," *Taipei Times*, August 23 2000, 4, www.taipeitimes.com/News/local/archives/2000/08/23/49186. See Ashley Esarey, "An Ami Couple Seeks Recognition For Their Music," *Travel in Taiwan Special* 1-3, accessed April 13, 2012, www.sinica.edu.tw/tit/special/0996_Innocence.html.

11. Deming Liu, "Can Copyright Lend Its Cinderellaic Magic to Chinese Folklore?" *John Marshall Rev. Intell. Prop. L.* 203, 214 (2006), 5. For a dissenting view, see Elisabetta LeJeune, "Mu-Lan, the Chinese Woman Warrior," *Southeastern Louisiana University,* 1–4. www2.selu.edu/Academics/Faculty/elejeune/mulan.htm (last visited Apr. 13, 2012).

12. The ayahuasca vine, native to the Amazon rain forest, was used by aboriginal shahmen to treat illnesses, commune with spirits, and foresee the future. Loren Miller, an American entrepreneur and scientist, obtained a patent on a purified version of the psychotropic substance in the ayahuasca vine, which led to tensions between the United States and Ecuador. See Danielle Knight, "An Enemy of Indigenous Peoples the Case of Loren Miller, COICA, the Inter-American Foundation and the Ayahuasca Plant," *Multinational Monitor*, accessed April 13, 2012, www.amazon.com/enemy-indigenous-peoples-Inter-American-Multinational/dp/B00098ALO8/ref=sr_1_37?s=books&ie=UTF8&qid=1327868393&sr=1-37; Leanne M. Fectaeau, "The Ayahuasca Patent Revocation: Raising Questions about Current U.S. Patent Policy," accessed April 13, 2012, www.bc.edu/bc_org/avp/law/lwsch/journals/bctwj/21_1/03_TXT.htm.

13. Factsheet, "Indigenous Peoples, Indigenous Voices," in United Nations Permanent Forum on Indigenous Issues, accessed June 5, 2012, www.un.org/esa/socdev/unpfii/documents/5session_factsheet1.pdf. See also United Nations Department of Economic and Social Affairs (UN-DESA), "State of the World's Indigenous Peoples," 2nd volume, no date, accessed December 3, 2015. www.un.org/esa/socdev/unpfii/documents/sowip2volume-ac.pdf; p. 3 ("[N]o such definition has ever been adopted by any United Nations body and the prevailing view today is that no formal universal definition is necessary for the recognition and protection of their rights"); Secretariat of the Permanent Forum on Indigenous Issues, "State of the World's Indigenous Peoples," accessed June 5, 2015. www.un.org/esa/socdev/unpfii/documents/SOWIP_introduction.pdf; p. 4 ("In the forty-year history of indigenous issues at the United Nations, and its even longer history at the ILO [International Labour Organization] . . . no such definition has ever been adopted").

14. Factsheet, "Indigenous Peoples, Indigenous Voices."

15. Ibid.
16. Ibid.
17. Ibid.
18. Ibid.
19. Ibid.
20. "State of the World's Indigenous Peoples," 4. See "The Concept of Indigenous Peoples," 1.
21. This historical continuity may consist of the continuation, for an extended period reaching into the present of one or more of the following factors:

a. Occupation of ancestral lands, or at least of part of them
b. Common ancestry with the original occupants of these lands
c. Culture in general, or in specific manifestations (such as religion, living under a tribal system, membership of an indigenous community, dress, means of livelihood, lifestyle, etc.)
d. Language (whether used as the only language, as mother-tongue, as the habitual means of communication at home or in the family, or as the main, preferred, habitual, general or normal language)
e. Residence in certain parts of the country, or in certain regions of the world
f. Other relevant factors ("State of the World's Indigenous Peoples," 4–5; "State of the World's Indigenous Peoples," 4).

22. "State of the World's Indigenous Peoples," 4. *See* "The Concept of Indigenous Peoples," 1.
23. "State of the World's Indigenous Peoples," 5.
24. Ibid.
25. "United Nations Declaration of Indigenous People," art. 33, GA Res 61/925, UN Doc A/RES/61/295 (13 September 2007), 46 *International Legal Materials* 1013 (2007). See also "International Labour Organization," Convention No. 169, Indigenous and Tribal Peoples Convention, art. 1 (27 June 1989) ("[i] ndicates that self-identification as indigenous or tribal shall be regarded as a fundamental criterion for determining the groups to which the provisions of [the] convention apply."), www.ilo.org/dyn/normlex/en/f?p=NORMLEXPUB:12100:3660859375172571::NO:12100:P12100_INSTRUMENT_ ID:312314:NO. See also "Indigenous People" OP 4.10(4), *The World Bank* (July 2005), web.worldbank.org/WBSITE/EXTERNAL/PROJECTS/EXTPOLICIES/EXTOPMANUAL/0,,contentMDK:20553653~menuPK:4564185~pagePK:64709096~piPK:64709108~theSitePK:502184,00.html. For a succinct comparison the World Bank's "official position" and the U.N. system's "modern understanding of [indigenous] on a variety of characteristics," see "Policy Brief: Indigenous Peoples," *The World Bank*, 2, accessed May 8, 2015, siteresources.worldbank.org/EXTINDPEOPLE/Resources/407801-1271860301656/HDNEN_ indigenous_clean_0421.pdf.
26. Benedict Kingsbury, "Indigenous Peoples' in International Law: A Constructivist Approach to the Asian Controversy," *American Journal of International Law* 92, no. 3 (1998): 414.
27. Ibid., 414.
28. Ibid.

29. Ibid.
30. Ibid., 414–15.
31. Ibid., 415.
32. Ibid.
33. Ibid.
34. Ibid.
35. Ibid., 415.
36. Ibid. (citing Mike Dodson, "Towards the Exercise of Indigenous Rights: Policy, Power and Self-Determination," in *Race and Class* [April–June 1994]: 65); Paul Coe, "ATSIC: Self-Determination or Otherwise," in *Race and Class* [April 1994]: 35.
37. Kingsbury, "Indigenous Peoples' in International Law," 415 (citing *Santa Clara Pueblo v. Martinez*, 436 US 49 [1978]).
38. Ibid. (citing Sarah Laird, A. B. Cunningham, and Estherine Lisginge, "Forests, Drugs, and Benefit Sharing: Putting the Formula to the Test—The Cameroon Case of Ansicstrocladus korupensis," in *People, Plants, and Justice*, ed. Charles Zerner [New York: Columbia University Press, 2000]).
39. Ibid. (citing Laird, Cunningham, and Lisginge, "Forests, Drugs, and Benefit Sharing").
40. Ibid., 416.
41. ILO Convention of 27 June 1989, No. 169, art. I, ¶1, accessed May 9, 2015, www.ilo.org/ilolex/cgi-lex/convde.pl?C169.
42. Hernandez-Truyol and Powell, *Just Trade*, 206–7.
43. World Bank Operational Directive 4.20, 2001, which was replaced by the revised policy OP/BP 4.10,2005. World Bank Operation Manual 4.10, July 2005, accessed May 9, 2015, web.worldbank.org/WBSITE/EXTERNAL/PROJECTS/EXTPOLICIES/EXTOPMANUAL/0,,contentMDK:20553664~menuPK:64701637~pagePK:64709096~piPK:64709108~theSitePK:502184~isCURL:Y,00.html.
44. Ibid.
45. Working Group on Indigenous Populations, Working Paper by the Chairperson-Rapporteur, Mrs. Erica-Irene A. Daes, on the concept of 'indigenous peoples,' U.N. Doc E/CN.4/Sub.2/AC.4/1996/2, accessed May 9, 2015, www.unhchr.ch/Huridocda/Huridoca.nsf/TestFrame/2b6e0fb1e9d7db0fc1256b3a003eb999?Opendocument.
46. The Secretariat is responsible for supporting meetings held under the Convention, including meetings of the Conference of the Parties, the Subsidiary Body on Scientific, Technical, and Technological Advice (SBSTTA), and the Working Group on the Implementation of Article 8(j) and Related Provisions. Among its other responsibilities include preparing documents and draft decisions for these meetings based on information provided by Parties as national reports, case studies, reports of experts, among others. Indigenous and local communities are particularly invited to contribute to the work of this process. The CBD Secretariat: "Role, Convention on Biological Diversity," accessed June 4, 2015, www.cbd.int/secretariat/role.shtml.
47. "Introduction," *Convention on Biological Diversity*, accessed June 4, 2015, www.cbd.int/traditional/intro.shtml.
48. Antony Taubman and Matthias Leistner, "Analysis of Different Areas of Indigenous Resources: Section 1: Traditional Knowledge," in Silke von Lewinski,

ed. *Indigenous Heritage and Intellectual Property: Genetic Resources, Knowledge and Folklore* (The Netherlands: Kluwer Law International BV, 2008), 59–60.

49. Ibid., 60.

50. Darrell Addison Posey, "Selling Grandma: Commodification of the Sacred through Intellectual Property Rights," in *Claiming the Stones; Naming the Bones: Cultural Property and the Negotiation of National and Ethnic Identity,* eds. Elazar Barkan and Ronald Bush (Oxford, UK: Oxford University Press, 2002), 201. For a general characterization distinguishing between Canadian first peoples' spiritual views versus the world view of their colonial conquerors, see Susan Marsden, "Northwest Coast Adawx Study," in *First Nations Cultural Heritage and Law: Case Studies, Voices, and Perspectives,* eds. Catherine Bell and Val Napoleon (Seattle, WA: University of Washing Press, 2008), 133.

51. Posey, "Selling Grandma," 201.

52. Annex to WIPO, The Protection of Traditional Knowledge: Revised Objectives and Principles, WIPO/GRTK/IC/11/5(c) (reproducing WIPO/GRTKF/IC/9/5) (26 April 2007) ("draft WIPO TK provisions," first circulated in this form as WIPO, The Protection of Traditional Knowledge: Revised Objects and Principles, WIPO/GRTKF/IC/8/5 (8 April 2005), Art. 3.

53. Antony Taubman, "Genetic Resources," in Silke von Lewinski, *Indigenous Heritage and Intellectual Property,* 209–10.

54. See, for example, Janice G. Weiner, *Protection of Folklore: A Political and Legal Challenge* 58 IIC (1987). This is in sharp contrast with Narayana Menon, "A Definition of Folklore," INTERGU Yearbook 209, vol. 4 (1979) (stating "I do not think it refers to anything of the lower strata of societies as such").

55. Universal Declaration of Human Rights, Art. 2, G.A. Res. 217A (III), U.N. Doc. A/RES/217(III) (10 December 1948) (hereinafter Declaration). See generally, International Covenant on Civil and Political Rights, Dec. 16, 1966, U.N.T.S. 3; S. Exec. Doc. D, 95-2 (1978) (hereinafter ICCPR); S. Treaty Doc. No. 95-19, 6 I.L.M. 360 (1967); International Covenant on Economic, Social and Cultural Rights, Dec. 16, 1966, 993 U.N.T.S. 3, S. Exec. Doc. D, 95-2 (1978); S. Treaty Doc. No. 95-19, 6 I.L.M. 360 (1967) (hereinafter ICESR).

56. Declaration, Art. 17.

57. ICESR, Art. 15(c); Declaration, Art. 27(2).

58. ICCPR, Art. 27.

59. Ibid., ICESR, Art. 2.; Declaration, Art. 2.

60. ICCPR.; ICESR, Art. 1.

61. ICCPR, Art. 1.; ICESR, Art. 1.

62. Hernandez-Truyol and Powell, *Just Trade,* 209.

63. *Convention No. 107,* International Labour Organization (hereinafter ILO), ¶3, (2012), accessed May 9, 2015, www.ilo.org/indigenous/Conventions/no107/lang--en/index.htm.

64. See generally, *Convention No. 169,* ILO, accessed May 9, 2015, www.ilo.org/indigenous/Conventions/ no169/lang--en/index.htm.

65. United Nations Declaration on the Rights of Indigenous Peoples, G.A. Res. 61/925, U.N. Doc. A/RES/61/925 (September 13, 2007), Art. 4, 46 I.L.M. 1013 (2007) (hereinafter UNDRIP).

66. Ibid., Art. 7.

67. Ibid., Art. 30.

68. For a description of the general workings and tensions between the Organisation Africaine de la Propriete Intellectuelle (OAPI) and African Regional Industrial Property Organisation (ARIPO), two African regional organizations, see generally, Adebambo Adewopo, "Developments in Intellectual Property in Africa," *International Association for the Advancement of Teaching and Research in Intellectual Property (ATRIP)*, accessed April 22, 2015, www.atrip.org/upload/files/activities/montreal2005/Adewopo%20Dev.%20of%20IP%20Africa.doc. Ayoyemi Lawal Arowolo, "A Continental Approach to Protecting Traditional Knowledge Systems and Related Resources in Africa," accessed April 22, 2015, papers.ssrn.com/sol3/papers.cfm?abstract_id=1313582.

69. African Intellectual Property Organization, Agreement Revising the Bangui Agreement of March 2, 1977, on the creation of an African Intellectual Property Organization, (Bangui [Central African Republic], February 24, 1999) accessed April 21, 2015, www.wipo.int/wipolex/en/other_treaties/details.jsp?treaty_id=227.

70. African Intellectual Property Organization, Agreement Revising the Bangui Agreement of March 2, 1977, on the creation of an African Intellectual Property Organization, (Bangui [Central African Republic], February 24, 1999) accessed April 21, 2015, www.wipo.int/wipolex/en/other_treaties/details.jsp?treaty_id=227.

71. African Intellectual Property Organization, Agreement Revising the Bangui Agreement of March 2, 1977, on the creation of an African Intellectual Property Organization, (Bangui [Central African Republic], February 24, 1999) accessed April 21, 2015, www.wipo.int/wipolex/en/other_treaties/details.jsp?treaty_id=227.

72. African Intellectual Property Organization, Agreement Revising the Bangui Agreement of March 2, 1977, on the creation of an African Intellectual Property Organization, (Bangui [Central African Republic], February 24, 1999) accessed April 21, 2015, www.wipo.int/wipolex/en/other_treaties/details.jsp?treaty_id=227.

73. African Intellectual Property Organization, Agreement Revising the Bangui Agreement of March 2, 1977, on the creation of an African Intellectual Property Organization, (Bangui [Central African Republic], February 24, 1999) accessed April 21, 2015, www.wipo.int/wipolex/en/other_treaties/details.jsp?treaty_id=227.

74. Gerard Bodeker, "Traditional Medical Knowledge, Intellectual Property Rights and Benefit Sharing," *Cardozo Journal of International & Comparative Law* 11 (2003–2004): 785, 786.

75. Anthony B. Cunningham, "Ethics, Biodiversity, and New Natural Products Development," *WWF-World Wide Fund For Nature* (Sept. 1996).

76. Convention on Biological Diversity, Art. 15, (5 June 1992), 1760 U.N.T.S. 79, 143; 31 I.L.M. 818 (1992) (hereinafter the CBD).

77. Hernandez-Truyol and Powell, *Just Trade*, 222 citing the CBD, Art. 15(5).

78. United Nations Declaration of Indigenous People, Art. 29.

79. See Ibid.

80. See generally, Agreement on Trade-Related Aspects of Intellectual Property Rights, Apr. 15, 1994, Marrakesh Agreement Establishing the World Trade Organization, Annex 1C, The Legal Texts: The Results of The Uruguay Round of Multilateral Trade Negotiations, 1869 U.N.T.S. 299, 22 I.L.M. 1197 (1994) (hereinafter TRIPS Agreement).

81. See generally, ibid. Berne Convention of the Protection of Literary and Artistic Works, Sept. 9, 1886, (revised in Paris, 24 July 1971, and amended in 1979), S. Treaty Doc. No. 99-27 (1986); Paris Convention for the Protection of Industrial Property, as last revised at the Stockholm Revision Conference, July 14, 1967, 21 U.S.T. 1583; 828 U.N.T.S. 303; Treaty on Intellectual Property in Respect of Integrated Circuits, May 26, 1989, 28 I.L.M. 1477.

82. Hernandez-Truyol and Powell, *Just Trade*, 216.

83. TRIPS Agreement, Art. 16.1.

84. Ibid., Art. 33.

85. Ibid., Art. 10.1.

86. World Trade Organization, Trade Related Aspects of Intellectual Property Systems (TRIPS) (2002), accessed April 22, 2015, www.wto.org/english/thewto_e/minist_e/min01_e/mindecl_e.htm.

87. World Trade Organization, Council for Trade-Related Aspects of Intellectual Property Rights, (8 February 2006), accessed April 22, 2015, www.wto.org/english/tratop_e/trips_e/ta_docs_e/4_ipcw368rev1_e.pdf.

88. World Trade Organization, Council for Trade-Related Aspects of Intellectual Property Rights, (8 February 2006), 3–9, accessed April 22, 2015, www.wto.org/english/tratop_e/trips_e/ta_docs_e/4_ipcw368rev1_e.pdf.

89. World Trade Organization, Council for Trade-Related Aspects of Intellectual Property Rights (8 February 2006), 13, 14–27, accessed April 22, 2015, www.wto.org/english/tratop_e/trips_e/ta_docs_e/4_ipcw368rev1_e.pdf.

90. World Trade Organization, Council for Trade-Related Aspects of Intellectual Property Rights (8 February 2006), 13, 28–67, accessed April 22, 2015, www.wto.org/english/tratop_e/trips_e/ta_docs_e/4_ipcw368rev1_e.pdf.

91. "About the Nagoya Protocol," *Convention on Biological Diversity* (2012), accessed May 9, 2015, www.cbd.int/abs/about/#objective.

92. Ibid.

93. "Nagoya gives new context to old views in intellectual property council," *World Trade Organisation* (1 March 2011) ¶8 (hereinafter Nagoya article). accessed May 9, 2015, www.wto.org/english/news_e/news11_e/trip_01mar11_e.htm.

94. "What is the Convention?" *Convention on Biological Diversity* (2012), accessed May 9, 2015, www.cbd.int/convention/.

95. "Introduction," *Convention on Biological Diversity* (2012), accessed May 9, 2015, www.cbd.int/ intro/.

96. Kabir Bavikatte and Daniel F. Robinson, "Towards a People's History of the Law: Biocultural Jurisprudence and the Nagoya Protocol on Access and Benefit Sharing," *Law, Environment and Development Journal* 35, vol. 7(1) (2011): 37.

97. Surendra J. Patel, "Can the Intellectual Property Rights System Serve the Interests of Indigenous Knowledge," *Valuing Local Knowledge Indigenous People and Intellectual Property Rights*, eds. Stephen B. Brush and Noreen Stabinsky (Washington, DC: Island Press, 1996), 306.

98. Veit Koester, "The Nagoya Protocol on ABS: ratification by the EU and its Member States and implementation challenges," *No. 3: Biodiversity, Institut du développement durable et des relations internationales [IDDRI]* (12 June 2012): 6.

99. Ibid.

100. Ibid.

101. United Nations Convention on Biological Diversity (1993) accessed April 21, 2015, www.cbd.int/convention/text/.

102. Koester, "The Nagoya Protocol on ABS," 6.

103. Ibid.; see also, United Nations Convention on Biological Diversity (1993), 98.

104. Simon West, "Institutionalized Exclusion: The Political Economy of Benefit Sharing and Intellectual Property," *Law, Environment and Development Journal* 8, vol. 1 (2012): 24.

105. Ibid. (citing Owain Williams, "Life patents, TRIPS and the international political economy of biotechnology," in *The International Politics of Biotechnology: Investigating Global Futuresi*, ed. Alan Russell and John Volger, (Manchester, U.K.: Manchester University Press, 2000), 67–68); Patel, "Can the Intellectual Property Rights System Serve," 308 (indigenous peoples preserved "[innovations and ideas] and passed them on to succeeding generations").

106. West, "Institutionalized Exclusion," 24 (citing Williams, "Life patents, TRIPS and the international political economy of biotechnology," 67–68).

107. Patel, "Can the Intellectual Property Rights System Serve," 318.

108. Ibid. "What is the Nagoya Protocol and what is its objective?"

109. Koester, "The Nagoya Protocol on ABS," 13.

110. Ibid.

111. Ibid.

112. Ibid.

113. Ibid. But, see West, "Institutionalized Exclusion," 40 ("However, the Protocol has omitted a list of potential 'checkpoints' . . .").

114. Bavikatte and Robinson, "Towards a People's History of the Law," 48.

115. Koester, "The Nagoya Protocol on ABS," 13. See also West, "Institutionalized Exclusion," 38 ("The relative success or failure of the Protocol . . . depends on the extent to which rules regarding access and benefit-sharing can be made to 'stick' on both user and provider countries . . ."); Bavikatte and Robinson, "Towards a People's History of the Law," 38 ("[m]any users of genetic resources and associated traditional knowledge have not necessarily felt obliged to follow principles of prior informed consent and benefit-sharing" [internal citations omitted]).

116. "Negotiations on CBD-TRIPS Relationship Still Deadlocked After Adoption of ABS Protocol," IISD Reporting Services, ¶2, (1 March 2010), accessed May 9, 2015, biodiversity-l.iisd .org/news/negotiations-on-cbd-trips-relationship-still -deadlocked-after-adoption-of-absprotocol/.

117. Nagoya article, ¶5.

118. "110301 Debate on Access to Medicine and Biodiversity at the WTO," Africa Europe Faith and Justice Network (undated) §2 ¶2 (hereinafter 110301 Debate), accessed May 9, 2015, www .aefjn.org/index.php/357/articles/id -110301-debate-on-access-to-medicines-and-bio diversity-at-the-wto.html.

119. Nagoya article, ¶5.

120. Ibid., ¶3.

121. Ibid.

122. Rodolphe Paternostre, Comment, "The Nagoya Protocol: A Legally Sound Framework for an Effective Regime?" (master's thesis, Utrecht University, 2011), 79, dspace.library.uu.nl/handle/1874/213518.

123. "Positions unchanged on biodiversity issues, 'Para 6' system," *TWN: Third World Network*, ¶9 (10 March 2011), accessed May 9, 2015, www.twn.my/title2/health.info/2011/health20110303.htm.

124. Nagoya article, ¶¶3 and 5.

125. Positions unchanged on biodiversity issues, "Para 6" system, ¶10.

126. Nagoya article, ¶7.

127. Ibid.

128. 110301 Debate, §2, ¶5.

129. Nagoya article, ¶9.

130. Report, *What Comes After Nagoya?* United Nations Conference on Trade and Development and International Center for Trade and Sustainable Development (3 March 2011), 3 (quoting Professor Carlos Correa, University of Buenos Aires/South Centre), accessed May 9, 2015, ictsd.org/downloads/2011/05/ictsd-unctad-what-comes-after-nagoya-report.pdf.

131. Bavikatte and Robinson, "Towards a People's History of the Law," 48.

132. West, "Institutionalized Exclusion," 41.

133. Ibid., 21.

134. Ibid., 22.

135. Ibid.

136. Ibid.

137. Ibid., 41.

138. Ibid., 23.

139. Ibid., 42–43.

140. Nagoya article, ¶14.

141. Paternostre, "The Nagoya Protocol," 28 (quoting S. Laird, *Biodiversity and Traditional Knowledge: Equitable Partnerships in Practice* (2002), xxvi.). See also generally, Kerry ten Kate and Sarah A. Laird, eds. *The Commercial Use of Biodiversity: Access to Genetic Resources and Benefit Sharing* (London: Earthscan Publications Ltd., 1999).

142. Bryan A. Liang, "Global Governance: Promoting biodiversity and protecting indigenous communities against biopiracy," *Journal Commercial Biotechnology* 17 (2011): 248, ¶6.

143. Ibid., ¶7. *See also* Koester, "The Nagoya Protocol on ABS," 11 ("[TRIPS] patent provisions are perceived by developing countries as potentially leading to biopiracy and misappropriation of [traditional knowledge].").

144. *What Comes after Nagoya?*, 3 (quoting Professor Carlos Correa, University of Buenos Aires/South Centre).

145. Nagoya article, ¶13 (Bolivia, with the support of Venezuela, went as far as submitting a proposal, first presented in March 2010, to amend TRIPS so that patenting of all life forms is banned. 110301 Debate, 115 at §2, ¶6; Nagoya article, ¶¶12 and 17).

146. Bavikatte and Robinson, "Towards a People's History of the Law," 29.

147. *What Comes after Nagoya?*, 4 (quoting Antony Taubman from the WTO).

148. Ibid. (quoting Antony Taubman from the WTO).

149. Ibid.

150. Ibid.

151. Koester, "The Nagoya Protocol on ABS," 11.

152. Mitsuo Matsushita, Thomas J. Schoenbaum and Petros C. Mavroidis, *The World Trade Organization: Law, Practice, and Policy* (Oxford, UK: Oxford University Press, 2003), 408.

153. Hernandez-Truyol and Powell, *Just Trade*, 217.

154. Convention on Biological Diversity, Art. 15, (5 June 1992), 1760 U.N.T.S. 79, 143; 31 I.L.M. 818 (hereinafter the CBD).

155. International Institute for Sustainable Development (hereinafter IISD) and ICTSD, "Intellectual Property Rights" (February 2003), compiled in *Doha Round Briefing Series* (February 2003): 4.

156. Ibid.

157. Silke von Lewinski, "Introduction," in *Indigenous Heritage and Intellectual Property*, 36.

158. WIPO, "Intellectual Property and Traditional Cultural Expressions/ Folklore," *Booklet* no. 1 (hereinafter WIPO Folklore): 3.

159. Von Lewinski, "Introduction," 36.

160. Ibid.

161. Ibid.

162. WIPO Folklore, 3.

163. Ibid.

164. Von Lewinski, "Introduction," 36.

165. WIPO Folklore, 3.

166. Ibid.

167. WIPO, "Intellectual Property Needs and Expectations of Traditional Knowledge Holders" (2001), June 5, 2015, www.wipo.int/tk/en/tk/ffm/report.

168. WIPO, "Roundtables in Intellectual Property and Traditional Knowledge," described in Agnés Lucas-Schloetter, "Folklore," in *Indigenous Heritage and Intellectual Property: Genetic Resources, Knowledge and Folklore*, ed. von Lewinski (The Netherlands: Kluwer Law International BV, 2008), 461.

169. WIPO Folklore, 3.

170. Ibid., 4.

171. von Lewinski, "Introduction," 37.

172. All these materials are available from the Secretariat of WIPO cited in WIPO Folklore, 4.

173. *See* Raj Bhala, *International Trade Law: Interdisciplinary Theory and Practice*, 3rd ed., (LEXISNEXIS, 2008), 474–78 (critical review of the exploitation of rhetoric purportedly aimed at assisting the poor in both developing and developed countries).

174. Kenneth J. Armour and Peter S. Harrison, "Indigenous Rights and IP Protection," *World Patent Information* 29 (2007): 261.

175. Thomas Kuhn, *The Structure of Scientific Revolutions* (Chicago: University of Chicago Press, 1970), viii.

176. Lieh-Ching Chang, "An Examination of Cross-Cultural Negotiation: Using Hofstede Framework," *Journal of American Academy of Business* 2 (March 2003): 567, accessed June 5, 2015, www.aeflup.com/ficheiros/Cultural%20Negotiation.pdf.

177. Ibid.

178. Rodolfo Stavenhagen, "Cultural Rights: A Social Science Perspective," in *Economic, Social and Cultural Rights*, 2nd ed., eds. Ashbjørn Eide, Catrina Krause and Allan Rosas (Kluwer Law International, 2001), 87.

179. Ibid.

180. Ibid., 88.

181. Ibid., 89.

182. Ibid., 89.

183. First Generation or "Civil and Political Rights" include the right to nondiscrimination based on race, gender, language, religion, culture, family, ethnicity, national origin, and social origin. Hernandez-Truyol and Powell, *Just Trade*, 59. Realistically, "first," "second," and "third" generation rights are inextricably intertwined but may be analytically parsed apart, to some extent.

184. Third Generation or "Solidarity Rights" include, ironically, the rights to both development as well as environment, peace, democracy, a common heritage, communication and humanitarian assistance. Hernandez-Truyol and Powell, *Just Trade*, 61.

185. *About the Nagoya Protocol*. There are other regionally based suggestions as well. For example, Latin American reforms, in relation to protecting the rights of indigenous peoples in general has led to the following recommendations: (1) support the U.N. indigenous programs that use the Human Rights model; (2) increase funding for legal education and human rights training for indigenous tribes; (3) advocate for increasing use of indigenous law for local use; (4) maintain and continue the attempts to develop even more effective international indigenous rights instruments. Justin Dargin, "Indian Question in Latin America: An Overview of the Legal and Social Position of Indigenous Peoples," Guild Practitioner 63, (2006): 149, 154–55. See also: "Right of Food of Indigenous People in Latin America," accessed May 9, 2015, www.fian.org/resources/documents/others/the-right-to-food-of-indigenous-peoples-in-latin-america/pdf.

2

Law In and As Culture[1]

CULTURE AND PARADIGMS

This chapter generally characterizes the paradigmatic nature of culture. The underlying method of this chapter (and book) may be characterized as having autoethnographic dimensions. This chapter specifically deals with case studies of two particular cultural clashes occurring between indigenous peoples and majoritarian cultures. To perform this analysis, this chapter adapts Hofstede, Hofstede, and Minkov's[2] cultural rubric of individualism versus communitarianism to dissect the cultural conflicts embedded in the disagreement between the German band, Enigma, and the Ami tribal couple, the Duanas, over the ownership of an Ami traditional folk song. In addition, this chapter also uses Hofstede, Hofstede, and Minkov's cultural schema of hierarchy versus egalitarianism[3] to draw out key elements of the cultural conflict between the Chilean government and the Mapuche/Pehuenche tribe over control of the right to build a dam that would flood the tribe's ancestral lands, and uses an intersectional approach to analyze the Australian Aboriginal artists' struggle for recognition and intellectual property protection. Then, this chapter concretely proposes general programs of action and specific strategies in potentially overcoming these cultural barriers in the attempt to protect, in a nuanced way, indigenous peoples' intellectual property rights.

REGARDING HUMOR AND CULTURAL LOGICS

The following miscommunications illustrate the intricacies of translating across languages and more importantly, translating the internal cultural logic of humor to an outsider or "foreign" culture.

> A few years ago, the Dairy Association led a wildly successful marketing campaign throughout the United States built on the slogan "Got Milk?" Unfortunately, when the campaign was exported to Mexico, the translation read, "Are you lactating?"[4]

> A U.S. software company suffered from having the name of its industry translated as an "underwear" company when launching internationally.[5]

> A European company couldn't succeed at selling its chocolate and fruit dessert called "Zit" in the United States nor could the Finns who attempted to sell "Super Piss," a Finnish product for unfreezing car door locks.[6]

To those of us who get the joke, to explain the joke, recontextualizing imagery from one of T. S. Eliot's poems, is to spread the joke out like a patient etherized on a table.[7] To dissect the joke is to kill the joke. As Arthur Koestler noted, the cultural logic of a joke comes from the sudden juxtaposition of two things that are normally kept separate; that sudden juxtaposition produces a certain tension that must be dispelled through laughter.[8] The "logic" that directs what is normally kept apart, as opposed to what usually accompany each other, resides in the culture that generates this matrix of meaning. The cathartic power of the joke lies precisely in the seamlessness or invisibility of its cultural logic, which, in humor, is momentarily disturbed, thus yielding a different way of viewing and experiencing reality.

Culture is "paradigmatic" in the sense in which Thomas Kuhn originally used the word in 1966—well before its explosion into ubiquity in several disciplines.[9] Simply described, a paradigm is the cultural matrix that directs attention to certain questions and ignores others, and maps acceptable methods of attempting to solve these selected problems for a particular community at a particular point in time.[10] A rough analogy to how paradigms (and cultures, as paradigmatic) operate is the child's game of seeing different "animals" in an unruly squiggle of lines, curves, and splotches of color. There is no foolproof way of interpreting a jagged line or a small dot. And yet, once the child has grown accustomed to interpreting these rather ambiguous markings in a roughly uniform and meaningful way (i.e., once she has acquired a mental "model" of how to interpret these markings), then these pictures are no longer random configurations. And as the child habitually refers to this mental "pattern," she grows more skillful at uncovering more and more "animals" carefully camouflaged by the tangled undergrowth of shapes and hues. And as more "animals" are successfully mentally "captured" via reference to this "model" or "pattern," the more the "model" or "pattern" becomes equated with the "obvious" or "common-sensical." An artful example of this is illustrated in M. C. Escher's *Sea and Sky*.

In Escher's *Sea and Sky*, the figures of the fowl and the fish are at the topmost and bottom portions are evident. The mid-line figures, however, are ambiguous and may be interpreted as either fish or fowl, depending upon which cultural lens is "common-sensically" referenced because culture is "the way in which a group of people solve problems and reconcile dilemmas."[11] And because our culture is "like water to fish,"[12] we are nourished and limited by it in ways that defy rational thought processes; we either "see" the "fish" or the "fowl" first as a hardwired, or amygdala-based response.[13] Culture is the "collective programming of the mind,"[14] and entails sharing "particular symbols, meanings, images, rule structures, habits, values and information processing and transformational patterns."[15]

More concretely illustrated in relation to traditional Indian medicines, Arjun Appadurai argues that meanings connected to material objects are dependent upon the social-cultural context in which they are situated and function.[16] For Appadurai, sociocultural contexts, which he terms "arenas" or "sites," are performatively given meaning by their transactions and meanings. Thus, different values emerge, in relation to the same object depending on the arena in which it is situated: for example, the same object is valued differently when it is a commercial item sold at an auction; a holy object worshipped in a temple; or a revered memento in a home viewed as a relic of one's ancestors. Appadurai's framework has yielded a host of scholarly works that argue that modern pharmaceuticals have different "life phases" (and different significations and commercial valuations) as they are manufactured, traded, prescribed, and consumed.[17] In addition to functioning essentially as coping strategies for a lack of well-being, generally understood, medicines signify cultural ideas about health, illness, and therapy. Thus, as Maarten Bode argues:

> Ayurvedic and Unani medicines are framed by a variety of arenas. For example, in the context of the family these substances are tokens of nurturance; in the national arena they are proof of Indian spirituality vis-a\`-vis Western materiality; and in the social context the consumption of Ayurvedic and Unani medicines testifies to a wholesome lifestyle and ecological awareness. And as prescriptions of traditional physicians of high repute and moral status, Ayurvedic and Unani medicines become signals of wisdom and are conceptualized as gifts to ailing humanity of Hindu rishis (seers) and Muslim

> tabibs (wise men). However, when Ayurvedic and Unani medicines feature on the price lists of manufacturers they are merchandi[s]e.[18]

While this chapter adopts many of Bode's insights, it refuses a reductionist focus on commodification, and retains Appadurai's broader framework, with its multiple cultural arenas of signification and valuation, in which the meanings and values of a "thing" are always already contested and negotiated even as they are rooted in multiple intersecting frames, some of which are capable of integration or reconciliation, and others of which remain fundamentally at odds with each other. Thus, this chapter's (and book's) method is, to some extent, as gestured to earlier, inevitably autoethnographic. It is written to explore how lawyers and clients could potentially interact effectively in legal negotiation and counseling situations, where cultural clashes between the client's and lawyer's cultures, the majoritarian culture, the culture of law, and other embedded layers of culture, could cause potential conflicts. It is an attempt to work across differences, while both respecting and acknowledging them.

"Autoethnography" is an offshoot of critical communication, sociological, and symbolic interactionist studies that explores how the study of culture ("ethnos") is always already intertwined with the self ("auto") that weaves the narration.[19] It is principally qualitative, rather than quantitative.

> Generally characterized, qualitative researchers stress the socially constructed nature of reality, the intimate relationship between the researcher and what is studied, and the situational constraints that shape inquiry. Such researchers emphasize the value-laden nature of inquiry. They seek answers to questions that stress how social experience is created and given meaning.[20]

Thus, this chapter (and book) starts from the conviction that there is no omniscient perspective from which one can record cultural interactions from a clinical distance. This does not mean there is no such thing as "objectivity," but that the notion of "objectivity" itself reflects a complex, historical, and sociological unfolding in which participant-observers are always already implicated, even as when such participant-observers function as lawyers and are trained to deal principally with facts.

These complexities are magnified even more when indigenous populations,[21] attempting to protect their traditional knowledge (TK), expressions of folklore (EoF),[22] ancestral lands, and cultural identities, come in contact with either the culture of international globalization, or the majoritarian culture of their own country. Yet the issue is even more complex, as what is at stake is not simply cultural difference, but cultural difference as imbricated with power differentials. As Christopher May has argued, there is an emergent global politics of intellectual property.[23] May points out how inequitable relations of power are camouflaged under the seemingly neutral rubric of "international standards" and in keeping with that façade, that there is a presumption of equality in the global politic that lies underneath multiple social and economic imbalances that mark relations between (and within) countries.[24] And indeed, May is not alone in arguing that the concept of intellectual property is culturally European in its historical genesis, and thus, Eurocentric assumptions inform its modes of classification, identification, and operation.[25]

In this chapter, two particular cultural clashes are analyzed, both in terms of general pragmatic strategies and a review of their actual resolution. First, the chapter analyzes the confrontation between an individualistic capitalist culture and a communitarian economically subsistent culture. Then, the chapter evaluates the clash between a hierarchical majoritarian government determined to join the race toward development at all costs, and a comparatively egalitarian coalition composed of tribal members (and sympathizers) equally determined to preserve their traditions and resources.

EXAMPLES OF CULTURAL CONFLICTS: INDIVIDUALISM VS. COMMUNITARIANISM AND HIERARCHY VS. EGALITARIANISM

Enigma versus Difang and Igay Duana: Individualism versus Communitarianism

The husband and wife team, Difang Duana (Kuo Ying-Nan) and Igay/Agay Duana (Kuo Hsiu-chu)[26] were betel nut leaf farmers and members of the Ami tribe from Taiwan.[27] In 1988, the couple traveled to France to sing on a tour, for which they, and approximately thirty other aboriginal Taiwanese artists, were paid fifteen dollars a day.[28] Their performances were recorded without their knowledge by the Institute for World Cultures, part of the French National Education Ministry. These recordings[29] were compiled into an "anonymous" collection of "Taiwanese aboriginal songs."[30] The French government sold the recording, again without seeking permission and devoid of any kind of notice or public announcement, to EMI Music, a large record company.[31] EMI then authorized Enigma, a German rock band, to use and edit an excerpt from the Duanas' "Elders' Drinking Song" or "Weeding and Paddyfield Song No. 1,"[32] (in other versions, described as "Palang," a host's welcoming song[33]) to become part of the background in Enigma's song, "Return to Innocence."[34] "Return to Innocence," which remixed two minutes of the Duanas' unauthorized recording, achieved a high media profile partly because it was used to promote the 1996 Olympic Games.[35] According to the Duanas'/Kuos' attorney, Huang Shui-Lan, the first nine seconds of both the Duanas' "Jubilant Drinking Song" and "Return to Innocence" were identical, and that over half of "Return to Innocence" incorporated some parts of the "Jubilant Drinking Song."[36] The song was so popular that it stayed for thirty-two weeks on Billboard Magazine's International Top 100 hits,[37] eventually resulting in the sale of more than six million copies of the album.[38]

From the very beginning, the contrast between Enigma's culture of individualism, infused with the forces of global capitalism, and the Duanas' culture of communitarianism and subsistent economics was clear. Nevertheless, to further dissect how legal conflicts entail cultural conflicts at numerous levels, this chapter adapts a schema initially developed by Hofstede, Pedersen, and Hofstede.[39] Hofstede, Pedersen, and Hofstede outlined basic communicative characteristics of extreme individualists and extreme communitarians[40] that are useful in analyzing the identity-related and economic-based conflicts captured in this case.

One of the dimensions of culture that Hofstede, Hofstede, and Minkov studied in their pioneering work is the dimension of individualism versus collectivism (which is rephrased as "communitarianism" in this chapter because of the negative connotations that accompany the word, "collectivism").[41] Individualistic cultures, such as the American culture, tend to value personal achievement, innovation, and autonomy above all other traits. In these cultures, individuals tend to exclusively look out for their own and their nuclear families' interests.[42] Thus, individualistic cultures place a high premium on "self-sufficiency, personal time, freedom, challenge, and extrinsic motivators such as material rewards, honesty, talking things out, privacy and individual rights."[43] In contrast, communitarian cultures are characterized by powerful group-oriented identities. They are "societies in which people from birth onward are integrated into strong, cohesive in-groups, which throughout people's lifetime continue to protect them in exchange for unquestioning loyalty."[44] Thus, communitarian cultures, such as Asian cultures, value "group responsibility, harmony, social order, relationships and loyalty."[45]

Using the cultural rubric of individualism versus communitarianism to analyze the rhetorical registers of both groups, Michael Cretu, the spokesperson for Enigma, the German rock band, epitomized the extreme individualist view through his motive, language and nonverbal communications throughout the conflict. In general, extreme individualists typically reflect a self-centered vernacular, frequently using the words "I" and "me."[46] Mr. Cretu emphasized that he thought the Duanas' recording was in the public domain and kept stressing his lack of deliberate intent in appropriating the Duanas' recording.[47] Nonverbally, an extreme individualist will make eye contact freely and when they are in groups, they are likely to stand out visually.[48] Correspondingly, Mr. Cretu stood out as the star and spokesperson for Enigma; other band members were never visible during coverage of this story.[49] Furthermore, Mr. Cretu rhetorically rationalized his extreme individualistic motivation to accumulate individual wealth and prestige by vehemently defending his individual innocence while seeking to maximize profit by minimizing reputational damage.[50]

In stark contrast, the Duanas, who spoke for the Ami tribe, embodied the extreme communitarian ideal. Extreme communitarians can be very silent, especially when in the company of a group of outsiders, and typically use the word "we" instead of "I."[51] Thus, the Duanas emphasized tribal ownership and heritage of the song, as an expression of folklore—a communal creation and property. The Duanas sought recognition, first for the Ami tribe and only secondarily for themselves as performers.[52] In addition, extreme communitarians tend to be physically very close with in-groups but reserved with out-groups.[53] Correspondingly, the Duanas always seemed networked with their community. They learned about Enigma's use of their recording only because a friend had told them about it; the Duanas always underlined their identities as members of the tribe.[54] Finally, an extreme communitarian will tend toward gaining recognition for the tribe first, honoring the connection with the tribe. As classic extreme communitarians, the Duanas only wanted to be allowed to perform the song at the Olympics principally as ambassadors of Ami culture initially and did not at first seek financial remuneration.[55]

Thus, in terms of general value systems, the key elements of the cultures of extreme individualists versus extreme communitarians may also be sketched comparatively. An extreme individualist will believe that honest persons will speak their mind to everyone and anyone while an extreme communitarian tends to believe that one's in-group constitutes the only audience who should be trusted.[56] While an extreme individualist communicates in low-context, explicit concepts where the listener must adapt to the speaker, an extreme communitarian uses an imprecise communication style with discreet, nonverbal cues such as crucial tonal cues and pauses wherein the speaker must adapt to the listeners, to make sure the audience understands the speaker.[57] Finally, an extreme individualist believes that the successful completion of a task takes precedence over relationships while an extreme communitarian believes that relationships are always more important than the task at hand.[58]

As a final note, although this book uses the Duanas and the Ami tribe as a key example to point out the clash between communitarian and individualist cultures, there are numerous examples of such clashes. For instance, *Milpurrurru & Others v. Indofurn Pty. Ltd. & Others* involved the importation into Australia of a number of carpets woven in Vietnam that incorporated Aboriginal designs.[59] Three living Aboriginal artists and the Public Trustee, acting on behalf of the estates of five deceased Aboriginal artists, mounted the claim. It is important to note that in this particular case, each of the artists raising a claim had works that were either reproduced in portfolios of Aboriginal art, which had been produced for the Australian National Gallery (ANG), or in portfolios published by the Australian Government Printer for the Australian Information Service (AIS).[60] As in the case of the Duanas, therefore, each of these claimants were recognized "authors" of aboriginal artwork; nevertheless, the grounds upon which they claimed relief were inextricably bound with communal traditions in the generation of the particular works of art. For instance, as part of the rationale for the grounds of relief from the clear infringements of their work, the claimants showed that the painting techniques and the adoption of totemic and other traditional images and symbols usually involved significant creation stories, strictly controlled by Aboriginal law and custom. Because artworks are an important venue of transmitting these stories, the claimants pointed out that errors in the reproduction of such sacred symbols could cause deep offense to the tribe. Furthermore, the claimants pointed out that traditionally, "the right to create paintings and other artworks depicting creation and dreaming stories and to use preexisting designs and clan totems resided in the traditional custodians of the stories."[61] Under Aboriginal law, because the creation and managements of such symbols were crucial to the very lifeblood of the tribe, it was the responsibility of the traditional "owners" to act in order to preserve the "dreaming" and to punish those who had endangered the integrity of this process.[62] Thus, it is clear that the justificatory mechanisms that shored up the claim were tied up with the appeal to a communitarian form of "ownership" of these symbols.

An even more recent case, *John Bulun Bulun & Another v. R & T Textiles Pty Ltd.*, attempted to carry the distinction between individual and communitarian ownership of traditional cultural expressions (TCEs) even more, and to authorize communitarian ownership as just as valid a legal ground for relief as individual ownership. This case, like *Milpurrurru & Others*, involved the importation and sale in Australia of printed clothing fabric that infringed the individual copyright of the known Aboriginal artist, Mr. John Bulun Bulun, in his nationally renowned work, "Magpie Geese and Water Lillies [sic] at the Waterhole."[63] The legal proceedings, initiated by Mr. Bulun Bulun and by Mr. George Mihpurrurru, began on February 27, 1997. Both claimants were members of the Ganalbingu people; Ganalbingu country is located in Arnhem Land, in the Northern Territory of Australia.[64] Mr. Bulun Bulun raised an individual claim as the legal owner of the copyright in the painting and sought remedies for infringement under the Australian Copyright Act 1968. On the other hand, Mr. Milpurrurru (one of the claimants in the *Milpurrurru & Others* case) mounted a claim based on his own individual ownership, and a communitarian-based claim, as a representative of the Ganalbingu tribe, based on the reasoning that the Ganalbingu people were the equitable owners of the copyright subsisting in the painting.

The basis for Mr. Milpurrurru's communitarian-based claim bore a striking resemblance to the ground for relief sought in the *Milpurrurru & Others* case. The waterhole depicted in Mr. Milpurrurru's painting was Djulibinyamurr, which served as the principal totemic well for the artist's clan. As a TCE, it depicted the sacred place from which Barnda, the legendary long-necked turtle creator ancestor of the Ganalbingu people, had emerged. As in the prior *Milpurrurru & Others* case, Mr. Bulun Bulun's affidavit explained that because his ancestors were granted the responsibility of maintaining and preserving the traditional "corpus of ritual knowledge," part of that duty lay in creating paintings in compliance with the laws and rituals of the Ganalbingu people. Thus, Mr. Bulun Bulun, though his was an individual claim, stated that unauthorized reproductions of his art work "[threaten] the whole system and ways that underpin the stability and continuance of [the artist's] society. [These reproductions interfere] with the relationship between people, their creator ancestors and the land given to the people by their creator ancestor."[65] Clearly, Mr. Bulun Bulun's individually based claim was tied up with a claim based on a communitarian ownership of the copyright that inhered in his painting.

I will reserve analyzing the legal resolutions of these two cases for a later chapter. Similarly, for organizational purposes, working across these differences in a negotiation or counseling context will be discussed later in this chapter. For now, the chapter turns to outlining the next cultural clash studied here: the clash between peoples with hierarchical values and those with more egalitarian values.

The Chilean Government versus the Mapuche/Pehuenche Tribe: Hierarchy vs. Egalitarianism

Briefly sketched, in the case of the Pangue/Ralco hydroelectric project, spanning roughly from 1990 to 2002, Chile's central government and domestic courts colluded with a Spanish transnational company, Endesa, to evict systematically the Mapuche/Pehuenche people from their traditional lands in order to create dams that would power Chile's attempts to join the race toward full economic development[66] (see figure 2.1). The cultural clash between the majoritarian elite and the tribe, lying at the margins of

Figure 2.1. Cornelio Saavedra, Chilean official, at a meeting with Mapuche caciques during the first phase of the Occupation of Araucanía, 1869, Biblioteca Nacional (National Library). Author: Manuel Olascoaga (segun Álbum Gráfico Militar de Chile, Campaña del Pacífico 1879–1884, Compiled by J. Antonio Bisama Cuevas, Sociedad Imprenta y Litografía Universo, Santiago, Huérfanos 1036, Chile. 1909, Página 66). The conflict between the Mapuche people and the Chilean government is long and complex; during the "Pacification of Araucania" (1861–1883), the Mapuche tribe were defeated by Chilean and Argentine armies, and were given "mercy titles," and confined to 3,000 communal lands out of the original 10 million hectares they previously occupied.

Chile, took place against the backdrop of the Chilean government's ambitious resolve to join the sphere of developed nations through the construction of the Pangue/Ralco Hydroelectric Project in Chile's Alto BíoBío.[67] Clearly, the majoritarian elite had control of the vertical structure of power and believed it was in the best interest of Chile, as a whole, to follow their lead. The construction of the Pangue dam was facilitated by the "leverage of international capital brokered by the World Bank Group's International Finance Corporation (IFC)."[68] But to the Pehuenche/Mapuche tribe, the building of the dam meant the flooding of their ancestral lands and resources, the loss of their semi-nomadic way of life, and their cultural identity.[69] Viewing themselves as equal to any other citizen of Chile, the Pehuenche simply sought to preserve their rights as citizens.

Again, Hofstede, Hofstede, and Minkov's schematization of the dimensions of culture is invaluable in this chapter's work of providing a contrast between hierarchical and egalitarian cultures. Hofstede, Hofstede, and Minkov used the term "power-distance"[70] to define the variable that determines the degree of hierarchy (or respect for rank) that is culturally accepted in a particular society. For Hofstede, Hofstede, and Minkov, power distance is the "*extent to which the less powerful members of institutions and organizations within a country expect and accept that power is distributed unequally. Institutions* . . . [include] the family, the school, and the community; *organizations* are the places where people work."[71] Thus, whereas high-power-distance (hierarchical) cultures emphasize the dependence of subordinates upon the discretion of their superiors, low-power-distance (egalitarian) cultures expect a comparatively higher interdependence between bosses and subordinates.[72] As Walters observes in a business context:

> High power distance results in little consultation between superiors and their subordinates and emphasizes formal hierarchy, resulting in an increased level of respect for each level. Low power distance cultures tend to view the hierarchy prevalent in any corporation as less important than high power cultures, with CEOs, managers and subordinates consulting with each other from the bottom-up and top-down.[73]

Again, Hofstede, Pedersen, and Hosftede's schematization of the key elements of hierarchical culture versus egalitarian culture[74] is instructive as a summary of the essential areas of conflict between the Chilean government and the Mapuche/Pehuenche tribe. An extremely hierarchical culture, like the Chilean government believes that "might makes right" and that power is good.[75] Such a culture has a strong conviction that privileges and status symbols are "natural" to those who have access to them and are sources of pride and power.[76] Furthermore, members of hierarchical cultures believe that power, status, and privilege go together.[77] Thus, extreme hierarchical cultures prefer a centralized structure, where less powerful people are dependent on those who are more powerful.[78] By contrast, an extremely egalitarian culture, characteristic of groups such as the Pehuenche tribe, believes that inequalities among people should be minimized and privileges and status symbols are frowned upon.[79] Extreme egalitarian societies prefer a decentralized structure where there is interdependence between less and more powerful people.[80]

Having outlined the key components of these two types of cultural clashes (individualism versus communitarianism and hierarchy versus egalitarianism), this book will move into an analysis of how to work across these two types of cultural clashes, within a negotiation context, both theoretically and pragmatically, in succeeding chapters. For the next section, this chapter continues to explore where an examination of law in and as culture, generally construed, can lead, in terms of general strategies of negotiating across cultural differences.

TRANSLATING ACROSS CULTURES, WORKING ACROSS DIFFERENCES

General Programs of Action

Although David Livermore's[81] program of developing "cultural intelligence"[82] is aimed at promoting international business and Iris Burke's[83] strategies for working across cross-cultural differences is geared toward legal counseling and negotiation, both feature an autoethnographic bent as well as similar methods and objectives.[84] They each begin with knowing the self as a cultural entity, freezing the impulse to stereotype and judge others/cultures that are radically different, moving outward to study and reflect upon cultural differences, and finally enabling better communication and possibly collaboration.[85] But that movement across the inner and outer selves is a never-ending spiral and requires a feedback loop of discovery, critique, and adaptation in order to potentially forge better communicative links across cultural chasms. Table 2.1 below illustrates how the two general schemas correlate with each other.[86]

Table 2.1. A Comparison of Livermore's and Burke's General Programs of Action for Working Across Cultural Differences

	Livermore's Schema	*Burke's Schema*
Internal	**Drive**: Show the interest and confidence to adapt cross-culturally.	Learn about yourself. Do not stereotype.
Internal-External	**Knowledge:** Understand how differences such as religion, family, education, and legal and economic influences affect the way people [yourself included] think and behave.	Understand what culture is and how it works [personally and generally]. Learn about your client.
External-Internal	**Strategy:** Monitor, analyze, and adjust plans in unfamiliar cultural settings.	**Work Across Differences:** Identify conflicts. Discuss differences. Avoid binaries of morality. Avoid making judgments. You do not have to justify or change your worldview.
External	**Action:** Choose the right verbal and nonverbal behaviors, depending on context.	**Work Across Differences:** Work within/prioritize the client's worldview. Be sensitive to power imbalances. Consider three worldviews: the client's, yours, and the law's.

In contrast, Tracy Novinger, a specialist in intercultural communication, created a detailed taxonomy of various obstacles to communication, such as culturally shaped perceptions (e.g., hierarchy) and personal perceptions within a cultural framework (e.g., adaptability); and she mapped out a series of factors to watch for in relation to verbal (e.g., accent and cadence) and nonverbal processes of communication (e.g., Kinesics or body motion and Proxemics or space sense).[87] While fascinating in its intricacy and thoroughness, Novinger's list can make it easy to lose sight of the larger picture. Novinger's approach comes closest to a quantitative approach, with its catalogue of variables and focus on decoding cultural expressions.[88] To counterbalance this tendency for cataloging minutiae, this chapter highlights some of the more pragmatic strategies suggested by Hofstede and his co-authors, as well as by Fons Trompenaars and Charles Hampden-Turner,[89] in relation to the specific cultural clashes discussed in the next section.

Negotiating the Individualist versus the Communitarian Divide: Specific Strategies

Hofstede and his co-authors catalogued words with positive connotations for both individualists and communitarians.[90] They noted that what is positive for an individualist is usually negative for a communitarian, and therefore proposed using words with positive connotations for addressing the appropriate groups in order to move from the "outer" circles to the "inner" circles.[91] Table 2.2 comparatively juxtaposes words with positive connotations for extreme individualists[92] and their correlates for extreme communitarians.[93]

Trompenaars and Hampden-Turner, in turn, suggest practical tips for negotiating with groups, as well as strategies designed to promote respect, create a sense of authenticity, and enhance overall long-term efficiency in dealing with the potentially conflicting impulses of other cultures.[94] They detail several guidelines for dealing with individualists

Table 2.2. A Comparison of Positive Words for Extreme Individualists and Extreme Communitarians

Words with Positive Connotations for Extreme Individualists	*Words with Positive Connotations for Extreme Communitarians*
self, friendship, "do your own thing," contract, litigation, self-interest, self-respect, self-actualizing, individual, dignity, I, me, pleasure, adventure, guilt, privacy	we, harmony, face, obligation, sacrifice, family (in a symbolic sense), tradition, decency, honor, duty, loyalty, shame

(when one is a communitarian) and communitarians (when one is an individualist).[95] When negotiating with an individualist, a communitarian must prepare for a quick decision or a sudden offer.[96] It is important to realize that individualist negotiators are conducting business alone and therefore must retain the respect of their group.[97] The main goal of the individualist negotiator is to make a quick deal.[98] In contrast, when negotiating with a communitarian, an individualist should show patience in the consent and consultation periods.[99] When communitarian negotiators are surrounded by helpers, they enjoy a high status in the group and their main goal is to build lasting relationships.[100]

Next, this chapter turns to applying a similar approach to working across the clash between hierarchical and egalitarian cultures.

Attempting to Bridge the Divide between Hierarchy and Egalitarianism: Specific Strategies

Table 2.3 distills Hofstede and his co-authors' discussion of positive words, core values, and core distinctions for cultures of hierarchy and egalitarianism from *Cultures and Organization: Software of the Mind*.[101] The goal is not simply to catalogue them, but rather to use them in order to break down barriers and boundaries that impede effective communication and, when possible, to enable problem-solving.[102] Table 2.3 catalogues some positive words, core values and core distinctions for those belonging to an extremely hierarchical culture[103] as opposed to an extremely egalitarian culture.[104]

There is some correspondence, in terms of value systems, between this dichotomy separating cultures of hierarchy versus cultures of egalitarianism, and that of Trompenaars and Hampden-Turner's dichotomy of "ascription-oriented" cultures versus "achievement-oriented" cultures). John Barkai,[105] in *Cultural Dimension Interests, the Dance of Negotiation, and Weather Forecasting: A Perspective on Cross-Cultural Negotiation and Dispute Resolution*, also notes that status, derived from either age or seniority,

Table 2.3. A Comparison of Positive Words, Core Values, and Core Distinctions Between Extremely Hierarchical and Extremely Egalitarian Cultures

Extremely Hierarchical	*Extremely Egalitarian*
Positive words: respect, father (as a title), master, servant, older brother, younger brother, wisdom, protect, obey, orders, pleasing	**Positive words:** rights, complain, negotiate, fairness, task, necessity, co[-]determination, objectives, question, criticize
Core value: respect for status	**Core value:** equality between people
Core distinction: powerful/dependent	**Core distinction:** responsible for task X/not responsible for task X

is very important to high-power-distance (hierarchical) cultures, while opportunity and equality are the norm for low-power-distance (egalitarian) cultures.[106] Noting these general intersections, this chapter moves into identifying the following practical pointers for dealing with cultures of hierarchy (when one is more egalitarian) and for interacting with egalitarian cultures (when one is more hierarchical).[107] For example, as an egalitarian negotiating with a hierarchical culture, make sure you have a clear figurehead who commands respect from within and outside of the group.[108] Additionally, you should display respect for status and influence, and use a title that reflects the degree of influence you possess.[109] In comparison, as a hierarchical negotiator working with an egalitarian culture, make sure your focus is on pragmatic solutions.[110] Furthermore, you should display respect for knowledge and skill, and use the title that reflects your competence.[111]

Although these guidelines provide detailed strategies, the next chapter will proceed to more specific analyses of the two cases, described earlier in this chapter, in order to assess whether and how factors that are more specific to interacting with indigenous populations can be delineated.

CULTURE AS PARADIGMATIC; PARADIGMS AS CULTURAL

In summary, this chapter concretely illustrates the paradigmatic nature of culture. The particular culture clashes this chapter deals with are those principally occurring between indigenous peoples and majoritarian cultures. It applies Hofstede, Hofstede, and Minkov's cultural schema of individualism versus communitarianism in order to sketch the cultural conflicts embedded in the conflict between the German band, Enigma, and the Ami tribal couple, the Duanas, over the ownership of an Ami traditional folk song. The chapter also briefly analyzes a similar clash between individual and communitarian cultures inherent in two Australian cases, *Milpurrurru & Others*, and *Bulun Bulun*. Additionally, the chapter uses Hofstede, Hofstede, and Minkov's cultural rubric of hierarchy versus egalitarianism to draw out key elements of the cultural conflict between the Chilean government and the Mapuche/Pehuenche tribe over control over the right to build a dam that would flood the tribe's ancestral lands.

The chapter closes by returning to the analogy of interpreting ambiguous figures in relation to encountering cultural conflicts. Ambiguous figures, such as the duck-rabbit illusion or the young woman-old woman illusion show us that we perceive phenomena as wholes, and that this process is not purely a rational step-by-step procedure. We either see the duck or the rabbit; we either recognize the shape of the young woman or the old woman. And we can alternate across them. But we cannot see them both at the same time.

NOTES

1. This chapter is adapted from a precursor published as: Caroline Joan "Kay" S. Picart, "Cross Cultural Negotiations and International Intellectual Property Law: Attempts to Work Across Cultural Clashes Between Indigenous Peoples and Majoritarian Cultures," *Southern California Interdisciplinary Law Journal* 23, issue 1 (January 2014): 37–65. The author thanks the *Southern California Interdisciplinary Law Journal* for prior permission granted to reprint and adapt this material.

2. Geert Hofstede, Gert Jan Hofstede, and Michael Minkov, *Cultures and Organizations: Software of the Mine*, 3rd ed. (New York: McGraw-Hill Education, 2010), 89–134.

3. Ibid., 53–88.

4. David Livermore, *Leading with Cultural Intelligence: The New Secret to Success* (New York: Amacon, 2010), 106.

5. Ibid.

6. Ibid.

7. Thomas Sterns Eliot, "The Love Song of J. Alfred Prufrock," *Prufrock and Other Observations* (1920; Bartleby, 2011), http://www.bartleby.com/198/1.html/.

8. Briefly sketched, the psychological "mechanics" of humor are essentially the same as other "creative" acts: these mechanics involve the sudden clash between two mutually exclusive codes of rules, or associative contexts, which are suddenly juxtaposed. "The conscious or unconscious processes underlying creativity are essentially combinatorial activities—the bringing together of previously separate ideas of knowledge and experience. The scientist's purpose is to achieve *synthesis;* the artist aims at a *juxtaposition* of the familiar and the eternal; the humorist's game is to contrive a *collision.*" Arthur Koestler, *Janus: A Summing Up* (New York: Random House, 1978), 129.

9. Thomas Kuhn, *The Structure of Scientific Revolutions* (Chicago: University of Chicago Press, 1970), viii.

10. Ibid.

11. Fons Trompenaars and Charles Hampden-Turner, *Riding the Waves of Culture: Understanding Cultural Diversity in Global Business*, 2nd ed. (New York: McGraw-Hill, 1998), 6.

12. Ibid., 20.

13. Iris Burke, "Introduction to the Basic Cultural Worldviews: The Neuroscience of Culture," (lecture, University of Florida Levin College of Law, Gainsville, FL, May 21, 2012). See also Hofstede, Hofstede, and Minkov, *Cultures and Organizations*, 4–7. For illustrations of how "hard wired" culture is, see Gert Van Hofsted, Paul B. Pedersen, and Geert Hofstede, *Exploring Culture: Exercises, Stories and Synthetic Cultures* (Yarmouth, Maine: Intercultural Press Inc., 2002), 8 (suggesting that an ambiguous picture yields different culturally based interpretations, ranging from "two women walking and a man threatens one of them with a piece of wood" to "gardening").

14. Lieh-Ching Chang, "An Examination of Cross-Cultural Negotiation: Using Hofstede Framework," *Journal of American Academy of Business* 2 (March 2003): 567, http://two.nitbj.com.cn/nit/content/references/Chang,%20L..pdf.

15. Ibid.

16. Arjun Appadurai, ed., "Introduction: Commodities and the Politics of Value," in *The Social Life of Things: Commodities in Cultural Perspective* (Cambridge: Cambridge University Press, 1986), 3–63.

17. Sjaak Van der Geest, Susan Whyte, and Anita Hardon, "The Anthropology of Pharmaceuticals: A Biographical Approach," *Annual Review of Anthropology* 25 (1996): 153–78. Susan Reynolds Whyte, Sjaak van der Geest, and Anita Hardon, *Social Lives of Medicines* (Cambridge, UK: Cambridge University Press, 2002), 3–19.

18. Maarten Bode, "Taking Traditional Knowledge to the Market: The Commoditization of Indian Medicine," in *Anthropology & Medicine* (London: Routledge, 2007), 227.

19. See generally, Arthur P. Bochner and Carolyn Ellis, eds., *Ethnographically Speaking: Autoethnography, Literature, and Aesthetics* (Walnut Creek, CA: AltaMira Press, 2002); Norman K. Denzin and Yvonna S. Lincoln, eds., *The Sage Handbook of Qualitative Research,* 3rd ed. (Thousand Oaks, CA: Sage Publications Inc., 2005).

20. Norman K. Denzin & Yvonna S. Lincoln, eds., "The Discipline and Practice of Qualitative Research," in *The Sage Handbook of Qualitative Research,* 3rd ed. (Thousand Oaks, CA: Sage Publications Inc., 2005), chapter 1.

21. Who are "indigenous peoples"? Article 1 of the ILO Convention Concerning Indigenous and Tribal Peoples in Independent Countries gives the following description: "those who inhabit a country or area within a country at the time of conquest, colonization, or establishment of the present state boundaries and who, irrespective of their legal status, retain some or all of their own social, economic, cultural and political institutions." ILO Convention No. 169 Concerning Indigenous and Tribal Peoples in Independent Countries, Article 1, Paragraph 1, June 27, 1989, last accessed May 12, 2015, http://www.zaoerv.de/59_1999/59_1999_2_s_543_592.pdf. See also chapter 1.

22. For simple analytic reasons, this book, as explained in chapter 1, distinguishes between indigenous peoples' "traditional knowledge" (TK), which has a more scientific basis—for example, a traditional cure for a disease, and "traditional cultural expressions" (TCE) or "expressions of folklore" (EoF), which seem more akin to artistic forms, such as tribal songs used in a ritual to heal a disease. Nevertheless, both TK and EoF appear imperiled and prone to exploitation by both multinational corporations (MNCs) and governments amidst the pressures of globalization.

23. Christopher May, "Why IPRs are a Global Political Issue," *European Intellectual Property Review* 25, no. 1 (2003): 1.

24. Ibid., 4. See also Jane Anderson, "The Politics of Indigenous Knowledge: Australia's Proposed Communal Moral Rights Bill," *University of New South Wales Law Journal* 27, no. 3 (2004): 585.

25. See generally Brad Sherman and Lionel Bently, *The Making of Modern Intellectual Property Law: The British Experience, 1760–1911* (Cambridge: Cambridge University Press, 1999); Mark Rose, *Authors and Owners: The Invention of Copyright* (Cambridge, MA: Harvard University Press, 1993); Ronan Deazley, *On the Origin*

of the Right to Copy: Charting the Movement of Copyright Law in Eighteenth-Century Britain (1695–1775) (Portland, OR: Hart Publishing, 2004); Peter Drahos, *A Philosophy of Intellectual Property* (Sudbury, MA: Dartmouth Publishing, 1996).

26. "Difang and Igay Duana," *Wikipedia*, last modified May 31, 2013, http://en.wikipedia.org/wiki/Difang_and_Igay_Duana; "0817 #80 Difang Duana & Enigma Copyrights Issue," YouTube video, 2:56, posted by "TiTV," on August 19, 2008, http://www.youtube.com/watch?v=EaVnHFHj6MM; Chiung-Wen (Michelle) Chang, "'Return to Innocence': In Search of Ethnic Identity in the Music of the Amis of Taiwan," *College Music Symposium* 49/50 (2009/2010): 327–32.

27. Ashley Esarey, "An Ami Couple Seeks Recognition for Their Music," *Travel in Taiwan Special*, accessed May 12, 2015, http://www.sinica.edu.tw/tit/special/0996_Innocence.html.

28. "Difang and Igay Duana," *Wikipedia*.

29. To see videoclips of the Duanas unadorned performances, *see* "Elders Drinking Song by Difang," YouTube video, 0:38, posted by "tnfshbest," on October 12, 2007, https://www.youtube.com/watch?v=uROdVAV1zQo; and "Difang & Igay singing 'Weeding and Paddyfield Song No. 1,'" YouTube video, 1:00, posted by "DebraShick," on August 3, 2012, https://www.youtube.com/watch?v=ePKKeXNZnaY.

30. "Difang and Igay Duana," *Wikipedia*; Richard Roper, "Taiwanese Settle Lawsuit Claiming Their Original Composition Was Stolen; They Will Now Set Up Foundation," *Business Wire*, June 23, 1999, accessed June 6, 2015, http://www.geocities.ws/enigmalair/rtiarticle4.html.

31. Ibid.

32. Ibid.

33. Esarey, "An Ami Couple." For additional factual information regarding the Duana case, see Agnès Lucas-Schoetter, "Folklore," in *Indigenous Heritage and the Intellectual Property: Genetic Resources, Traditional Knowledge and Folklore* 2nd ed., ed. Silke von Lewinski (The Hague, Netherlands: Kluwer Law International, 2008), 342. Chong Hui-Yeung, "IPR Draft Law for Aborigines Under Attack," *Taipei Times*, August 23, 2000, accessed May 12, 2015, http://www.taipeitimes.com/News/local/archives/2000/08/23/49186.

34. "Difang and Igay Duana," *Wikipedia*.

35. Esarey, "An Ami Couple."

36. Shiu-Lan Huang, "Aborigines Sue for Justice and Recognition: Justice for the Kuos," *Law News Network*, accessed June 6, 2015, http://www.taiwanfirstnations.org/Difang.htm.

37. Esarey, "An Ami Couple."

38. "Lost in Music," *Far Eastern Economic Review 158*, no. 4 (1999), accessed June 6, 2015, http://newint.org/features/1996/02/05/update/.

39. Gert Jan Hofstede, son of Geert Hofstede, is a senior researcher and assistant professor in information technology at Wageningen University in the Netherlands. Hofstede, Pedersen, and Hofstede, "Exploring Culture." Paul B. Pedersen, a well-known author and authority in the field of cross-cultural counseling, is professor emeritus at Syracuse University and a visiting professor in the Department of Psychology at the University of Hawaii. Geert H. Hofstede is an international authority in the field of cross-cultural social psychology and is cofounder

of the Institute for Research on Intercultural Cooperation at Tilburg University, where he also serves as a senior fellow. Clearly, their groundbreaking work on understanding and pragmatically negotiating across cultures is of paramount importance to structuring the theoretical foundations of analysis of this chapter.

40. Hofstede, Pedersen, and Hofstede, *Exploring Culture*, 94, 96.

41. Hofstede, Hofstede, and Minkov, *Cultures and Organizations*, 91 (discussing that Hofstede and his co-authors disavow any political connotations of the word).

42. Ibid., 92.

43. John Barkai, "Cultural Dimension Interests, the Dance of Negotiation, and Weather Forecasting: A Perspective on Cross-Cultural Negotiation and Dispute Resolution," *Pepperdine Dispute Resolution Law Journal* 8, no. 3, (2008): 403.

44. Hofstede, Hofstede, and Minkov, *Cultures and Organizations*, 92.

45. Cristina Walters, "Cross-Cultural Negotiations: A Role Evaluation of Four Cultural Dimensions and Two Cultural Components," *Michigan Business Law Journal* 37, issue 2, (Summer 2007): 39.

46. Hofstede, Pedersen, and Hofstede, *Exploring Culture*, 94.

47. "Difang and Igay Duana," *Wikipedia*.

48. Hofstede, Pedersen, and Hofstede, *Exploring Culture*, 94.

49. "Difang and Igay Duana," *Wikipedia*.

50. Ibid.

51. Hofstede, Pedersen, and Hofstede, *Exploring Culture*, 96.

52. Esarey, "An Ami Couple."

53. Hofstede, Pedersen, and Hofstede, *Exploring Culture*, 96.

54. Esarey, "An Ami Couple."

55. Ibid.

56. This is condensed and adapted from Hofstede, Pedersen, and Hofstede, *Exploring Culture*, 94, 96.

57. Ibid.

58. Ibid.

59. (1995) Australian Institute of Professional Counsellors (AIPC), 91–116; cited in: Michael Blakeney, "Communal Intellectual Property Rights of Indigenous Peoples in Cultural Expressions," *The Journal of World Intellectual Property* 1, no. 6 (November 1998): 987.

60. Ibid.

61. Ibid., 988.

62. Ibid.

63. [1998] 1082 Franchise Council of Australia (FCA) (3 September 1998), cited in: Blakeney, "Communal Intellectual," 992.

64. Ibid.

65. Ibid.

66. Marcos O. Orellana, "Indigenous Peoples, Energy and Environmental Justice: The Pangue/Ralco Hydroelectric Project in Chile's Alto BíoBío," last modified 2004, accessed May 12, 2015, http://www.ciel.org/Publications/Ralco_Brief_22Jul04.pdf, 1–8.

67. Ibid., 1.

68. Ibid., 3.

69. Ibid.

70. Hofstede, Hofstede, and Minkov, *Cultures and Organization*, 61.

71. Ibid.

72. Ibid.

73. Walters, *Cross Cultural Negotiations*, 40.

74. Paraphrased and adapted from Hofstede, Pedersen & Hofstede, *Exploring Culture*, 98, 100.

75. Ibid.

76. Ibid.

77. Ibid.

78. Ibid.

79. Ibid.

80. Ibid.

81. David Livermore is a pioneer in cultural intelligence and global leadership. Livermore, *Leading with Cultural Intelligence*. He is president and partner at the Cultural Intelligence Center in East Lansing, Michigan and a visiting research fellow at Nanyang Technological University in Singapore. Prior to leading the Cultural Intelligence Center, Livermore spent twenty years in leadership positions with a variety of nonprofit organizations around the world and taught in universities. He is a frequent speaker and adviser to leaders in Fortune 500s, nonprofits, and governments and has worked in more than one hundred countries across the Americas, Africa, Asia, Australia, and Europe. Livermore's experientially based and highly acclaimed program, used by international business practitioners, make it an invaluable resource for this chapter.

82. Livermore, *Leading with Cultural Intelligence*, 30–31.

83. Iris A. Burke is a professor emeritus at the University of Florida Levin College of Law who specializes in family law (particularly multidisciplinary and nonadversarial approaches), interviewing and counseling, pro se litigation, legal research and writing, and appellate advocacy. "Iris A. Burke," *Levin College of Law, University of Florida*, last accessed May 12, 2015, http://www.law.ufl.edu/faculty/iris-a-burke. In 1997, Burke, together with Legal Skills Professor Peggy F. Schrieber, the Pro Se/Unbundling Family Law Advice Clinic, to work with the Family Court Self Help of the Eighth Judicial Circuit and assist low income pro se litigants in family law cases. "History of the Clinics," *Levin College of Law, Univeristy of* Florida, last accessed May 12, 2015, http://www.law.ufl.edu/academics/clinics/about-the theclinics/history-of-the-clinics. The author owes a great deal to Professor Burke's mentorship in formulating the initial version of this section.

84. Iris Burke, "A Short Summary of Strategies for Working Across Cultural Differences," (lecture, University of Florida Levin College of Law, May 21, 2012). This general approach is also one practiced in many fields, going far beyond purely legal uses. See, for example, Randall Bass and Joy Young eds., introduction to *Beyond Borders: A Cultural Reader* 2nd ed. (New York: Houghton Mifflin Harcourt, 2003); Thomas A. Schwandt, "Three Epistemological Stances for Qualitative Inquiry: Interpretivism, Hermeneutics, and Social Construction," in *Handbook of Qualitative Research*, ed. Norman K. Denzin and Yvonna S. Lincoln (Thousand Oaks, CA: Sage Publications, 2000); Gloria E. Anzaldua, "Preface: (Un)natural bridges, (Un)safe spaces," in *This Bridge we Call Home: Radical Visions for Transformation*, eds. Gloria Anazaldua and Analouise Keating (New York:

Routledge, Taylor and Francis Group, 2002), 3. To see this approach as applied to law and culture (especially of indigenous peoples), see generally Rosemary J. Coombe, "Intellectual Property, Human Rights and Sovereignty: New Dilemmas in International Law Posed by the Recognition of Indigenous Knowledge and the Conservation of Biodiversity," *Indiana Journal of Global Legal Studies* 6, no. 1 (Fall 1998): 59, http://www.repository.law.indiana.edu/ijgls/vol6/iss1/3; Rosemary J. Coombe, *The Cultural Life of Intellectual Properties: Authorship, Appropriation and the Law* (Durham, NC: Duke University Press, 1998), 18; Jane E. Anderson, *Law, Knowledge, Culture: The Production of Indigenous Knowledge in Intellectual Property Law* (Cheltenham, UK: Edward Elgar Publishing Limited, 2009), 5.

85. See Livermore, *Leading with Cultural Intelligence*, 30–31; Burke, "A Short Summary of Strategies."

86. See Livermore, *Leading with Cultural Intelligence*, 30–31; Burke, "A Short Summary of Strategies."

87. Tracy Novinger, *Intercultural Communication a Practical Guide* (Austin, TX: University of Texas Press, 2001), 24.

88. Ibid.

89. Fons Trompenaars is a world-renowned expert on international management and the author of the global bestseller *Riding the Waves of Culture*. Trompenaars and Hampden-Turner, "Riding the Waves of Culture," introduction. He is also the cofounder and director of Trompenaars Hampden-Turner and is the author or coauthor of eleven bestselling books on culture and business, innovation, and leadership. Charles Hampden-Turner is a research associate with Trompenaars Hampden-Turner in Amsterdam. Recognized as a key business thinker, Hampden-Turner has worked as a consultant for Shell, BP, Digital Equipment, the BBC, Nissan, and many other companies. Their pragmatic, experientially based program of strategies in negotiating across cultural differences is crucial to this chapter.

90. Hofstede, Pedersen and Hofstede, *Exploring Culture*, 94, 96.

91. Ibid.

92. Ibid., 94.

93. Ibid., 96.

94. Trompenaars and Hampden-Turner, *Riding the Waves of Culture*, 68.

95. See Ibid.

96. Ibid.

97. Ibid.

98. Ibid.

99. Ibid.

100. Ibid.

101. See generally Hofestede, Hofstede, and Minkov, *Cultures and Organizations*.

102. Hofstede, Hofestede, and Minkov, *Cultures and Organizations*, 4–7.

103. See Hofstede, Pedersen and Hofstede, *Exploring Culture*, 98.

104. Ibid., 100.

105. Professor John Barkai joined the faculty of the William S. Richardson School of Law, University of Hawai'i at Manoa, in 1978. "John Bakai," *Williams S. Richardson School of Law, University of Hawai'i at Manoa*, accessed May 12, 2015, https://www.law.hawaii.edu/personnel/barkai/john. Prior to coming to

Hawai'i, he was a criminal trial lawyer in Detroit and a tenured faculty member at Wayne State University Law School. Professor Barkai also served previously as Associate Dean at the law school. Barkai currently directs the clinical program and teaches Alternative Dispute Resolution (ADR), Evidence, and Prosecution Clinic. In addition, he teaches conflict resolution and international negotiations for the University of Hawai'i College of Business Administration. Thus, like Professor Burke of the University of Florida Levin College of Law, Professor Barkai has spent a lifetime practicing skills of negotiating cultural differences and teaching these to generations of students.

106. Barkai, "Cultural Dimension Interests," 411.

107. Ibid.

108. See Trompenaars and Hampden-Turner, *Riding the Waves of Culture,* 121.

109. Ibid.

110. Ibid.

111. Ibid.

3

Cultural Meanings of Intellectual Property[1]

CHARACTERIZING "CULTURE" AS OPERATIVE IN INTELLECTUAL PROPERTY LAW

This chapter begins with Rodolfo Stavenhagen's three underlying conceptions of culture, implied in the practice of international and intellectual property law. The first, of culture as "capital," conceives of culture as "the accumulated material heritage of humankind in its entirety, or of particular human groups, including monuments and artifacts."[2] This view, most compatible with free trade markets, views the "right to culture" as "equal access by individuals to . . . accumulated cultural capital"[3] and can be viewed as an extension of the right to development.

The second, of culture as "creativity," is the more traditional characterization of culture in intellectual property law: as the "process of artistic and scientific creation."[4] This view of what "culture" is, is infused with Eurocentric and colonial assumptions—assumptions that undergird distinctions made between "high" culture (which is deemed genuinely creative and therefore protectable) and "low" culture (which is deemed not truly "original" and therefore in the public domain).

Finally, the third description, of culture as a "total way of life," is more anthropological and, therefore, integrative. In this third meaning, culture is "the sum total of the material and spiritual activities and products of a given social group which distinguishes it from other similar groups."[5] This description is probably the one most useful in protecting indigenous peoples' ancestral lands, traditional knowledge, and traditional cultural expressions as constitutive of as an indivisible whole—that is, as "a coherent self-contained system of values, and symbols as well as a set of practices that a specific cultural group reproduces over time and which provides individuals with the required signposts and meanings for behavior and social relationships in everyday life."[6]

Rosemary Coombe adopts the same descriptions as Stavenhagen and points out certain tensions between the different descriptions.[7] For example, the second description, culture as "creation," protects individual rights whereas the third description, culture as a "total way of life," protects "collective rights; even more significantly, how broadly one must draw the boundaries of the collective is vague."[8] The resultant clash in definitional interpretations leads to conflicting policy choices.

> If culture is viewed as the sum total of a society's cultural capital, then "cultural development" may mean "more culture" in the sense of encouraging more creative activity, more cultural products, and thus more intellectual properties . . . However, if the right to culture is understood as the right to "one's own culture" then cultural development may have a different meaning. Under the third understanding of culture, the right of a group to maintain its cultural integrity might take precedence over the rights of cultural creators in the wider society, and the group might choose to restrict access to and use of elements of its cultural heritage in the expressive and scientific work of others if doing so was deemed necessary to preserve the group's identity. Certain exercises of these cultural rights and rights to cultural identity, however, might also be seen to restrict improperly freedom of expression and the free flow of information in the larger society and thus to violate significant political and civil rights.[9]

CURRENT INTELLECTUAL PROPERTY LAW'S EUROCENTRIC AND COLONIALIST ASSUMPTIONS: SOME CHALLENGES IN ATTEMPTING TO USE INTELLECTUAL PROPERTY LAW TO PROTECT INDIGENOUS PEOPLES' RIGHTS

Numerous examples of biopiracy, which involves the misappropriation of traditional knowledge (TK) by multinational corporations (MNCs), devoid of any benefit to or recognition of the tribes that initially generated the source of the TK, exist. Instances include: U.S. pharmaceutical Eli Lilly's patenting of the cancer-fighting drugs vinblastine and vincristine from the rosy periwinkle plant in Madagascar;[10] American timber exporter Robert Larson's receipt of a patent for importing India's Neem tree (India's "curer of all ailments") into the United States and commercialization of a pesticide derived from the Neem extract called Margosan-O;[11] American agricultural executive Larry Proctor's patenting of the "Enola" bean, derived from the traditional Mexican bean, the Mayacoba.[12] In each of these instances, thousands of dollars of profit were involved, sometimes leading to a severely negative impact on the livelihood of the local communities that were the original source of the TK from which the MNC developed the patented drug. For example, Proctor's appropriation of the Enola bean led to export sales of the Mexican traditional bean dropping over 90 percent, "causing severe economic damage to more than 22,000 farmers in Northern Mexico who depended on sales from this bean."[13]

On a slightly more positive note, such patents can be revoked, usually through a challenge raised by an NGO. For example, in 2008, the U.S. Patent and Trademark Office (USPTO) revoked Proctor's patent of the Enola bean based on Columbia-based International Center for Tropical Agriculture (CIAT)'s formidable seven-year challenge to Proctor's patent.[14] Despite the NGO's victory, Proctor and his company managed to exploit the patent for seven years—about a third of the twenty-year patent term.[15] Similarly, the ayahuasca case resulted in ambiguous and temporary gains. Ayahuasca is a South American vine with hallucinogenic properties; as TK, it is used to treat sickness, contact spirits, and foresee the future. Customary law, usually engaging the assistance of a shaman,[16] typically guides the preparation and administration of the drink, which has significance both as an embodiment of TK and as an instance of traditional cultural expression (TCE) because it is associated with religious rituals.[17] Following the typical pattern, the patent holder brought a particular variety of the vine back to the United States in the 1970s and claimed a patent on it that was approved in 1986.[18] The Coordinating Body of Indigenous Organizations of the Amazon Basin (COICA) opposed the patent based on nonnovelty and nonutility.[19] Initially, the USPTO revoked the patent; however, the USPTO later reinstated it because the variety was not identical to specimens in the U.S. herbarium.[20] This is because U.S. patent law excludes unpublished foreign sources when determining what constitutes "novelty" or "prior art." Nevertheless, the patent, covering only the specific genome of that plant sample and its asexually reproduced progeny, lapsed on June 17, 2003. [21]

At an initial level, there are clear analytic reasons, embedded in the assumptions of what "counts" as "protectable," that explain why current intellectual property (IP) law is a blunt instrument in attempting to protect TK and expressions of folklore (EoF) as property of the tribe, rather than the MNCs. First, as Berta Hernandez-Truyol and Stephen J. Powell point out, TK is the "product of *collective* experimentation, which makes impossible associating a resource use with *one individual* [italics mine].[22] Intellectual property law requires an identifiable inventor or author (who could be an employee or agent of an MNC, for example); in contrast, TK and EoF draw from the collective therapeutic and pragmatic knowledge of the tribe, as well as the collective cultural and artistic heritage of the group.

A second factor is associated with that difference between the emphasis on the individual and the focus on the collective. As required by TRIPS

Article 27(1),[23] patent protection can be granted only if inventions and ideas are "new," "nonobvious," and "useful." In addition, patent protection has a requirement called "enablement"[24]—which simply means that the application for a patent must describe the new idea by a physical manifestation or display a newly discovered type through a sample, and in written form. The written format is especially important if it is a method patent, for instance, in order to be able to describe the invention so clearly that potentially, anyone wishing to replicate or exploit that knowledge once patent protection has lapsed, can do so. This is very much in keeping with patent protection's policy of balancing the desire to incentivize inventors into innovating by granting them temporary monopoly rights over their inventions with the attempt to make such knowledge eventually generally available, to promote public welfare.

Unfortunately, again, patent protection's emphases on "novelty," "nonobviousness," and "usefulness" are radically opposed to TK's valuation of what is collectively familiar, intuitively obvious and "useful" (though not in a Western sense) to the tribe. And TK, much like EoF, as exemplified in traditional crafts, music, or dances, rely more on an oral mode of transmission, not a written method. As such, TK is usually regarded as not patentable, belonging to the public domain. Even more disturbingly, as Hernandez-Truyol and Powell point out, even if TK were to meet patent law's "originality" requirement, most instances of TK do not fit patent law's requirements of being "profitable" and "capable of 'industrial application.'"[25] Again, the prevailing viewpoint's requirements of being "profitable" and "capable of industrial application," though applicable in a capitalist market-driven society, may constrain the IP rights of indigenous peoples.

Consequently, convergent problems attend the attempts to use intellectual property law to protect the EoF of indigenous peoples, which are compounded by stereotypes of primitivism and racism.[26] For instance, the Western notion of "folklore" often implies clichés of the (merely) "collected" and (already) "dead" or "dying."[27] In sharp contrast, for the communities whose identities are bound up with TCEs, folklore is nothing short of a living heritage, which is inextricably intertwined with daily realities and as such, necessarily evolves.[28] Nevertheless, two principal characteristics of EoF make it immediately evident why intellectual property law make it difficult to use copyright, for example, to protect EoF as tribal property. Two consistent features are: anonymity and traditional character (oral transmission).[29] In consonance with this general description, the WIPO characterization of EoF or TEC includes the following features:

(i) being handed down from one generation to another, either orally or by imitation;

(ii) reflecting a community's cultural and social identity;
(iii) consisting of characteristic elements of a community's heritage;
(iv) being made by "authors unknown" or by communities or by individuals communally recognized as having rights, responsibility or permission to do so;
(v) being constantly evolving, developing and being created within the community.[30]

However, these precise features make it difficult to demarcate EoF as "property" separate from the public domain. Copyright law, akin to patent law in some ways, creates a binary between private property (usually individually owned and exploited) and the notion of a "commons" (usually not owned by any individual and free for use by all in the community). "Copyright law matured in the classical era of liberalism, which formally enshrined the ideal of the abstract individual freely exercising his or her creative capacity protected by a neutral system of natural rights, the most important of which was the right of property."[31] The converse to these clearly delineated individual rights is the amorphous "public domain," which is "usually equated with the non[-] propertied general welfare of the common people of a particular nation-state or, more generously, with the larger welfare of the undifferentiated global community as a whole."[32]

Yet what that binary hides are precisely the assumptions behind copyright law and its historical origins. Much as patent law requires an inventor, copyright law requires an author; in addition, both invention and the creation of literary texts (as copyright's origins lie in the attempt to protect the production of books) became regarded as testaments to the creativity and "genius" of a particular individual. Historically, within the context of eighteenth-century England, a book rose to becoming "the intellection of a unique individual,"[33] rather than a product of mastering the rules of craftsmanship. Because a book is a particular embodied or "fixed" expression of the author's unique mind, originally expressed, it is private intellectual property; thus, the right to exploit this identifiable piece of property belongs purely to this unique individual.

Yet as James Boyle points out, such an idealized view of authorship "blinds us to the importance of the commons—to the importance of the raw material from which information products are to be constructed."[34] Hardly surprisingly, given this binary, EoF, like TK, become discredited as "not original"—to borrow a monstrous metaphor, they become as the anonymous and interchangeable or "unfixed" body parts that the genius, Dr. Frankenstein, stitches together to breathe life into his creature. Within this context, "[i]ndigenous knowledge and generations of indigenous labor—mental and physical—are discredited. All that is credited is the 'chop-shop' labor of individual corporate and academic scientists who interject 'novelty' into what they have taken."[35]

In a parallel but different example, Russell Lawrence Barsh points out how within the context of the Human Genome Diversity Project—also termed the "vampire project" by some human rights activists, in the 1990s, partly because of its perceived threat to indigenous and tribal peoples[36]—Big Pharma's shift to "gene mining" resulted in the covert gathering of samples from indigenous and tribal communities, often without consent.[37] Despite the existence of an admirable protocol for the harvesting of human tissue samples, requiring genuine informed consent and theoretically consistent with the standards advocated by the Indigenous Peoples Council on Biocolonialism,[38] enforcement of these requirements has been weak. For example, in 1993, the University of Pennsylvania collaborated with Argentine public health clinics to utilize blood samples harvested from the Tobas and Matacos; however, national indigenous organizations protested against the procedure.[39] Despite an alleged ceasing of the covert harvesting, Mapuche DNA sequences have been published.[40] Furthermore, Barsh claims:

> [N]o patents appear to have resulted [from these harvesting of indigenous peoples'genetic material], at least in the United States. Researchers have generally not experienced any difficulties re-sampling communities that were sampled in the past. The Yanamamö, for example, were sampled repeatedly from the 1960s to the 1990s by many of the same researchers.[41]

The result, hardly surprisingly, tasked indigenous communities with the burden of providing much of the data needed for the development of new pharmacological technologies, without necessarily giving them access to its benefits, essentially reducing them to a mere "academic sideshow."[42]

Hardly unexpectedly, the justificatory rhetoric for rendering invisible the contributions of TK and EoF to the development of highly profitable pharmaceutical inventions or musical innovations partakes of the patterns of colonialist reasoning.

> [A]ppeals to common property, private property, and usually both in succession constitute the legitimating rationale of cultural imperialism. It enables the dominant culture to secure political and social control as well as to profit economically from the cultural and genetic resources of indigenous cultures. Just as the concept of *terra nullius* once provided legal and moral cover for the imperial powers' treatment of indigenous peoples, the concept of public domain plays a comparable role within late capitalism.[43]

Within a contemporary framework, the persistence of these colonialist notions of "originality" and "novelty" may be traced to the General

Agreement on Tariffs and Trade (GATT)[44] and its provisions on Trade-Related Aspects of Intellectual Property Rights (TRIPS), which were forged by the dominant powers, among which was the United States. "According to the U.S. initiative in the GATT, if other nation-states want to engage in trade with the United States, they must adopt U.S. stipulations regarding intellectual property which are contrary to their customary practice and which enable acquisition of their genetic and cultural resources."[45] Once again, the same pattern emerges: as Darryl A. Posey and Graham Dutfield remark, TRIPS refuses to recognize "the more informal, communal system of innovation through which Third World farmers produce, select, improve and breed a plethora of diverse crop varieties."[46] At this point, we have come full circle, seeing how interconnected TK and EoF are, and how tricky it comes to fully demarcate them, and thus to come up with pragmatic solutions to the issue of breaking past the two master narratives of Fear and Optimism discussed in chapter 1.[47]

Thus, one problem with relying purely on Stavenhagen's first and second characterizations of culture (i.e., culture as "capital" and culture as "creativity") lies in unearthing these descriptions' colonialist assumptions, with the familiar theme of bringing enlightenment to "ignorant" indigenous communities, whose benefits are both economically advantageous and morally gratifying to the "torch-bearers." In a similar manner, the same pattern emerges—as Posey and Dutfield observe, TRIPS refuses to recognize "the more informal, communal system of innovation through which the Third World farmers produce, select, improve and breed a plethora of diverse crop varieties."[48]

ATTEMPTING TO NEGOTIATE CULTURAL DIFFERENCES: CONCRETE CASE STUDIES OF THE AMI TRIBE IN TAIWAN, THE MAPUCHE TRIBE IN CHILE, AND THE GANALBINGU PEOPLE IN AUSTRALIA

The Duanas versus Enigma: Successful Rapprochement in Negotiating Culture as Creativity

This chapter now returns to the case of the Duanas versus Enigma and examines how this particular conflict was resolved; this chapter also traces how the resolution of this case is tied up with Stavenhagen's second description: of culture as "creativity." After about two years of litigation (and, more importantly, significant press coverage), the Duanas' battle for recognition of the Ami tribe's ownership of the "drinking" / "welcoming" song yielded a settlement.[49] Based on press releases, the deal contained several incentives for both groups to settle the matter amicably. For example,

Enigma/Virgin Records was able to clear the names and reputations of the band and recording company, and cut back the financial losses due to bad press.[50] Correspondingly, the Duanas and the Ami Tribe were given a foundation to preserve the tribe's culture and, as to the tribe's music, granted full attribution on all future releases, and given a platinum copy of "Cross of Changes" (which included the single, "Return to Innocence").[51]

Crucial to motivating the financially powerful parties, Enigma and Virgin Records, to come to the negotiating table, was the unrelenting press coverage in favor of the Duanas, particularly when the song was used to promote the 1996 Summer Olympics.[52] The Taiwanese reaction to the story, especially when the promo began to be featured heavily on CNN and other networks, catalyzed Magic Stone Record Company ("Magic Stone") to offer the Duanas a contract and also to lend them the services of the "hot shot copyright lawyer," Huang Hsiu-lan.[53] In keeping with their communitarian culture, the Duanas initially only sought recognition for both the tribe and themselves as the specific performers of the song. At first, Difang Duana made the following declaration: "All I want is for the people of the world to know that part of the music they hear is performed by the Ami aboriginal tribe in Taiwan and the singers are Kuo Ying-nan and Kuo Hsiu-chu."[54] In terms of the couple's original intent when they initially recorded the folk song, another attorney speaking for them, Patrick Ellison, claimed: "Mr. and Mrs. Kuo made this recording for cultural preservation purpose[s] only. At no time did they grant anyone permission to commercialize their song."[55] The Duanas had originally only wanted to perform the song at the Olympics, but when Enigma and the Olympic Committee snubbed their request, Huang, Magic Stone's lawyer, began collaborations with the Dewey Ballantine Law Firm and used more aggressive tactics.[56]

Even more significantly, a precedent for successfully pressuring Enigma/Virgin Records into negotiation already existed. In 1994, Munich-based choir, Capella Antigua, and its record label, Polydor Germany, sued Enigma/Cretu for similarly using samples from Capella Antigua's 1976 LP *Paschale Mysterium*, which was clearly copyrighted.[57] However, Capella Antigua appeared to have a stronger case because European law acknowledges a broad array of moral rights (*droit moral*)[58] while American law does not (save in the case of "visual works of art").[59] Thus, Capella Antigua's claim that Enigma/Cretu had infringed its "right of integrity" by distorting the original excerpt and embedding it in the derivative works, "Sadness (Part I)" and "Mea Culpa"[60] initially seemed stronger than the Duanas' claim, which was eventually filed in the United States.[61] Nevertheless, in both cases, Enigma/Virgin Records settled.[62] On June 23, 1999, via the efforts of the international law firm Oppenheimer Wolff & Donnelly LLP, Enigma/Virgin Records and the Duanas arrived at a settlement acceptable to both parties, described above.[63] Perhaps the fact that the Duanas had achieved a stardom of their own, even if limited to Taiwan and Japan, was sufficient to tip the negotiating power in their direction and eventually force Enigma/Virgin Records to settle out of court.[64]

Interestingly, the facts of this case lined up with Stavenhagen's description of culture as "creativity" easily. First, there were clearly individual "artists" (rather than a faceless collective) whose original interpretations of the songs were clearly appropriated without due credit. Second, the Duanas had produced hybridized musical forms in between the original ethnic form and more commercial Western forms, thus creating a following for them. Third, although the Duanas had repeatedly stressed that they simply wanted to draw recognition to the tribe, the final resolution not only produced a foundation dedicated to preserving the culture of the tribe but also produced clear legal and material artifacts attesting to the Duanas' ownership of copyrightable musical property. This negotiated settlement included the promise of full attribution on all future releases, and a platinum copy of "Cross of Changes" (that includes the single, "Return to Innocence.")

In a fascinating interpretative twist, Nancy Guy claimed that because there was a high degree of creativity in the recording the Duanas had made because of the couple's "improvisational skill," thus attesting to the "creative process" inherent in the process of recording the Duanas' version of the traditional folk song, "Jubilant Drinking Song."[65] Guy stressed that the resultant distinctiveness of the recorded song, due to the couples' improvisational skill, added to the strength of the arguments made by the Duanas' lawyer. Yet as we shall see in chapter 4, within the context of dance for example, improvisational skill does not necessarily lead to the creation of copyrightable material. Being a distinctive performer is not necessarily the same as being an author.

Nevertheless, in keeping with their communitarian culture, the Duanas purportedly used some of the money from the settlement to set up a scholarship fund for Ami children.[66] In addition, although Magic Stone's attorney was also successful in a suit against the French government, the government insisted on giving the money to a folk art foundation in trust, and not to the Duanas, as individuals;[67] this, in keeping with their communitarian culture, was more in keeping anyway with the Duanas' explicitly stated aspirations. However, in response to the lawsuits, a Taiwanese recording industry representative from the Association of Recording Copyright Owners affirmed that traditional folk music was indeed in the public domain and claimed that legally, performers or arrangers of traditional folk music could not claim any copyright on it.[68] Nevertheless, probably because the Duanas already had a public presence, they have been credited on all subsequent releases of the song.

On March 29, 2002, Difang passed away. After Difang was bitten by a venomous centipede in 2001, he never fully recovered and his health had continued to decline. After a few months, Igay joined him. Nevertheless, the legacy of the Duanas lies in having made "translatable" in legal terms, the Amis communitarian ownership of its traditional folk songs by becoming effectively the identifiable representatives of their tribe, and as such, standing in as the "authors" and rights-bearers of copyright in these folk songs.

More cynically, the very same mechanisms of globalization that allowed Enigma's appropriation of the Ami folk song also allowed its commercial re-appropriation, absorbing and reinterpreting the Duanas identities to become part of the commercial rubric. For Taylor, this re-appropriation came in the form of the New Formosa Band's album, "Circle of Life."[69] This album was created, unlike the single, "Return to Innocence," with collaboration and permission from the Duanas; under the aegis of the Duanas' consent, the album's jacket reimagined Difang as a "World Musician," strategically visually surrounded by a lush green backdrop and overtly connected to nature. "The album also incorporated modern (almost Enigma-like) beats and instruments (which could, arguably, be a form of subtle reverse appropriation) and even the title suggests the cyclical nature of re-appropriation in a world where both globalization and glocalization occur."[70] Within this metamorphic transformation of the Duanas' identities, there is little discernible difference between the Duanas and Enigma.[71] Ultimately, as a final note, Chiung-Wen Chang notes that traditional Ami culture is matrilineal; that within this society, women "hold a higher position than men"; that many Ami songs make women their subject; and that in the Ami people's "lead-and-responsorial songs, such as 'Jubilant Drinking Song,' a female usually takes part in singing the soprano voice, because women have the naturally higher vocal range than the men and can easily render the beautiful, soft soprano vocal texture."[72] However, in the remake, "Circle of Life," and in subsequent publicized representations, it is clearly Difang, the man, who is given central prominence, with Igay/Agay, the woman, who is given a secondary role. For example, the remixed 3:58 youtube video of the couple singing featured three solo photographs of Difang and one photograph of the couple together, in traditional dress, against a backdrop of idyllic landscapes; additionally, Difang's voice was also made visibly louder than Igay's/Agay's, which was reduced to an echo in the background.[73] This is in sharp contrast to the earlier unadorned recordings, where, whether in traditional dress or in more Westernized clothing, Igay's/Agay's physical presence and powerful voice tended to overpower Difang's.[74] In that sense, as well, the repackaging of the Duanas' identities and relationship had to be recast to be in keeping with majoritarian cultures' expectations, in the attempt to reach (and market to) a more globalized commercial audience.

The Mapuche Tribe versus the Chilean Government: Settlement of Differences regarding Culture as a Way of Life via an International Regional Court

Unlike the battle of the Duanas, the Mapuche tribe's comparatively less publicized fight against its own government lasted over ten years[75] (see figure 3.1). As a last legal resort, the tribe and its sympathizers appealed

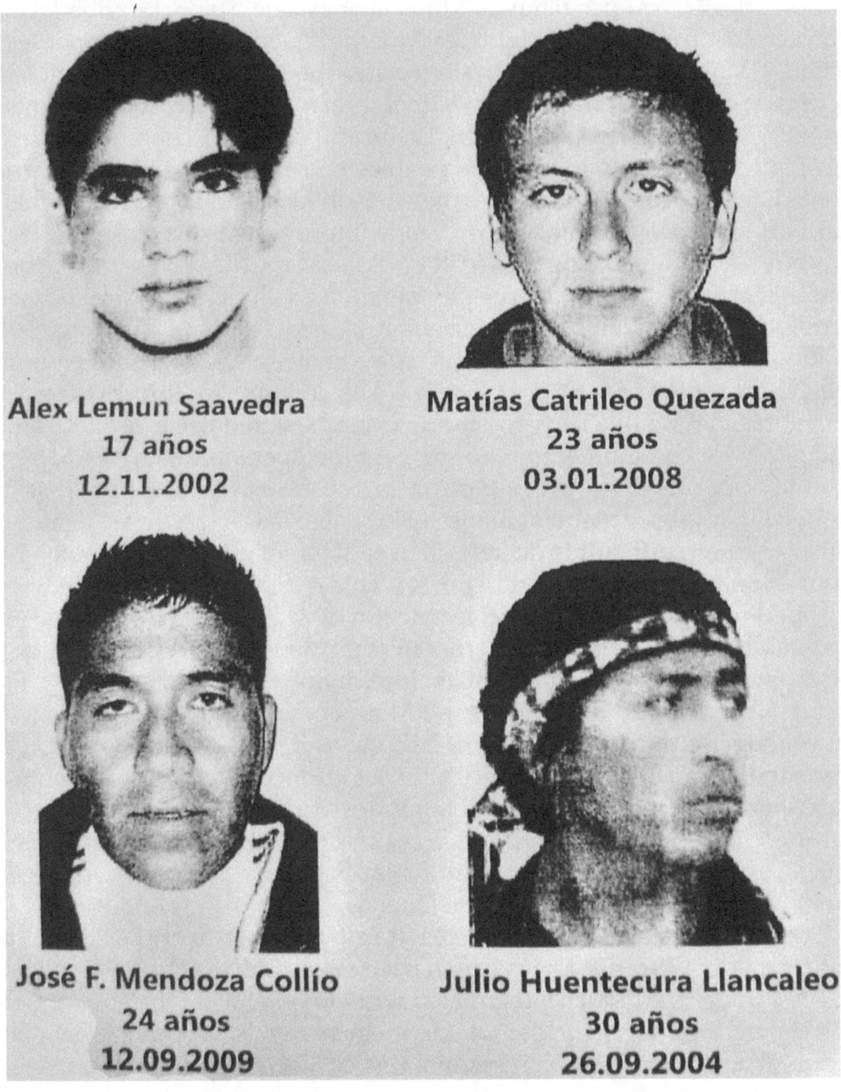

Figure 3.1. Young Mapuche Who Have Died in the Conflict with the Chilean Government in the 2000s; Posted: 21 January 2010, 11:37:13.
Photograph by Fabio Malk.

to the Inter-American Human Rights Commission (IACHR), which, in October 2003, forged a "friendly settlement."[76] The settlement included reparations to the Mapuche families for their legal rights to natural resources projected to be flooded by dams, as well as additional protections for the Mapuche tribe.[77] For example, the government granted the tribe ownership over "lands of good quality, technical support to promote agricultural productivity, educational scholarships, and monetary compensation . . . of US $300,000 per family."[78] In exchange, the Mapuche tribe legally transferred their ancestral rights and discontinued the international legal action.[79] More generally and systemically, the Chilean government also agreed to strengthen national laws that guarantee respect for indigenous rights.[80] This included constitutional reform that would culminate in legal recognition of Chile's indigenous peoples and ratification of the International Labor Organization Convention 169 on indigenous peoples' rights.[81] Furthermore, the government resolved to improve and strengthen the legal procedures for delineating the territory of the Mapuche/Pehuenche people and ensuring their meaningful participation in the official development process.[82] Additionally, the government agreed to create a municipality in the upper BíoBío and promulgate specific measures to ensure environmental protection of the upper BíoBío.[83] The government further agreed to guarantee that no other hydro-electric projects would occur in the region, and allow for community monitoring over the operation of the dam.[84]

What emerges from a comparison of the cases are two principal insights. First, rapprochement along a vertical axis (hierarchy vs. egalitarianism) is more difficult to achieve than settlement along a horizontal axis (individualism vs. communitarianism). This is because power differences within a hierarchical cultural construction of reality are "naturalized" as inevitable and even moral in terms of the ruling elite.[85] Second, in both cases, media coverage and popular international support were key factors.[86] Nevertheless, the facts of the Mapuche case lined up easily with Stavenhagen's third description of culture: as a "total way of life." Given that all-encompassing characterization of culture, the conflicts Coombe described, involving the rights of a minority group's right to preserve its culture, and the majority group's right to development, came into clear relief, resulting in an arduous path towards uneasy and temporary resolution, compared to the case of the Duanas.

Despite the gains of the 2003 IACHR settlement, as early as 2002,[87] the government of Ricardo Lagos began to wield an antiterrorist law, created in 1984, under the Pinochet regime, in order to quell what the government has characterized as a dangerous Mapuche revolt. This antiterrorism law grants the judiciary and the criminal justice system additional powers.[88] Although this law was allegedly tailored so as not to violate democratic standards, it still has provisions that defy international indigenous and human rights standards. For example, the law triples ordinary criminal sentences and those arising under the state security law.[89] Moreover, the law revokes the accused person's right to due process, and allows the government to hold the person in prison without arraignment for a long period of time.[90] Additionally, the law also allows witnesses to testify anonymously,[91] thus negating the accused individual's right to confront his or her accusers or to undergo the essential process of cross-examination, effectively making accusation tantamount to proof.

Chilean Deputy Secretary of the Interior Patricio Rosende gave assurances that the legislation was not racist in its application (i.e., that it does not specifically target Mapuche people because of their race), but rather, focuses on "serious" crimes that could be classified as "terrorist" in nature.[92] Nevertheless, the international view of the law has been far from positive. For example, the United Nations and Human Rights Watch have condemned the use of the law; the Inter-American Court of Human Rights found the antiterrorism legislation unlawful under international law.[93] Additionally, the U.N. Committee for the Elimination of Racism has urged the Chilean government not to use the legislation because the antiterrorism law discriminates specifically against the Mapuche, and attempts to de-legitimate their demands.[94]

To be fair, there was a period during which the Chilean government, under the leadership of President Michelle Bachelet, appeared to be open to the protection or return of the Mapuche's ancestral lands. According to Human Rights lawyer Juan Jorge Faundes, President Bachelet, who left office in March, 2011, had approved 115 requests from the Mapuche population for restitution of ancestral lands; unfortunately, however, her administration was unable to fulfill that promise and had purchased only 60 percent of those ancestral lands prior to her leaving office.[95]

Similarly, then-President Bachelet had also promised, during a trip to Austria in 2006, that she would not deploy the antiterrorist law during her presidency.[96] However, in March 2009, Bachelet's promise was broken with the arrest and prosecution, under the authority of the antiterrorism law, of Miguel Tapia Huenulef, a Mapuche construction worker accused of involvement in a January arson attack on a private estate near the town of Lautaro, in the Araucanía Region. Among the items allegedly seized during the police raid on Tapia's home in Santiago, and later presented as evidence of terrorist activity, were a submachine gun, ammunition clips, two grenades and bomb-making materials; in contrast, the accused's family claimed these items were planted during a five-hour ordeal in which their home was raided, they were racially abused and threatened, and items ranging from money, tools and cell phones were stolen.[97]

In addition to her initial intent to purchase and redistribute 33,000 hectares (81,500 acres) of land to the Mapuche through the end of her term, then-President Bachelet had also announced the creation of two government bodies: the Indigenous Ministry and the Council of Indigenous Peoples, to be comprised of forty-four members chosen by popular vote to represent the eight different ethnic groups in the country.[98] However, then-President's Bachelet's initiatives were met with strong criticism by both her political opponents and the Mapuche, the latter of whom claimed they had not been consulted in the formation of these initiatives.[99] As Chilean history attests, the narrative of the Mapuche's call for political self-determination and regional autonomy is long and complex; thus, the difficulties inherent in the attempt to resolve a dispute around culture functioning as a "total way of life," in relation to the Mapuches' property and intellectual property rights, must be contextualized and grounded within the realities of this history.

The Ganalbingu Tribe versus Foreign Infringement of TCEs: *Milpurrurru & Others* and *John Bulun Bulun & Another* and the Issue of Communitarian Ownership of TCEs

This section now returns to two landmark cases in Australia regarding aboriginal copyright ownership of TCEs. These cases are particularly instructive because they illustrate the need for an intersectional approach, as culturally, it entailed plotting differences along both the individualist versus communitarian axis (in the clash between tribal culture and majoritarian culture and copyright law) as well as the egalitarian versus hierarchical axis (within the tribal culture itself).

As discussed in chapter 2, both the *Milpurrurru & Others v. Indofurn Pty. Ltd. & Others*[100] and the *John Bulun Bulun & Another v. R & T Textiles Pty Ltd.*[101] cases hinged on attempts to acquire legal recognition for communitarian claims for copyright protection for TCEs. In *Milpurrurru & Others*, the first four artists who mounted claims were well-known proponents of bark paintings visualizing legends of the peoples of Central Arnhem Land. Among them was Mr. George Milpurrurru, whose painting "Goose Egg Hunt" had been copied. The others were members of the Papunya school of Aboriginal art from the western desert areas of Central Australia, and Ms. Marika, a linocut printmaker who also happened to be the first Aboriginal person appointed to the Australian National Gallery (ANG) and also to the Board of the Northern Territory Museum and Art Gallery.[102] As in the case of the Duanas, the artists involved, despite their grounding their claims for relief in communitarian claims of ownership and stewardship, were known artists and spokespersons of their respective tribes, and in this case, with legitimate links to authorized Australian entities associated with the art world.

What was distinctive about the resolution of this case, after a finding of clear infringement, was that the relief given was based, not on palpable monetary loss based on sales of their art (as the conversion of their art into commercial carpets was not a use that the tribe would have even contemplated, and so there was no loss of any market potential).[103] Nevertheless, the court noted that given the circumstances of that case, the damages sustained, especially in the case of the living artists, extended beyond the commercial potential for monetary return.[104] Given the artwork's grounding as a TCE, the court acknowledged that the infringements had caused great personal distress and potentially exposed the artists to embarrassment and contempt within their communities, as well as to the foreseeable risk of diminished earning potential and physical harm.[105] Traditionally, as the claimants pointed out, the punishments for breaches of the sacred process of the reproduction of these images had included death, but more recently, ranged from "preclusion from the right to participate in ceremonies and removal of the right to reproduce the stories of the clan, as well as in some cases spearing or ostracism."[106] Thus, the basis for relief, in this particular case, was not from the diminishment of value of the copyright by virtue of its infringement (Stavenhagen's characterization of culture as capital in copyright law), but rather from grounds resembling a tort-based claim, in which punitive damages could be awarded based on flagrant copyright infringement.

This analysis was particularly salient to the harms that resulted from the infringement of Ms. Marika's artwork; Ms. Marika's artwork visually interpreted her ancestral creator Djang'Kawu and his two sisters, the Wagilag sisters at the end of their journey from Burralku to Yelangbara.[107] Her right to deploy this imagery arose from her membershp of the Yolgnu Clan, the land-owning group in that area. As she explained by affidavit: "[A]s an artist, whilst I may own copyright under Western law, under Aboriginal law I must not use an image or story in such a way as to undermine the rights of all the other Yolngu."[108] Of particular significance to the court was that the commercial use of the images—as things to be walked on by their purchasers—was completely at odds with the intended traditional cultural usage of her images. Even more importantly, were she not to protest or to fail in her protest, Ms. Marika would be subject to a range of indigenous sanctions that varied from being an outcast to prohibition from further artistic production. Phrased slightly differently, "*Milpurrurru* establishes the principle that where the unauthorized reproduction of such works involves a breach of copyright, customary Aboriginal laws on the subject may be taken into account in quantifying the damage [that] has been suffered."[109] Thus, having found an infringement in the copyright of Ms. Marika's works, the court also considered the potential sanctions/harms to which Ms. Marika may have been subject by her people in the calculation of her damages. The court thus distinguished between copyright law that functioned to compensate economic loss to an owner (Stavenhagen's description of "culture as capital") and copyright law that acknowledged the cultural rootedness of these TCEs and that their infringement had far-ranging negative consequences for the particular artists whose exploitation of these works hinged on a responsible stewardship of these images (Stavenhagen's characterization of "culture as a way of life").

The court innovatively relied upon Section 115(4) of the Copyright Act, which provides for the additional grant of damages in cases of "flagrant infringement."[110] Additionally, *Williams v. Settle*[111] served as precedent (authorizing the substantial award of "vindictive damages" for the commercial sale of photographs of a plaintiff, whose father had been murdered in notorious circumstances, by a wedding photographer). In that case, damages awarded were computed to reflect the brazenness of the infringement and the "total disregard not only of the legal rights of the plaintiff regarding copyright but of his feelings and his sense of family dignity and pride. It was an intrusion into his life, deeper and graver than an intrusion into a man's property."[112] In other words, the court upheld the legal adage that one must not profit from a crime, which, in this case, was seen as more than an easily quantifiable property violation.

The facts in *Milpurrurru* showed ample evidence that the respondents had flagrantly disregarded the aboriginal artists' intellectual property rights. Prior to the importation of the carpets, Mr. Horrocks, an office manager of the Aboriginal Legal Service of Western Australia Inc., gave legal notice to the respondents that the importation would clearly constitute a copyright infringement and that advice should be sought from the Aboriginal Arts Management Association (AAMA), which had been set up under the auspices of the Aboriginal Arts Unit of the Australia Council.[113] The respondents failed to consult with the AAMA, which subsequently became aware of the circumstances of the case when a New South Wales Aboriginal art dealer made an inquiry, with the AAMA, as to whether the carpets had received copyright approval. After conducting its own investigation, the AAMA contacted the respondents, informing them of their copyright infringements and breaches of Sections 52 and 53 of the Trade Practices Act; the AAMA demanded an immediate cessation of the respondent's activities, a surrender of all carpets, and an accounting of profits.[114] Instead of responding in good faith, the respondents chose to deny infringement and to continue with their activities, claiming that the AAMA was not acting in the best interest of the aboriginal artists and that the works were actually in the public domain. The court took issue with the respondents' tactical positions and held that the infringements were "plainly deliberate and calculated," based on the facts that, from the beginning, the respondents knew of the source of the imagery that they reproduced on the carpets and that the respondents had repeatedly been given prior notice by Mr. Horrocks and the AAMA. Additionally, the court also took into consideration that the respondents had created a false impression that the carpets, with aboriginal artwork on them, were endorsed by prominent artists.[115] Interestingly, the court's calculation of damages placed greater weight on the communitarian-based harms rather than the individual economic loss that resulted from the infringement. Blakeney summarized the court's final ruling elegantly:

> In his computation of damages the trial judge awarded an amount of AUS $ 1,500 per artwork against each of the respondents under Section 115(2) of the Copyright Act, reflecting the low quantum of damage attributable to the commercial depreciation which had been suffered. However, to mark the seriousness of the infringements he awarded an additional sum, under Section 115(4), of AUS$ 70,000 to be apportioned in the amounts of Am$ 15,000 to each of the living applicants to "reflect the harm suffered [by them] in their cultural environment."[116]

In comparison, as preliminarily introduced in chapter 2, the case of *John BulunBulun & Another v. R. &T Textiles Pty Ltd.*[117] emerged because of the unauthorized importation and sale in Australia of printed clothing fabric that infringed the copyright of the Aboriginal artist, Mr. John Bulun Bulun, in his work "Magpie Geese and Water Lillies [sic] at the Waterhole." As in the Duana case, Mr. Bulun Bulun had achieved some recognition for his work as an artist. Mr. Bulun Bulun mounted an infringement suit as the legal owner of copyright in the painting and sought remedies for infringement under the Australian Copyright Act of 1968.[118] Mr. Milpurrurru applied for relief on a two-fold basis, both in in his own name and as a representative of the Ganalbingu people, claiming that they were the equitable owners of the copyright subsisting in the painting.[119]

It is important that in this case, the basis for the relief not only relied upon an appeal to communitarian grounds of ownership or stewardship, but also upon a traditional aboriginal concept of hierarchy. In specific, geographically and sociopolitically, the Ganalbingu people are divided into two groups. Mr. Bulun Bulun was the most senior person of the "bottom" Ganalbingu. According to tribal custom, Mr. Bulun Bulun was second in seniority to Mr. Milpurrurru, who was a "top" Ganalbingu.[120] Thus, by virtue of that hierarchy, any copyright that inhered in Mr. Bulun Bulun's individual ownership eventually inhered in Mr. Milpurrurru as the principal representative of the tribe, and the Ganalbingu people on a communitarian basis, as it is the practice of their traditions that generated and authorized Mr. Bulun Bulun's art work. Thus, it is important to see that an axis of individualism versus communitarianism can be plotted along an axis of egalitarianism versus hierarchy, depending on the circumstances. Although Geert Hofstede, Gert JanHofstede, and Michael Minkov's framework[121] is deployed along a single axis, for simple analytic parsing in several of the chapters of this book, it is just as useful using an intersectional approach.

It is striking that in this case, Mr. Bulun Bulun's individual ownership of copyright in his artwork was never contested. At the start of the proceedings, the respondents, unlike those in *Milpurrurru*, admitted to infringing Mr. Bulun Bulun's copyright and voluntarily consented to permanent injunctions against future infringement. This was probably a tactical attempt at avoiding the severe punitive actions that resulted from *Milpurrurru*'s respondents' refusal to acknowledge the individual original artists' ownership of their copyright in their works of art. However, in its defense to Mr. Milpurrurru's actions, the *Bulun Bulun* respondent pleaded that because Mr. Bulun Bulun's individual claim had been satisfied, it was not necessary to consider the question of the equitable ownership of the copyright.[122] The *Bulun Bulun* respondent therefore sought to emphasize the conventionally held copyright wisdom that copyright inheres in an individual author, not a communitarian entity. Nevertheless, Mr. Milpurrurru sought to persist in mounting the action as an experiment on testing how far the communitarian intellectual property rights of indigenous Australian peoples extended under Australian copyright law.[123]

In this confrontation, what eventually resulted was an unambiguous retreat from the vindication of communitarian ownership of copyright in TCEs. The principal issue for the court to address hinged on whether the communitarian-based interests of traditional indigenous owners in cultural works of art or TCEs, affirmed as such under Aboriginal law, created binding legal or equitable obligations on persons outside the relevant Aboriginal community. Historically, the court conceded that at the time of the first British settlement of Australia in 1788, some legitimate forms of copyright existed under the common law of England, such as an author's property right in an unpublished composition.[124] However, with the codification of copyright law in Australia, these ownership claims based upon common law claims lost their legal basis as the court reasoned that Section 8 of the Copyright Act of 1968 states that "copyright does *not* [italics added] subsist otherwise than by virtue of this Act."[125]

The Ganalbingu claim of rights in equity in Mr. Bulun Bulun's artwork hung on there being a trust grounded in expressions of ritual knowledge or TCEs, as exemplified in Mr. Bulun Bulun's "Magpie Geese and Water Lillies at the Waterhole." The court acknowledged that among African tribal communities, tribal property was regarded as being held on trust by the customary head of a tribal group, thus affirming a hierarchical cultural component to this form of ownership.[126] However, the court distinguished between the case of these African tribes and the circumstances of the *Bulun Bulun* case in that, based on the facts of the case, in the court's view, there was no evidence of an express or implied trust, as evidenced, for example, in customary tribal practices, that existed in relation to Mr. Bulun Bulun's art.[127]

In attempting to find an equitable remedy, the court found, despite the non-existence of a trust, the subsistence of a fiduciary relationship between Mr. Bulun Bulun and the Ganalbingu people. In the court's view, this relationship found its genesis in the trust and confidence held by the Ganalbingu people that Mr. Bulun Bulun's artistic creativity would be used, not for individual gain, but to protect the "integrity of the law, custom, culture and ritual knowledge of the Ganalbingu."[128] The court's ruling followed the jurisprudence expressed in the holding of *Hospital Products Ltd., v. United States Surgical Corporation* (holding that "the fiduciary undertakes or agrees to act for or on behalf of or in the interests of another person in the exercise of a power or discretion which will affect the interests of that other person in a legal or practical sense").[129]

Nevertheless, the court reasoned that this finding did not position Ganalbingu Aboriginal law and custom as an integral part of the Australian legal system; rather, the conclusion regarding the existence of a fiduciary relationship arose not from a legal question but from a factual set of circumstances peculiar to this particular case. Hence, the court found that a pre-existing fiduciary obligation imposed on Mr. Bulun Bulun required that he refrain from exploiting his artistic work in a manner that is "contrary to the laws and custom of the Ganalbingu people, and, in the event of infringement by a third party, [that Mr. Bulun Bulun] take reasonable and appropriate action to restrain and remedy infringement of the copyright in the artistic work."[130] Thus, any relief the tribe sought for infringement against Mr. Bulun Bulun's artwork based on a communitarian claim had to be limited to *in personam* actions against Mr. Bulun Bulun to enforce his copyright in works against third-party infringers because as a fiduciary, he had the duty to always act in the best interests of the Ganalbingu people. Since Mr. Bulun Bulun had successfully enforced his copyright, the court reasoned that no further equitable remedy was necessary.[131] The court's holding is interpreted to mean that the Ganalbingu people did not possess an equitable interest in the copyright inherent in Mr. Bulun Bulun's artwork, but instead, given the facts of the case, the Ganalbingu people were the beneficiaries of the fiduciary obligations owed to them by Mr. Bulun Bulun.

Bulun Bulun's holding can be viewed as a retreat from the holding of *Milpurrurru* because of *Bulun Bulun*'s unambiguous upholding that copyright inheres in an individual's authorship. Nevertheless, it is evident that even in *Milpurrurru*, the awarding of punitive damages lay in harms done to prominent and known individual artists and spokespersons, not in the recognition of communitarian-based copyright claims. This shows how resilient and deeply entrenched the Eurocentric convention of valuing individual creativity over communally generated cultural expressions is. This is a topic that recurs, in various forms, throughout this book.

PARADIGM SHIFTS AS CULTURAL SHIFTS

In summary, this chapter used Stavenhagen's and Coomb's characterizations of "culture" as implied in intellectual property law. Additionally, it also applied Hofstede and his co-authors' cultural schema of individualism and communitarianism in order to sketch how cultural conflicts embedded in the controversy over ownership of a partially incorporated folk song between the German band, Enigma, and the Ami tribal couple, the Duanas, were successfully negotiated. Furthermore, the chapter also applied Hofstede and his co-authors' cultural rubric of hierarchy versus egalitarianism to draw out key elements that made the cultural conflict between the Chilean government and the Mapuche/Pehuenche tribe over the right to build a dam that would flood the tribe's ancestral lands, so difficult to negotiate, ultimately requiring an intervention by the IACHR. Finally, the chapter also briefly sketched general programs of action and specific strategies and incentives for negotiation in overcoming cultural clashes (understood both in terms of intellectual property law's descriptions of cultures and Hofstede and his co-authors' autoethnographic dimensions of culture) between indigenous cultures (such as the Ami tribe in Taiwan and the Mapuche/Pehuenche tribe in Chile) and various majoritarian cultures.

In explaining how a paradigm shift occurs in science, Thomas Kuhn had two insights that are relevant to this chapter. First, when one has begun to see the formerly "invisible" rabbit (as opposed to the "obvious" duck), it is as if one now lives in a different world; objectively, it is the same world, but it is one that can now be glimpsed from multiple vantage points.[132] Second, when a scientific "revolution" occurs (e.g., the shift from Newton's model to Einstein's model in physics), it occurs not so much because the Einsteinians have rationally convinced the Newtonians they are correct. Rather, a crucial factor is that the prior generation (the Newtonians) have died off, and the younger generation has grown up within the Einsteinian way of questioning and finding answers and continues using that paradigm.[133] The replacement of one paradigm by another occurs not necessarily purely by rational argumentation and persuasion than, to some extent, by a generational and sociological shift. This is not to reduce such a shift to pure irrationalism and contingency, but to attempt a model of complexity, neither purely rational, nor purely a-rational or irrational.

The insight is crucial as it underlines how opening one's self up to cross-cultural negotiation necessitates openness and an awareness and acceptance of limitations. "Reality" is not just the "duck" or the "rabbit." It is both (and more), seen through different lenses, and even more fundamentally, lived, through different modes of relationality. Cross-cultural work is difficult. As Tracy Novinger's book illustrates through a startling story, the significance of tapping into a common cultural set of norms can sometimes have dramatic consequences.

> A well dressed Mexican pulled up in a taxi to the Palacio de Justicia in Lima, Peru. Armed guards were standing on the steps ascending to the building. The passenger paid and thanked the driver and opened the door of the cab, intent on the information he had come to get. As he leaned forward and put one foot onto the pavement, a cold rifle muzzle jabbed him in the temple and jerked his attention to matters at hand. The Peruvian guard holding the rifle shot two harsh words at him. The Mexican reddened, emerged from the taxi, and drew himself erect. With a sweep of his arm, he retorted three words: "¡Qué! ¿Nos *conocemos?*" (What! Do we know each other?) With a half bow the guard lowered the rifle and courteously gestured the man up the steps, speaking in deferential tones.[134]

What occurred, as described, was an exchange that tapped into a set of norms regarding formality and hierarchy shared between the Mexican civilian and Peruvian guard. The Peruvian guard had used the words "¿Que *quieres?*" (What do you want?)—but using the familiar form: one normally used for family members, close friends, former classmates, or children.[135] The Mexican appears to have replied reflexively in indignation, despite the rifle muzzle on his neck. "Do we know each other?" served as a powerful cultural rebuke,[136] probably reminding the guard of class/status differences (and masculinity) also embedded in the differences between the formal and informal modes of address. Chastened, the guard amended his discourtesy. The Mexican man's response, in Novinger's view, was risky because the guard could have easily pulled the trigger. But the hard-wired nature of the Mexican man's response awoke a corresponding cultural instinct in the Peruvian guard, leading him to recognize the Mexican as not an "outsider" but as someone deserving of respect and deference. The story emphasizes that studying and working across cultural differences is indeed challenging work but it is through such endeavors that lived reality can potentially become, in the words of J. R. R. Tolkien, simultaneously "wide and deep and high."[137]

NOTES

1. This chapter has been adapted from Caroline Joan "Kay" S. Picart, "Negotiations and International Intellectual Property Law: Attempts to Work Across Cultural Clashes Between Indigenous Peoples and Majoritarian Cultures," *Southern California Interdisciplinary Law Journal* 23, no. 1 (January 2014): 37–65. The author thanks the *Southern California Interdisciplinary Law Journal* for permission to adapt this material.
2. Rodolfo Stavenhagen, "Cultural Rights: A Social Science Perspective," in *Economic, Social and Cultural Rights*, 2nd ed., ed. Ashbjørn Eide, Catrina Krause, and Allan Rosas (The Hague, Netherlands: Kluwer Law International, 2001), 87.
3. Ibid.
4. Ibid., 88.
5. Ibid., 89.
6. Ibid., 89.
7. Rosemary J. Coombe, "Intellectual Property, Human Rights and Sovereignty: New Dilemmas in International Law Posed by the Recognition of Indigenous Knowledge and the Conservation of Biodiversity," *Indiana Journal of Global Legal Studies* 6, no. 1 (Fall 1998): 59, 73–74.
8. Ibid., 74.
9. Ibid.
10. Lorna Dwyer, "Biopiracy, Trade, and Sustainable Development," *Colorado Journal of International Environmental Law and Policy* 19 (2008): 219, 226.
11. Ibid., 216–17.
12. Ibid., 228–29.
13. Ibid.
14. Ibid., 229–30.
15. Ibid.
16. Leanne M. Fecteau, "The Ayahuasca Patent Revocation: Raising Questions about Current U.S. Patent Policy," *Boston College Third World Law Journal* 21 (2001): 69, 70–71.
17. Daniel Wüger, "Prevention of Misappropriation of Intangible Cultural Heritage through Intellectual Property Laws" in *Poor People's Knowledge: Promoting Intellectual Property in Developing Countries*, ed. J. Michael Finger and Philip Schuler (Washington, DC: World Bank Publications, 2004), 183.
18. Ibid.
19. Ibid., 194.
20. Ibid.
21. 35 U.S.C. § 102(a) and (b) (2002); Steve Beyer, "The Ayahuasca Patent Case," Singing to Plants, www.singingtotheplants.com/2008/01/ayahuasca-patent-case/, January 3, 2008.
22. Berta Hernandez-Truyol and Stephen J. Powell, *Just Trade: A New Covenant Linking Trade and Human Rights* (New York: New York University Press, 2009), 218–19.
23. Trade Related Aspects of Intellectual Property Rights, Article 27(1), Annex 1C, 1995, in Daniel C. K. Chow and Thomas J. Schoenbaum, eds., *International Trade Law: Documents Supplement* (2010), 297–98.

24. USPTO, The Enablement Requirement, Section 2164, 35 U.S.C. 112 in Manual Patent Examining Procedure (MPEP) (8th ed., August 2011), www.uspto.gov/web/offices/pac/mpep/documents/2100_2164.htm (last visited May 14, 2015).

25. Hernandez-Truyol and Powell, *Just Trade*, 219.

26. See, for example, Rosemary J. Coombe's analysis of the controversy over a malt whiskey company's appropriation of Lakota statesman Crazy Horse's name as the trademark for its product in Rosemary J. Coombe, *The Cultural Life of Intellectual Properties: Authorship, Appropriation, and the Law* (Durham, NC: Duke University Press, 1998), 199–204.

27. Janice G. Weiner, "Protection of Folklore: A Political and Legal Challenge" 18 *IIC: International Review of Industrial Property and Copyright Law* (1987), 56, 58.

28. Terri Janke, "UNESCO-WIPO World Forum on the Protection of Folklore: Lessons for Protecting Indigenous Australian Cultural and Intellectual Property" *Copyright Reporter* 15 (1997): 104, 109.

29. Agnés Lucas-Schloetter, "Folklore," in *Indigenous Heritage and the Intellectual Property: Genetic Resources, Traditional Knowledge and Folklore* 2nd ed., ed. Silke von Lewinski (The Hague, Netherlands: Kluwer Law International, 2008), 346.

30. WIPO, *Intergovernmental Committee on Intellectual Property and Genetic Resources, Traditional Knowledge and Folklore* no. 50, WIPO/GRTFK/IC/6/3 (1 December 2003), 17.

31. Thomas Streeter, "Broadcast Copyright and the Bureaucratization of Property" in *The Construction of Authorship: Textual Appropriation in Law and Literature*, ed. Martha Woodmansee and Peter Jaszi (Durham, NC: Duke University Press, 1994), 306.

32. Marlon B. Ross, "The New Negro Displayed: Self-Ownership, Proprietary Sites/Sights, and the Bonds/Bounds of Race" in *Claiming the Stones, Naming the Bones: Cultural Property and the Negotiation of National and Ethnic Identity*, ed. Elazar Barkan and Ronald Bush (Los Angeles, CA: Getty Publications, 2002), 259.

33. Martha Woodmansee, "The Genius and the Copyright," *Eighteenth Century Studies* 17, no. 4 (1984): 434, 447.

34. James Boyle, *Shamans, Software, & Spleens: Law and The Construction of the Information Society* (Cambridge, MA: Harvard University Press, 1996), xiv.

35. Laurelyn Whitt, *Science, Colonialism and Indigenous Peoples: The Cultural Politics of Law and Knowledge* (New York: Cambridge University Press, 2009), 162.

36. Lori Andrews and Dorothy Nelkin, *Body Bazaar: The Market for Human Tissue in the Biotechnology Age* (New York: Crown Publishers, 2001); L. Lone Dog, "Whose Genes Are They? The Human Genome Diversity Project," *Journal of Health and Social Policy* 10, no. 4 (1999): 51–66; Michael Dodson and Robert Williamson, "Indigenous Peoples and the Morality of the Human Genome Diversity Project," *Journal of Medical Ethics* 25 (1999): 204–8; Henry T. Greely, "Legal, Ethical, and Social Issues in Human Genome Research," *Annual Review of Anthropology* 27 (1998): 473–502; Hilary Cunningham, "Colonial Encounters in Postcolonial Contexts: Patenting Indigenous DNA and the Human Genome Diversity Project," *Critique of Anthropology* 18, no. 2 (1998): 205–33. For a lucid overview of aims of human genetic diversity research generally see Michael H. Crawford, "Anthropological Genetics in the 21st Century: Introduction," *Human Biology* 72, no. 1 (2000): 3–13.

37. Russell Lawrence Barsh, "Pharmacogenomics and Indigenous Peoples: Real Issues and Actors," *Cardozo Journal of International and Comparative Law* 11, no. 2 (2003–2004): 365, 385.

38. "Indigenous Research Protection Act," *Indigenous Peoples Council on Biocolonialism*, accessed April 20, 2015, www.ipcb.org.

39. Barsh, "Pharmacogenomics," 385.

40. See, for example, A. S. Goicoechea et al., "Genetic Relationships Between Amerindian Populations of Argentina," *American Journal of Physical Anthropology* 115 (2001): 133–43; Mauricio L. Moraga et al., "Mitochondrial DNA Polymorphisms in Chilean Aboriginal Populations: Implications for the Peopling of the Southern Cone of the Continent," *American Journal of Physical Anthropology* 113 (2000): 19–29.

41. Barsh, "Pharmacogenomics," 385.

42. Barsh, "Pharmacogenomics," 385.

43. Whitt, *Science, Colonialism*, 162.

44. "General Agreement on Tariffs and Trade 1947" in *International Trade Law: Documents Supplement* 2010–2011 ed., Daniel C. K. Chow and Thomas J. Schoenbaum, eds. (New York: Aspen Publishers, 2010), 38–101.

45. Whitt, *Science, Colonialism*, 164.

46. Darryl A. Posey and Graham Dutfield, *Beyond Intellectual Property: Toward Traditional Resource Rights for Indigenous Peoples and Local Communities* (Ontario, Canada: International Development Research Centre, 1996), 103.

47. For a detailed assessment of the strengths and limitations of intellectual property rights as a tool for protecting TK and EoF, see a recent joint study by UNCTAD and the International Centre for Trade and Sustainable Development. See UNCTAD-ICTSD Project on IPRs and Sustainable Development, Intellectual Property Rights: Implications for Development Ch. 8 (Geneva: ICTSD and UNCTAD, 2003).

48. Posey and Dutfield, *Beyond* Intellectual, 103.

49. Richard F. Roper, "Taiwanese Settle Lawsuit Claiming Their Original Composition Was Stolen; They Will Now Set Up Foundation," *Business Wire*, last updated June 23, 1999, accessed January 1, 2014, www.angelfire.com/az/MizSpiffysLair/article3.html.

50. Ibid.

51. Ibid.

52. Ashley Esarey, "An Ami Couple Seeks Recognition for Their Music," *Travel in Taiwan Special*, accessed May 12, 2015, www.sinica.edu.tw/tit/special/0996_Innocence.html.

53. Ibid.

54. Ibid.

55. Victor Wong, "Taiwanese Aboriginal Singers Settle Copyright Lawsuit," *Billboard* 31, issue 11 (July 31, 1999): 14.

56. Esaray, "An Ami Couple."

57. "Enigma (Musical Project)," *Wikipedia*, accessed January 9, 2013, en.wikipedia.org/wiki/Enigma_%28musical_project%29. See also "Difang and Igay Duana," *ZIKKIR*, last modified September 19, 2011, zikkir.net/words/Difang_and_Igay_Duana; Yvonne Lin Mei-Jung, "Intellectual Property Rights of the

Aboriginal Peoples of Taiwan," *Taiwan First* Nations, last accessed May 14, 2015, www.taiwanfirstnations.org/TFNIPR.html.

58. See, for example, Cour d'appel [CA][regional court of appeal] Paris, Apr. 10, 1995, RIDA 1995, 166 (Fr.) (affirming the artist's right to divulgation). See generally André Françon and Jane C. Ginsburg, "Authors' Rights in France: The Moral Right of the Creator of a Commissioned Work to Compel the Commissioning Party to Complete the Work," *Columbia-VLA Journal of Law and the Arts* 9 (1985): 381. In general, artists' moral rights have been codified in the Berne Copyright Convention, Rome, 1928; Berne is the oldest and most comprehensive international treaty giving authors rights outside their home countries and the protection of the artists' moral rights is enshrined in article 6bis. See Berne Convention for the Protection of Literary and Artistic Works, art. 6bis, Sept. 9, 1886, amended on Sept. 28, 1979, available at www.wipo.int/treaties/en/ip/berne/trtdocs_wo001.html#P123_20726. The United States did not sign the Berne Convention until 1988 (effective March 1, 1989) and refused to adopt article 6bis. See Ann M. Garfinkle, J. Fries, D. Lopez, and L. Possessky, "Art Conservation and the Legal Obligation to Preserve Artistic Intent," *Journal of the American Institute for Conservation* 36 (1997): 165.

59. The Visual Artists Rights Act (VARA) protects the rights of integrity and attribution of artists of "work[s] of visual art." Visual Artists Rights Act, 17 U.S.C. § 106A (1990). However, "a work of visual art" is narrowly defined as "a painting, drawing, print, sculpture, existing in a single copy, in a limited edition of 200 copies or fewer that are signed and consecutively numbered by the author, or, in the case of a sculpture, in multiple cast, carved, or fabricated sculptures of 200 or fewer that are consecutively numbered by the author and bear the signature or other identifying mark of the author." 17 U.S.C. § 101 (2010). The Duanas' "moral rights" would clearly not be protected under U.S. law. See Ibid.

60. "Enigma (Musical Project)," *Wikipedia*.

61. Ibid.

62. Ibid.

63. Roper, *Taiwanese Settle*, 1.

64. Ibid.

65. Nancy Guy, "Regaining their Voices: Music, Cultural Ownership, and the Amis Copyright Struggle," *Copyright and Conceptions of Intellectual Property in Cross-Cultural Perspective*. Austin, TX: Popular Music Section of the Society for Ethnomusicology, 1999, accessed February 21, 2008, orpheus.tamu.edu/pmssem/copyright.htm#guy cited in Chiung-Wen Chang, "'Return to Innocence': In Search of Ethnic Identity in the Music of the Amis of Taiwan," *College Music Symposium* 49/50 (2009/2010): 327–32, accessed June 6, 2015, symposium.music.org/index.php?option=com_k2&view=item&id=9238:%E2%80%9Creturn-to-innocence%E2%80%9D-in-search-of-ethnic-identity-in-the-music-of-the-amis-of-taiwan&Itemid=124.

66. "Difang and Igay Duana," *Project Gutenberg Self-Publishing Press*, accessed June 5, 2015, self.gutenberg.org/articles/difang_and_igay_duana#cite_note-2.

67. Ibid.

68. Ibid.

69. Timothy D. Taylor, "A Riddle Wrapped in a Mystery: Transitional Music Sampling and Enigma's 'Return to Innocence,'" in *Music and Tenchoculture*, ed.

René T. A. Lysloff and Leslie C. Gay, Jr. (Middletown, CT: Wesleyan University Press, 2003), 64.

70. Emily Nott, "Appropriation, Re-appropriation, and the Musical Fourth World: The Politics of 'Borrowing,'" *Emily Nott Presses* Words (blog), April 2011, nottemil.wordpress.com/2011/04/18/appropriation-re-appropriation-and-the-musical-fourth-world-the-politics-of-%E2%80%9Cborrowing-%E2%80%9D/.

71. To view the Duanas' more polished reconstruction of identity and performance, see "Elders Drinking Song by Difang," YouTube video, 0:38, posted by "tnfshbest," on October 12, 2007, www.youtube.com/watch?v=uROdVAV1zQo.

72. Chang, "'Return to Innocence.'"

73. See, for example, Difang, "Elders' Drinking Song."

74. See, Difnag "Elders Drinking Song" and "Difang & Igay singing 'Weeding and Paddyfield Song No. 1,'" YouTube video, 1:00, posted by "DebraSchick," on August 3, 2012, www.youtube.com/watch?v=ePKKeXNZnaY.

75. Beroiza, "Case No. 4617/02," *Comisión Interamericana de Deroches* Humanos, Report No. 30/04 (2004), www.cidh.oas.org/Indigenas/Chile.4617.htm.

76. Marcos O. Orellana, "Indigenous Peoples, Energy and Environmental Justice: The Pangue/Ralco Hydroelectric Project in Chile's Alto BíoBío 9" (2004), accessed May 14, 2015, www.ciel.org/Publications/Ralco_Brief_22Jul04.pdf. See also "Chile: Mapuche Increase Opposition to Bío Bío River Dam," *Toward* Freedom, last modified December 1, 2008, accessed January 1, 2014, towardfreedom.com/home/content/view/1470/1/.

77. Ibid., 525.

78. Ibid.

79. Ibid.

80. Ibid. See generally "The Mapuche People of South America," *Human Rights Research Center*, accessed May 14, 2015, www.hrusa.org/indig/reports/mapuche.pdf; James Langman, "Indigenous Fight to Keep Land in Chile," *Washington Times*, February 11, 2003, accessed May 14, 2015, www.latinamericanstudies.org/chile/pehuenches-03.htm.

81. Ibid. See also The Coalition of Concerned NGOs on Bakun (Gabungan), Malaysia, "The Resettlement of Indigenous People affected by the Bakun Hydro-Electric Project, Sarawak, Malaysia," Prepared for Thematic Review I.2: Dams, Indigenous People and vulnerable ethnic minorities, in *World Commission on Dams*, (December 1999), accessed June 26, 2015, www.internationalrivers.org/files/attached-files/resettlement_of_indigenous_people_at_bakun.pdf.

82. Ibid.

83. Orellana, "Indigenous Peoples: Energy," 525.

84. Ibid. The battle for control over indigenous ancestral lands and dam building continues. See James Langman, "Company Vows More Chilean Dams on the Way," *Ecoamericas* (May 2013): 5, accessed May 14, 2015, www.futaleufuriverkeeper.org/wp-content/uploads/2013/06/EcoAmericas-Futaleufu-Dams May-2013.pdf.

85. For an example, on the use of antiterrorism laws against the Mapuche, see Gale Courey Toensing, "Inter-American Court Hears Mapuche Human Rights Case Against Chile," *Indian Country* Today, last modified June 3, 2013, accessed May 14, 2015, indiancountrytodaymedianetwork.com/2013/06/03/

inter-american-courthears-mapuche-human-rights-case-against-chile-149677. See also Luis Carcamo-Huechante, "Mapuche Political Prisoners Hearing at the Inter-American Court of Human Rights," *Cultural Survival*, May 29–30, 2013, www.culturalsurvival.org/news/mapuche-politicalprisoners-hearing-inter-american-court-human-rights-may-29-30-2013; Ryan Seelau, "Mapuche Testify Against Chile Before Inter-American Court of Human Rights," *Indigenous News*, May 31, 2013, indigenousnews.org/2013/05/31/mapuche-testify-against-chile-before-inter-american-court-ofhuman-rights-oas/.

86. The activists opposing the construction of the Belo Monte dam in Brazil seem to have learned the value of recruiting and deploying star power (especially that of director James Cameron) in drawing media attention to their cause. See Alexei Barrionuevo, "Tribes of Amazon Find Ally Out of 'Avatar,'" *New York Times*, April 10, 2010, New York Edition, A1, www.nytimes.com/2010/04/11/world/americas/11brazil.html.

87. Tian Spain and Mike Gatehouse, "Chile Accused of Racist Use of Anti-terrorism Laws Against Mapuches," *Latin American Bureau Council on Hemispheric Affairs*, accessed June 8, 2015, www.coha.org/chile-accused-of-racist-use-of-anti-terrorism-laws-against-mapuches/.

88. "Chile Invokes Pinochet-Era Anti-Terrorism Law Against Mapuche Demonstrators," *Council on Hemispheric Affairs*, last modified November 19, 2009, accessed June 8, 2015, www.coha.org/chile-invokes-pinochet-era-anti-terrorism-law-against-mapuche-demonstrators/.

89. Ibid.

90. Ibid.

91. Ibid.

92. Ibid.

93. Ibid.

94. Ibid.

95. Tian Spain and Mike Gatehouse, "Chile Accused of Racist Use."

96. Ibid.

97. Ibid.

98. "Chile Invokes Pinochet-Era," *Council on Hemispheric Affairs*.

99. Ibid.

100. Australian Institute of Professional Counsellors (AIPC) (1995), 91–116; cited in: Michael Blakeney, "Communal Intellectual Property Rights of Indigenous Peoples in Cultural Expressions," *The Journal of World Intellectual Property* 1, no. 6 (November 1998): 987.

101. "[1998] 1082 Franchise Council of Australia (FCA)," modified September 3, 1998, Mvw.austlii.edu.au/au/cases/cth/federd-ct/1998q082.html; cited in Blakeney, "Communal Intellectual Property," 992.

102. Blakeney, "Communal Intellectual Property," 987–88.

103. Ibid., 989.

104. Australian Institute of Professional Counsellors (AIPC) (1995), 91–116, at 39,081; cited in Blakeney, "Communal Intellectual Property," 989, n. 12.

105. Ibid., 989.

106. Ibid., 988.

107. Ibid., 989.

108. Ibid.
109. Ibid., 988.
110. Ibid., 990.
111. "[1960] 1 The Weekly Law Reports (WLR) 1072, at 1087–87"; cited in Michael Blakeney, "Communal Intellectual Property," 990, nn. 13, 16.
112. Ibid.
113. Ibid., 990.
114. Ibid., 991.
115. "(1995) Australian Institute of Professional Counsellors (AIPC), 91–116, at 39,065"; cited in Blakeney, "Communal Intellectual Property," 991.
116. Ibid.
117. [1998] 1082 Franchise Council of Australia (FCA) (3 September 1998), cited in: Blakeney, "Communal Intellectual," 992.
118. Ibid.
119. Ibid.
120. Ibid.
121. Geert Hofstede, Gert Jan Hofstede, and Michael Minkov, *Cultures and Organizations: Software of the Mine*, 3rd ed. (New York: McGraw-Hill Education, 2010), 89–134.
122. [1998] 1082 Franchise Council of Australia (FCA) (3 September 1998), cited in: Blakeney, "Communal Intellectual," 992.
123. Ibid.
124. Ibid., 993.
125. Ibid.
126. The court cited S. K. B. Asante, "Fiduciary Principles in Anglo-American Law and The Customary Law of Ghana," *International and Comparative Law Quarterly* 14, no. 4 (1965): 1145. Cited in Blakeney, "Communal Intellectual Property," 993, n. 26.
127. Blakeney, "Communal Intellectual Property," 993.
128. Ibid., 994.
129. "(1984) 156 Commonwealth Law Reports (CLR) 41"; cited in Blakeney, "Communal Intellectual Property," 993.
130. Cited in Blakeney, "Communal Intellectual Property," 994.
131. Ibid.
132. Thomas Kuhn, *The Structure of Scientific Revolutions* (Chicago: University of Chicago Press, 1970), 18–19.
133. Ibid. For a similar observation regarding generational change, see generally Robert D. Putnam, *Bowling Alone: The Collapse and Revival of American Community* (New York: Simon and Schuster Paperbacks, 2000).
134. Tracy Novinger, *Intercultural Communication: A Practical Guide*, (Austin, TX: University of Texas Press, 2001), 1.
135. Ibid., 5.
136. Ibid.
137. J. R. R. Tolkien, *Tree and Leaf: Smith of Wotton Major; The Homecoming of Beorhtnoth Beorthelm's Son* (London: Unwin Paperbacks—Allen & Unwin Book Publishers, 1975).

4

Colonial Appropriations of Marginalized Cultures and Possible Strategies of Resistance[1]

REFLECTIONS ON INTERSECTIONALITIES: STRATEGIES OF RESISTANCE IN RELATION TO NARRATIVE, PROPERTY, AND COLLECTIVE IDENTITY

Numerous critical legal and cultural scholars have analyzed how law creates a discourse that simultaneously levels (cultural) differences so that these differences seem invisible, while, paradoxically, it implicitly relies upon these underlying differences to weigh the differing pressing requirements required for effective legal interpretation, mediation, and remedy, among other functions.[2] All these are part of how law functions in and as culture. However, while law shuns difference that is submitted to it in a profoundly different way, law attempts to come to terms with difference provided this difference is presented using law's own categories and terms of reference.[3] Elizabeth Povinelli, for instance, has demonstrated how, in the context of land rights and native titles in Australia, this essential translation of difference can result in the innovation of particular categories of cultural differences, wherein a measure of "authenticity" inheres and that measure of authenticity in turn demands a specific "performance" of legal subjectivity, for this performance to be considered "authentic."[4] Thus, law, *de facto*, sets up the conditions of possibility within which particular legal subjectivities can become recognized, which then dictate the parameters within which "genuine" or "authentic" representative individuals can act within legal contexts. Nevertheless, this is not a reductive process as persons or groups can always strategically reconfigure or innovate the way in which the law is interpreted to suit certain purposes, as this book generally argues.[5] Thus, phrasing an interest in protecting indigenous peoples' intellectual property rights in a manner that makes this initiative intelligible, within law's own categories and using law's own terms, allows the initiative to become audible, and to some extent, cognizable. Precisely because the initiative is phrased using law's own language games, it cannot ignore the initiative since law cannot overturn its own internal coherence as a cultural system of meaning that claims to be universalist. Within this context, therefore, there is an emancipatory potential, alongside a grounding or repressive force, that is embedded in law in and as culture, and in this particular instance, intellectual property law. As Rosemary Coombe astutely observes: "It would be reductionist to see the power of intellectual property in purely prohibit[ive] terms. The law is always simultaneously prohibitive and productive: it creates realities and constitutes possibilities."[6]

Thematically, this chapter continues an analysis of law as a culture, and law in culture to examine a broad spectrum of different, but convergent, strategies of resistance and adaptation, to the prevailing power differentials embedded in law and culture. One model, principally ethnographic, deploys narrative as a medium capable of being a vessel of ambiguity and ambivalence, particularly within the context of reflecting the personal experiences, for example, of young immigrants, or others, whose outsider status remains uncertainly inscribed despite their apparent integration through formal legal processes.[7] Another model, principally politico-legal, deploys narrative as employing two sides: first, a "front-stage" side which projects a narrative of legal coherence and apparent integration; and second, a hidden "back-stage" view, which reveals a narrative of legal inconsistencies and the persistence of insidious culturally maintained discriminatory castes based on race, class, and gender.[8]

Correspondingly, the first narrative usually leads to a strategy of description—of attempting simply to draw attention to the ambivalences and ambiguities of occupying an insider-outsider position, or the status of an outsider within, or the process of apparently successfully crossing a border only to find more barriers within. In contrast, the second narrative generally leads to a strategy of deconstruction—of unveiling hidden binaries that require the privileging of one class against its required other; of drawing attention to the continued proliferation of monstrous metaphors in relation to women and minorities; of unmasking how legal systems can reify culturally conditioned categories of discrimination. Nevertheless, the two types of narratives, and strategies of resistance, are not necessarily mutually exclusive. More realistically, they remain porous. Indeed, most accounts usually fluctuate between these two modes of framing (ethnographic and politico-legal), and thus successfully deploy both strategies (descriptive and deconstructive).[9]

Although there are certainly important differences, principally because of its use of a third person point of view, and a focus on legal principles, Berta Hernandez-Truyol's[10] sympathetic account of the Brazilian indigenous tribe's continuing, and still peaceful, battle to maintain control over its lands, its traditional knowledge, its ancestral property, and collective identity, against the onslaught of Brazil's determined efforts to join the hallowed ranks of fully developed nations through building the Belo Monte Dam, has affinities with the approaches detailed above. This is not surprising because critical focus on the subject positions that minorities and indigenous people, in particular, occupy within the law (and as embedded in social norms and relationships) is crucial to unveiling modes of historical injustice. This critical strategy provides a context for the multitude of ways in which laws treat difference and relationships, which are crucial to unveiling modes of historical injustice.

As prior chapters have shown, the ways in which minorities and indigenous peoples have been constructed and produced within the dominant legal system is a result of social and political forces in which law has always been integrally engaged. This insight leads to the realization that law is deeply and inseparably imbricated with politics, and that law does not operate in a vacuum. The impetus, in critical legal studies, among other fields, to acknowledge the "special" circumstances under which indigenous peoples in particular can fully enter legal discourse and political life has spurred debates regarding the extent to which law can accommodate difference.[11]

One potentially creative area of tension for law is that indigenous peoples present the possibility of presenting arguments that could also be made in favor of groups in similar positions of displacement and marginality due to evolving cultural experiences, circumstances, and relations. The key issue is that indigenous differences, in relation to some laws such as those concerning land, property, and traditional knowledge, are localized and particular.[12] Thus, moving from the particular to the general concerning what would best protect a particular tribe's rights, compared to the collective rights of indigenous peoples, at the national level, requires a nuanced and complex approach. For example, in a country like the Philippines, which has over one hundred ethno-linguistic groups, the determination of the collective rights of indigenous peoples, at the national level, requires careful negotiation.[13]

As the Belo Monte struggle shows, the language of property has become a touchstone of the ways in which indigenous traditional knowledge and traditional cultural expressions have become positioned in law. Beginning first with land rights and ownership of material cultural products, such discussions also engage issues of intellectual property. The power of property is that it is both in law, and beyond law; it is both a legal and social trope. Property, as Joseph Singer points out, is less about "things" than about relationships among legal entities.[14] As such, the concept of property mediates the way people and other legal entities, such as legal, governmental, or nongovernmental institutions, interact.

Very clearly, modern Western notions of property are fundamentally shaped by the narrative of Locke's theory of labor and private property. A crucial source, often cited, for the current interpretation of Lockean notions of property, is the following passage:

> Though the Earth, and all inferior Creatures be Common to all Men, yet every Man has a *Property* of his own *Person*. This nobody has any right but himself. The *Labour* of his body and the *Work* of his hands, we may say are properly his. Whatsoever then he removes out of the State that Nature hath provided, and left it in, he hath mixed his *Labour* with, and joined to it something that is his own and thereby makes it his *Property*.[15]

Locke's theory of the primacy of private property rests on a tripartite foundation. First is an iteration of natural law: that "every Man has a *Property* of his *Person*," and that "*Labour* of his body and *Work* of his hands" form the first spoke.[16] The second and third spokes are bound up with how labor creates value. The second foundation is that it is via that expenditure or investment of individual labor, mingled with the state of nature that produces something new, which thus becomes the private property of the investor.

Yet the contemporary emphasis on property as relational is less a Lockean concept than a contribution by Jeremy Bentham.[17] For Bentham, it is less natural rights that generate value in property, than the fact that relations of property constitute social relations and power differentials.[18] The narrative of the "value" of property therefore is defined by the complex constellation of these relationships, and not by some objective measure, which can be calibrated apart from these social relations.

Yet these social regulations are maintained and upheld through the rule of law; it is law that provides the frameworks guiding the conceptions of what is "naturally" owned, and the entitlement of what certain types of persons can "naturally" expect to possess. Nevertheless, there is one more layer to add: the economic transformation of property, creating new forms of expectations and entitlements. Writ large, cumulative property relations become infused with a systemic drive to generate revenue or capital, and government influences demarcate political spheres of interaction. The workings of the market generate new expectations or new assumptions concerning what is collectively culturally "natural," and it is the law that regulates and maintains these expectations, which cement the foundations of society.

One insight that emerges from these reflections is that the law appears most capable of moderating difference when these differences are translated into a semblance or a close enough guise of its own categories or frameworks. Both indigenous movements', as well as minority groups', attempts to protect their cultural integrity and cultural expressions, as well as their autonomies, often first appear to integrate into the system, only to attempt to re-imagine the system from within—exploring what Michel Foucault has described as the lacunae and flows of power.[19] Coombe observes:

> The enabling power of law . . . is not simply that it provides instruments and discursive resources through which social groups may seek to have their differences legitimated or their needs addressed . . . but also that law generates the signs and symbols—the signifying forms—with which difference is constituted and given meaning. . . . It invites and shapes (although it does not determine) activities that legitimate, resist, and potentially rework the meanings that accrue to these forms in public spheres.[20]

Strategies of resistance are not linear but adaptive, and there are multiple ways of resisting the circulations of power, both collectively and individually, and thus generating new forces of political impetus.[21] Michel de Certeau has argued that it is possible to subvert hegemonic cultural representations and laws, "not by [overtly] rejecting or altering them, but by using them with respect to ends and references foreign to the system."[22] What de Certeau proposes is, in some ways, as old as a central tenet of Zen and the martial arts—that one can use the energy of one's opponent against him by following that flow, and then at a crucial point, using it as a pivot to redirect the flow.[23]

Failure to integrate into a narrative or a rhetoric that the majority can translate or "read" leads to the production of "monstrous" narratives, in which difference constitutes radical otherness.[24] Though different in degree, the law's encounter with the threat of terrorism has affinities with law's conflicts in attempting to address the otherness of indigenous cultures. It is tragic but unsurprising that in parallel, and more militant indigenous movements, such as those of the Mapuche tribe in Chile, the Chilean government has begun to deploy anti-terrorism laws against these indigenous movements.[25]

The primacy of law and legal frameworks in mediating some political struggles is a part of the fulcrum that grounds an analysis of law in and as culture. In the context of property, as we have seen, law operates as a locus where conflicting, competing positions gain circulation. This holds true, not only in the case of sovereignty claims, as in the Brazilian indigenous peoples' attempts to preserve fundamental control of their lands, but also in terms of value systems and intellectual traditions in relation to knowledge use, management, access, and circulation.[26]

As we shall see in the next sections of this chapter, especially in the realm of intellectual property, some incommensurable differences in knowledge production, ownership, and protection constitute some of the seemingly insurmountable obstacles that prevent closure or even rapprochement on some topics of discussion. Nevertheless, keeping in mind the complex relationship between knowledge and power, subjects of emergent forms of property, especially intangible intellectual property, once created, begin to generate their own frameworks of interpretation, by adapting the dominant culture's tools to strategic uses. Thus, such hybrid embryonic forms of legal expression are not simply artifacts of the colonizer's or majority culture's or powerful group's tools, but also, as modified and adopted by minorities, marginalized groups, and indigenous peoples, become a feature of these outsider-insiders' means of self-governance. For even if concepts like "property" and "ownership" may not fully encompass indigenous and minority aspirations, relationships, and perspectives, these Western concepts at least provide a readily recognized and accepted set of terms through which indigenous and minority aspirations may be given voices.

STRATEGIES OF RESISTANCE IN RELATION TO COPYRIGHT AND CHOREOGRAPHY IN AMERICAN DANCE

Given law's embeddedness in culture, and functioning as a culture, possible avenues of resistance are multiple. One option lies in attempting to restore voice to those normally silenced, with their ambivalent alliances and their porous identities as members of several communities. Another possibility lies in deconstructing front-stage myths of civic order and equality to unveil back-stage realities of prejudice and hegemony. Yet another possibility lies in adapting prevailing legal and cultural categories to give voice to, as well as recast, new legal expectations for justice and equality. This section attempts to review and assess strategies of resistance in relation to a critique of the evolution of American dance choreography in relation to a history of copyright law.

This section transplants many of the insights of the prior sections, concerning narrative, principles of property law, the cultural functions of law, and strategies of resistance, into an evolving analysis of the development of federal copyright protection for choreography in the United States. The next sections of this chapter, derived from a larger project,[27] illustrates that the effort to win federal copyright protection for dance choreography in the United States was simultaneously racialized and gendered. As applied in this section, "whiteness" is about having property (both tangible and intangible), being privileged enough to be considered an "artist," and consistently being protected by the law in a seemingly "neutral" process. All these certainly implicate an analysis of the assumptions about "authorship," "creativity," and "property" behind American copyright law, as it has evolved, mirroring the potentials and tensions of its historical moorings.

As the cases of Loïe Fuller, Josephine Baker, and Katherine Dunham show, white privilege often sustains its privileged position through an ambivalent posture of negation. As Jacques Derrida's analysis of the mechanics of deconstruction illustrate,[28] white privilege requires its "other" to demarcate itself, and to establish its (comparative) superiority. Nevertheless, whiteness is not monolithic. Furthermore, possessors of white privilege are not uniformly protected culturally; law is both embedded in a broader cultural backdrop, and functions as culture, legally. Ultimately, I mean that "whiteness," functioning as "property," is not a monolithic stable "thing" but a site of complex political and cultural contestation. Additionally, white privilege's underside is a fascination with, and envy of, that which is nonwhite, which it appropriates unto itself through its characterization of the "exotic."

This section limits itself to briefly tracing Loïe Fuller's rise to stardom[29] in Paris as "La Loïe" and her failure to secure copyright protection in the landmark trial, *Fuller v. Bemis* (1892).[30] But the bulk of the section, as an exploration of possible alternative copyrightable choreographic aesthetics, analyzes Josephine Baker's equally phenomenal rise to becoming Europe's "Black Venus,"[31] and Katherine Dunham's eventual enshrinement as the "Matriarch of Black Dance" in the United States.[32]

More significantly, as a way of theorizing the complex questions of resistance in relation to race, gender, and choreographic authorship, this section examines why, if Baker had dared mount a claim for copyright protection for her dance improvisations like Fuller, such a claim would have failed even more miserably, despite her celebrity. Crucial to the differences between the conditions of possibility within which Fuller, as opposed to Baker, could attempt to claim ownership of her choreographic works was her possession of an aesthetic of whiteness and of whiteness as status property, even if her sex and gender trumped her whiteness. Compared with Baker, Katherine Dunham succeeded in establishing copyright ownership of her choreography through a complex set of factors, some of which include her whitened academic credentials,[33] her embodiment of Caucasian beauty ideals, her comparatively lightly complexioned skin (even as she embraced her African American heritage), and her savvy understanding of the dance community's norms of hierarchy.[34] The norms in place then generally held that any choreographic contributions by black choreographers were rendered invisible and attributed to white choreographers.[35] Dunham upheld these norms, in relation to Balanchine, but shortly thereafter, building upon the fame that followed her successful apprenticeship, established her own company and choreographic identity.[36]

Generally sketched, to understand how the history of the ability to copyright choreography maps on its invisible underside, whiteness as status property, one must turn, arguably, to its master template. Unlike Loïe Fuller, also a pioneer of American modern dance, George Balanchine, a Russian émigré, succeeded in gaining and maintaining full control of his choreographic creations.[37] A hyper-whitened aesthetic and Balanchine's authority as a white, male ballet-master—both manifestations of whiteness as status property, were crucial to that success.

In contrast, Fuller, who predated Balanchine by almost a hundred years, was the first white woman choreographer in the United States to attempt to establish an infringement claim in response to what she saw as the stealing of her "original" dance material, and failed.[38] As a choreographer, Fuller's genius lay in her appropriation of the general aesthetic of the skirt dance,[39] to "whiten" it beyond its burlesque, working-class roots to become an iconic image of Art Nouveau. Fuller's serpentine dance, at the height of her artistic career, became immortalized as a metaphor for a powerful, abstract expressiveness beyond language and corporeality. As opposed to the illusion of her stage presence, Fuller, then already thirty years old, hardly the conventional beauty, and knowing that her theatrical career and financial stability hinged on her ability to control ownership of the serpentine dance, turned to the legal apparatus for protection against copyright infringement,[40] rather than relying on community norms within the dance community.

However, in an opinion that has become much quoted, Judge Lacombe of the New York Circuit Court dismissed Fuller's serpentine dance as unworthy of copyright protection because of its lack of "narrative" or "dramatic" content.[41] This opinion became virtually enshrined as the legal basis for denying dance choreography (or anything that was merely "spectacle" or "decorative") copyright protection. What the judge did not explicitly address was Fuller's class status as a vaudeville performer and her proximity to the purely "popular," merely "illusory," or "decorative" forms of entertainment, such as belly dancing, for example.

In contrast to Fuller's ethereal stage presence, Baker stepped into a series of historical convergences that iconized her as the "Ebony Venus," the "Black Venus," the "Jazz Empress," and the very embodiment of "Black Womanhood."[42] In compliance with the image projected on her by her promoters and audiences, Baker wielded five performance strategies of image and identity construction, which included: exoticizing race and gender; overturning racial and cultural codes and meanings; performing

Figure 4.1. Josephine Baker in Banana Skirt from the Folies Bergère production "Un Vent de Folie," 192.
Photograph by Lucien Waléry (French, 1863–1935).

"difference" through nudity, cross-dressing, song, and dance; exploiting these images of difference; and generalizing the outcome to allow the performance messages to reach larger popular audiences[43] (see figure 4.1).

Ironically, in order to remain "the same"—as an "exotic" sexualized object of fascination—Baker would have to constantly remake herself.[44] And a key component to Baker's many transformations is her consistent "whitening" as a wild child civilized into Parisienne culture. This process of transformation occurred both personally and professionally, as Baker moved from being a body acted upon, to becoming a specular projection of the star system.[45] Choreographically, the roots of the "authentic Africanist" dance style Europe venerated[46] were African American street dances magnified through Baker's hyperbolic and flamboyant exaggerations. More precisely, they lay in Baker's spontaneous improvisational reinterpretations of popular American "street" dance steps.

But in terms of choreographic protection, like Fuller, Baker's claim to ownership of her choreographic improvisations, if she had dared to mount such a claim, would have failed, not simply because it would probably have been dismissed, like Fuller's claim, as pure "spectacle." Even more significantly, because given Baker's performances' overt eroticism and closeness to vaudeville traditions and "popular" dance steps, Baker's claim would probably also have been roundly dismissed as "obscene," lacking originality, and not "promoting the advancement of science and the useful arts,"[47] which is the principal objective of patent and copyright protection. Even more problematically, improvisation, because it is not movement fixed in a replicable flow, is not copyrightable.[48] These rules, as shown in prior chapters, are historically grounded in copyright's rootedness in Eurocentric conventions,[49] which set apart the "genius" required for an individual artist/author/choreographer's work to be protected as private intellectual property from the merely "popular" entertainment or "folk" conventions for which no individual can take credit.

Given this historical context, had Baker attempted to follow Fuller's example, her claim would have failed. Nevertheless, traces of a nonwhite aesthetic, even if hyperbolically rendered a spectacle through colonialist and commercialist lenses, can be glimpsed through her dance legacy. As Samir Dayal remarks:

> [Baker's] legacy may not be that of a profoundly subversive and parodic cultural activist. But no one can deny her immense performative breadth or the role she played in the "blackening" of the European cultural scene. Nor can it be denied that her presence in that scene brought to the fore how intimately "blackness" was sutured to the construction of modern white European subjectivity.[50]

In comparison with Josephine Baker, Katherine Dunham's rise to stardom coincided with Baker's decline as the embodiment of the erotic and primal "savage" and Martha Graham's (among other white women) deployment of a then-principally sexless model of modern dancing (this was prior to Graham's involvement with Erick Hawkins).[51] In the face of these pre-existing and often stereotyped and racialized templates, Dunham was noteworthy in her self-proclaimed project of integrating "African dance traditions that featured more forthright acceptance of sexual elements in dance."[52]

And indeed, Dunham's choreography and dance technique, unlike Baker's, not only consciously used "whitened" (and established) elements of ballet and modern dance, but also a vocabulary of movement that had clear "nonwhitened" elements, derived from her interpretative recall of her fieldwork as an anthropologist in the West Indies (Jamaica, Trinidad, Cuba, Haiti, Martinique[53]).[54] Dunham's dance technique had clear non-European elements, but she hybridized it with white traces, which, like her academic credentials, served to authorize her work, particularly in Europe. The technique she developed "emphasized the torso movements of the primitive ritual of Caribbean-African dance and jazz rhythms."[55] 54

Though Dunham self-identified herself as black, and declared a social activist impetus to her work,[56] Dunham, in terms of her physical appearance, was clearly of a mixed racial heritage, and her own autobiography emphasized that hybridity (see figure 4.2). Dunham fiercely described

Figure 4.2. Katherine Dunham, American dancer, choreographer, songwriter, anthropologist, author, educator, and activist, January 25, 1956.

Photography by Phyllis Twachtman, *World Telegram* staff photographer.

herself as a "black woman" when her physical features placed her in a liminal sphere—one that tended to be in line with white ideals of feminine beauty. The point is not that "blackness" or "whiteness" is easy to demarcate, but that her choice to position herself as a black woman was a political and aesthetic choice—not a description of biology. In addition, Dunham's combination of academic credentials of the highest caliber,[57] her practical fieldwork experience, and her visually arresting reinterpretation of ethnographic experience into choreographic staging yielded refractory responses from the dance world, critics, and the public.[58] Nevertheless, unlike Baker, whose lack of education was apparent from the start, making Baker the perfect iconic colonial subject requiring French civilization, Dunham was portrayed as someone with both sophistication and eloquence, as well as the exotic primitivism Baker had come to symbolize. The fact that Dunham's second husband, John Pratt—the man who costumed her[59]—was also white, probably helped to further "whiten" Dunham, which worked to her unambiguous advantage in Europe but elicited more ambivalent responses in the United States.

Choreographically, Dunham is notable for incorporating not only "folkloric" material derived from a broad variety of "exotic" sources, but also the familiar street-derived U.S. social dance steps characteristic of African American entertainers that Baker surreptitiously drew from and exaggerated, either in a comedic or sensual fashion[60] (see figure 4.3). But despite Dunham's eclecticism, she did privilege the Caribbean as the ethnographic cradle from which she sought to discover and rearticulate a basic vocabulary that seemed, to her, to be common to African-derived dances in the United States.[61] One difference between Baker and Dunham was that while Baker sought to conceal the Americanness of the genealogy of her dance steps, wrapping them in the shroud of the "eternal primitive" so precious to the European imaginary, Dunham sought to unveil and celebrate the uniqueness of African American street dances, as expressions of African and American culture.[62]

Dunham cemented her career and reputation through what she called "revues"—staging her re-memory of her anthropological experiences and Caribbean dance and music together with the opulent settings, brightly colored costumes, orchestral reinterpretations of the Caribbean rhythms and folk music, and the polished look of American showbiz (see figure 4.4). But it was only after she was already professionally established that Dunham "collaborated" with George Balanchine on *Cabin in the Sky* (1940).[63] Ironically, the 1940 Broadway production of *Cabin in the Sky* did not give Dunham any credit as a choreographer.[64]

Nevertheless, in Dunham's extended interview with Constance Valis Hall conducted on November 1999 and January 2000, Dunham revealed, after much prodding, that she not only choreographed most, if not all, of

Figure 4.3. Josephine Baker dancing the Charleston at the Folies-Bergère, Paris, 1926.
Photography by Lucien Walery (French, 1863–1935).

the numbers, but also, as Aschenbrenner remarks, that "she staged most of the show, although she was not given credit for it."[65] Nevertheless, overall, it is clear that Dunham's credentials as an academic, her glamorized image, and the very manner in which she staged her ethnographic research as performances, did privilege and protect her to some extent.

However, there appears to be an anxiety that repeatedly surfaces in relation to both white and black American critics' reception of Dunham's work. In relation to the question of "authenticity," Dunham's work, her image, and even her looks, seemed whitened, compared to, for example, Pearl Primus. Primus was a contemporary who pursued similar goals and scholarly interests as Dunham in the 1940s, but who did not have Dunham's numerous liminalities, inclusive of Dunham's looks, which conformed more to whitened standards of beauty, as opposed to Primus's physical appearance.[66] In relation to this question of "authenticity," Dunham's choreographic interpretation of her ethnographic research has also undergone some critique as being overly reliant on hybridization, losing specificity, and perhaps even stereotyping Caribbean culture in general.

Figure 4.4. Katherine Dunham, dancer, full-length portrait, facing right, wearing dance costume, October 16, 1943.

Photograph by Alfredo Valente.

Contrastively, in the hands of someone like Martha Graham or George Balanchine, even if devoid of the intense ethnographic fieldwork Dunham had accomplished, such "inappropriate cultural appropriation" would probably have been interpreted as "artistic innovation," passing copyright's "modicum of originality" test easily.[67] But that Dunham strategically deployed the established kinesthetic techniques and body vocabularies of ballet and modern dance would probably have made any overt legal claim she might have raised, especially given the circumstances of *Cabin in the Sky*, more likely to survive.[68]

But given the raced, sexed, and gendered nature of the politics of the dance world, Dunham wisely refrained; that savviness is what eventually cemented her commercial success and artistic independence. Like Baker, Dunham, instead of banking on copyright protection, relied on her ability to "curate" her image through the numerous interviews she gave the media.

But unlike Baker, Dunham did have some access—even if not full access—to whiteness as status property, and as such, was able to achieve some acclaim as a choreographer in her own right—but only after loyal apprenticeship to the ballet master and legally and culturally enshrined genius, George Balanchine. Thus, similar to the struggle of the Brazilian indigenous tribe at the Belo Monte dam to realize their human rights, Baker's and Dunham's strategies of survival both entailed various degrees of adaptation to, and recasting of, recognized Western legal and choreographic inscriptions. To render their "traditional knowledge" or "traditional cultural expressions" legible within systems that still maintain their Eurocentric roots, indigenous peoples and marginalized groups use a variety of strategies—not only partially resisting or protesting against the current hierarchy, but also balancing that imperative with the need to communicate with, and establish, communities of sympathy and solidarity, or at the very least, the pragmatic compunction of not alienating those who are not adamantly pro-establishment.

It is fascinating that Baker's and Dunham's struggles for recognition as artists to some extent mirrors the tensions and paradoxes that underlay Australian indigenous populations' struggles to achieve intellectual property protection for their own expressions of folklore (EoF). Jane Anderson points out that a genealogy of the events that led to a consciousness and acceptance of the imperative to protect Australian Aboriginal art leads to an awareness of the potential marketability of these artworks.[69] In addition to the Australian policy changes made during the 1970s, in relation to indigenous people, of moving from assimilation to self-government and the establishment of statutory land rights, along with the advocacy of numerous individuals, the increasing market value of Aboriginal art led to the establishment of the first National Seminar on Aboriginal Arts in 1973.[70] This seminar "prompted renewed calls for consideration of Aboriginal art as legitimate art in a Western sense complete with market signifiers,"[71] which in turn spurred further economic entitlements for both Indigenous and non-indigenous groups involved in the sale or marketing of Aboriginal art.

Nevertheless, paradoxically, despite the increased marketability and the willingness to concede that Aboriginal art is truly original art, there still persisted the dual tendencies of viewing indigenous peoples as necessarily "primitivist" and requiring that their art meet the standard of being "authentically primitivist." This was a posture that indigenous artists themselves embraced. "The circulation of Indigenous products as commodities within a marketplace remained countenanced by the (mythological) position held by Indigenous people themselves, who remained popularly represented in romantic, traditionalist, and communal guises, these imagined subject positions paradoxically enhanced and increased the value of the art as commodity."[72]

Similarly, Baker, in particular, rose to stardom astride the clearly colonialist and primitivist myth of being a "Black Venus." Despite clearly drawing from African American street dances in her dance improvisations, Baker cloaked the origins of the movements that became part of her public persona as she cultivated the image of becoming transformed, through immersion in primal rhythms, to becoming an unthinking vessel of the "Spirit of the Savage," in sensual, corporeal form.[73] That Baker was poorly educated[74] and therefore not literate, particularly in French, ironically enhanced this image even more, and contributed, for a while, to her marketability, because it seemed to shore up her "identity" as an "authentic primitive."

Dunham also, to some extent, rode the wave of celebrity that Baker had established. But unlike Baker, Dunham strategically fluctuated across several registers—as both "authentically primitivist" and "authentically educated";[75] as a "goddess of the hips" who had also been trained in classical ballet;[76] as someone canny and literate enough to charmingly control interviews and her image, while knowing when to simply allow her movements do the "talking" onstage. And unlike Baker, Dunham proudly claimed the origins of her dance movements, whether they were African American, Caribbean, or European.[77] Partly precisely because she was so literate at explaining her choreographic re-imaginations of ethnographic work, Dunham, unlike Baker at her prime, faced controversy regarding how "authentic" her work was,[78] as the assumption was that "true" primitives, such as Baker, had to remain safely harnessed within the realms of the savage, primordial, and carnal.

In other words, the situations both Baker and Dunham faced bore a striking resemblance (without leveling the differences) to the dilemmas

Australian Aboriginal artists faced, in their attempts to gain respect and recognition for their work as artists. Anderson notes that

> there existed a noticeable disjuncture where Indigenous cultural products circulated within a contemporary framework, while the Indigenous creators remained on the periphery occupying subject positions that were difficult to transcend, because they were informed by a range of colonial knowledges that produced particular images of Indigenous people and interpretations of Indigenous subjectivity.[79]

Furthermore, the issue of what was not only "authentic" but also what was "original" was a crucial issue in both the cases of Australian Aboriginal artists and both Baker and Fuller. However, what made "originality" such an issue in these cases, lay less with laws' standard processes of determining originality (which, in practice, had a low threshold, as all that is required is a "modicum" of originality and there is no definition of "originality" as such in the American[80] and Australian[81] statutory copyright acts) but rather rested in the particular subject matter at hand—Aboriginal art and dance improvisation and choreography that set themselves against Eurocentric traditions of dance and movement—as enacted by their particular creators.

In these cases, the particular subject matter and their creators could be interpreted in a two-fold sense—as simultaneously relying on the importance of originality as a legal category crucial to demarcating what is copyrightable subject matter and yet as also acknowledging the irreducible difference inherent in Aboriginal or minority cultures that render them, to some extent, incommensurable with standard legal categories. The result was a tense compromise that located these Aboriginal artists,[82] and to a different degree, Baker and Dunham, as legal subjects astride two worlds whose revolutions seemed at odds with each other: a world of tradition, in which "originality" seemed logically impossible; and a world of modernity, in which an individual author and an original work of art were logically required. This insight, in some ways, is hardly surprising, given choreography's general recalcitrance to fitting into the statutory requirements of copyright,[83] and in practice, choreography's tendency to freely "borrow" or "steal" steps on a communal basis.[84]

This is not to collapse the cultural spaces occupied by Australian Aboriginal artists, compared with Baker and Dunham, into the same critical locus as there are clear differences. While Australian Aboriginal art has achieved some degree of copyright protection, Baker still remains relegated to the realm of the improvisational performer. Although Australian Aboriginal artists have become nationally recognized as artists, they do not have the international celebrity status that both Baker and Fuller enjoyed. And while the Australian Aboriginal artists' struggles to achieve copyright protection for their EoF seems more overtly tied up with Rodolfo Stavenhagen's third description of culture, as operative in intellectual property law, as a total way of life, Baker's and Dunham's struggles for respect seem tied up more with Stavenhagen's first and second descriptions of culture, as operative in intellectual property law: of culture as capital, and culture as creativity. Nevertheless, a critical review of the similar challenges they faced is instructive as they illustrate the tensions that underlie current copyright law's emphasis on the existence of an individual author, originality, and fixation.[85]

LEVERAGING LIMINALITIES AND INTERSECTIONALITIES

This chapter has focused specifically on the themes of strategies of resistance in relation to narrativity, property and intellectual property, and collective identity. Given law's embeddedness in culture, and functioning as culture, possible avenues of resistance are multiple. One such avenue involves simply giving voice to those normally silenced, with their ambivalent alliances and their porous identities as members of several communities. Another avenue involves deconstructing front-stage myths of civic order and equality to reveal back-stage realities of prejudice and hegemony. A third alternative lies in adapting prevailing legal and cultural categories to give voice to, as well as recast, new legal expectations for justice and equality. This third alternative appears to be similar to the strategy Australian Aboriginal artists chose to deploy in their attempts to gain copyright protection for their EoF, and there appear to be some illuminating similarities that can be drawn regarding the subject positions these Australian Aboriginal artists occupied and those in which Baker and Fuller found themselves, in relation to copyright law's requirements for legal protection.[86] Nevertheless, the narratives concerning Baker's and Dunham's attempts to forge ownership over their identities and dance choreographies or improvisations fluctuated, contextually and dynamically, across versions of all three strategies.

Throughout the chapter, law has been analyzed as partaking of an evolving cultural life: that as legal meaning is circulated, such meaning is communicated in a nonlinear manner, and that the direction can be shifted, depending on who frames the narrative for specific audiences, and who receive and interpret these circulations of meaning, in different contexts. Baker shifted meaning through parodic and hyperbolic appropriations of the exotic and racialized stereotypes that populated her image as a Black Venus. Dunham both owned and overturned her celebrity image as a sexualized woman of color whose choreographic movements emphasized the movement of the hips by simultaneously hybridizing her choreography and her professional identity with whitened elements. Such whitened elements included the incorporation of choreographic movements derived from classical ballet and the strategic buttressing of her choreography with her academic credentials from the prestigious University of Chicago.

Re-evaluating the construction of categories of law in relation to differing collective identities and individual subjectivities has generated new and diverse ways of reflecting upon the law, legal processes, and legal power that reshape the multitude of legal engagements and interactions within various social contexts. Baker and Dunham, through their examples and choreographic improvisations and creations, forged news ways of resisting, expanding, and transforming the boundaries of prevailing conventional matrices of power, law, and culture. Dunham, in comparison to Baker, enjoyed greater freedom and success in her deployment of strategies of resistance, largely because of her partial possession of whiteness as status property.

Thus, extending these insights to include intangible intellectual property in circulation, the social force of signification and the material weight that meanings may forge, form natural pivot points for a study of law as and in culture that is alert to issues of power and meaning, structure and agency, and symbolic forms and interpretive practice. Attempting to leverage a system entails the insight that law generates and operates in lacunae in which hegemonic struggles occur, and signs and symbols are always contested, and always at risk. Legal strategies and legal institutions may lend weight to some interpretations while tending to deny such privileged status to others, often forming hegemonic binaries, which can be potentially leveraged, as both Baker's and Dunham's examples show, although Baker was forced to move within a more tightly circumscribed space than Dunham. Similarly, the relationships binding authorship, agency, and alterity bear closer examination, with greater sensitivity to the politics of textuality, metaphorics, and materiality in various social circles. Law's constitutive or generative power, in addition to its prohibitive or punitive possibilities, must therefore always be kept in mind, if one is to attempt to continually re-engage what effective strategies of resistance are possible to enact, within multiple contexts, as Baker's and Dunham's examples illustrate.[87]

NOTES

1. Part of this chapter is adapted from an article, originally published as: Caroline Joan "Kay" S. Picart, "Rethinking Resistance: Reflections on the Cultural Lives of Property, Collective Identity, and Intellectual Property," *John Marshall*

Law Review 47 (November 2014): 1349–69. The author thanks the *John Marshall Law Review* for its permission to adapt and expand the original article.

2. See, for example, Peter Fitzpatrick, *The Mythology of Modern Law* (London: Routledge, 1992); Elizabeth Mertz, *A New Social Construction for Sociolegal Studies,* Law and Society Review 28 (1994): 1243, 1246; Susan Hirsch and Mindie Lazarus-Black, eds. *Contested States: Law Hegemony and Resistance* (New York: Routledge, 1994), 1–2, 8, 9; Carol Greenhouse, "Constructive Approaches to Law, Culture and Identity," *Law and Society Review* 28 (1994): 1240.

3. See generally, Fitzpatrick, *The Mythology of Modern Law*; Peter Fitzpatrick, *Modernism and the Grounds of Law* (Cambridge: Cambridge University Press, 2001).

4. See generally Elizabeth Povinelli, "The State of Shame: Australian Multiculturalism and the Crisis of Indigenous Citizenship," *Critical Inquiry* 24 (1998): 575–610; Elizabeth Povinelli, "Consuming Geist: Popontology and the Spirit of Capital in Indigenous Australia," in *Millenial Capitalism and the Culture of NeoLiberalism*, ed. Comaroff and Comaroff, 241–70 (Durham, NC: Duke University Press, 2001); Elizabeth Povinelli, *The Cunning of Recognition: Indigenous Alterities and the Making of Australian Multiculturalism* (Durham, NC: Duke University Press, 2002).

5. See generally, for example, Kathy Bowrey, *Law and Internet Cultures* (Cambridge, UK, and Sydney, Australia: Cambridge University Press, 2005).

6. Rosemary Coombe, *The Cultural Life of Intellectual Properties: Authorship, Appropriation and the Law* (Durham, NC: Duke University Press, 1998), 87.

7. For a principally ethnographic approach to the study of law, both in the United States and internationally, see generally June Starr and Mark Goodale, eds. *Practicing Ethnography in Law: New Dialogues, Enduring Methods* (New York: Palgrave MacMillian, 2002).

8. See generally Lina Newton, *Illegal, Alien, or Immigrant: The Politics of Immigration Reform* (New York: New York University Press, 2008). Newton focuses on the social construction of immigrants (both legal and illegal) as well as other target groups (employers, the INS, U.S.-born children of illegal immigrants, and state and local governments). Newton eventually argues that public discourses are actually policy narratives designed to attempt to persuade the polity that the value judgments embedded in policy and legal discourses justify who should be beneficiaries of, and who are burdens to, the government and society.

9. For a deconstructive analysis of immigration law, see generally Leo R. Chavez, *The Latino Threat: Construction Immigrants, Citizens and the Nation* (Stanford, CA: Stanford University Press, 2008). Briefly and generally summarized, Chavez analyzes the "Latino Threat Narrative"—a pernicious and pervasive popular cultural myth that contemporary Latino immigrants (which targets principally Mexican immigrants, U.S.-born Mexicans, and Mexico itself, but also extends to include all Latino groups) are unlike earlier (European) immigrants and pose a serious danger to the nation. However, using data gathered through surveys and interviews done in Orange County in the 1990s and early 2000s, Chavez debunks popular destructive stereotypes regarding Latinos, such as their unassimilability, their stubborn language retention, their goal of "re-conquering" the southwestern United States, and their (especially female) hyper-fertility. Unlike the narratives that invisibly shape immigration law, Chavez's data shows that, for example, Latino immigrants increase English language

usage and reduce their Spanish usage from the first to the third generation; that they achieve significant upward mobility in terms of education and income and eventually marry and integrate into more ethnically and racially diverse communities the longer they live in the United States; and that Latina women engage in intercourse at a later age, and have fewer sexual partners, than white women in the United States.

10. See Berta Esperanza Hernandez-Truyol, "Culture Clashes: Indigenous Populations and Globalization-The Case of Belo Monte," *Seattle Journal for Social Justice* 12, no. 3 (2014): Article 3, digitalcommons.law.seattleu.edu/sjsj/vol12/iss3/3; see generally Berta Hernandez-Truyol and Stephen J. Powell, *Just Trade: A New Covenant Linking Trade and Human Rights* (New York: New York University Press, 2009), 206–30 (speaking on For Hernandez-Truyol's general framework in interpreting International Human Rights Law, trade, and the indigenous peoples' struggles to protect their rights).

11. For critical interpretations that analyze and deconstruct the position that indigenous peoples occupy within the law, see generally P. Hanks and B. Keon-Cohen, *Aborigines and the Law* (Sydney, Australia, Unwin Hyman Press, 1984) (discussing the struggles of indigenous people and their competition with a developing nation); Russell Lawrence Barsh, "Indigenous Peoples: An Emerging Object of International Law," *The American Journal of International Law* 80, no. 2 (1986); E. Johnson, M. Hinton and D. Rigney, eds. *Indigenous Australians and the Law* (Sydney, Australia: Cavendish Publishing, 1997); and Chris Cunnean and Terry Libesman, *Indigenous People and the Law in Australia* (Sydney, Australia: Butterworths, 1995): 240 (all stating critical interpretations that analyze and deconstruct the position that indigenous peoples occupy within the law).

12. Jane E. Anderson, *Law, Knowledge, Culture: The Production of Indigenous Knowledge in Intellectual Property* (Cheltenham, UK: Edward Elgar Publishing, 2009), 3. Anderson focuses on a social theory of law, and on an alternative epistemology of knowledge embedded in indigenous culture, especially those of tribes in Australia. See generally Silke von Lewinski, ed., *Indigenous Heritage and Intellectual Property: Genetic Resources, Knowledge and Folklore* (The Hague, Netherlands: Kluwer Law International, 2008). This edited collection, in its second edition, has eight contributors, all of whom argue, using different case studies that the commercial exploitation of indigenous knowledge and resources occur amid a significant clash of cultures. All eight contributors explore ways in which intellectual property law potentially can expand to accommodate the interests of indigenous people as applied to the ownership and control of their traditional knowledge, genetic resources, indigenous names and designations, and folklore.

13. "Indigenous Peoples/Ethnic Minorities and Poverty Reduction, Philippines," *Environment and Social Safeguard Division, Regional and Sustainable Development Department* (Manila, Philippines: Asian Development Bank, June 2002), 7, accessed July 13, 2015, adb.org/sites/default/files/pub/2002/indigenous_phi.pdf. Although there is no reliable and formal census, the National Commission on Indigenous Peoples (NCIP) "estimates the population of indigenous peoples in the Philippines to be between 12–15 million, but the actual population may be higher. Indigenous peoples roughly constitute between 10–15 percent of the total population of the Philippines and are present in 65 of the country's 78 prov-

inces." Jacqueline K. Cariño, "Country Technical Notes on Indigenous Peoples' Issues, Republic of the Philippines," *International Fund for Agricultural Development (IFAD)*, 1, last updated November 2012, accessed July 13, 2015, www.ifad.org/english/indigenous/pub/documents/tnotes/philippines.pdf. Additionally, a United Nations Committee on the Elimination of Racial Discrimination (UN CERD) Report states: "The Philippines is a country of diverse cultures with its multi-linguistic, multiethnic, mu[lt]i faith and geographically dispersed population estimated at 89 million as of 2007. It is estimated that 17 percent of the population fall within the definition of Indigenous Peoples under the IPRA [Indigenous Peoples Rights Act]." United Nations Committee on the Elimination of Racial Discrimination (UN CERD), "Reports Submitted by States Parties Under Article 9 of the Convention," International Convention on the Elimination of all Forms of Racial Discrimination, July 8, 2008, p. 8.

14. Joseph William Singer, *Property Law: Rules Policies and Practices* 2nd ed. (New York: Aspen Law and Business,1997), xli.

15. John Locke, *Two Treatises of Government* (New York: Everyman Paperbacks, 1990), 136.

16. Ibid.

17. Jeremy Bentham, "Chapter VIII—Of Property," *Property: Mainstream and Critical Positions*, 51–52 (originally printed in 1789, Crawford Brough Macpherson, ed., reprinted 1978).

18. Ibid.

19. See generally Michael Foucault, *Discipline and Punish: The Birth of the Prison*, 2nd ed. (New York: Vintage, 1995) (discussing the ebb and flow of power).

20. Rosemary J. Coombe, "Contingent Articulations: A Critical Cultural Studies of Law," *Law in the Domains of Culture*, eds. Austin Sarat and Thomas R. Kearns (Ann Arbor, MI: University of Michigan Press, 2000), 37.

21. See generally Arun Agrawal, "The Politics of Indigenous Knowledge," in *Australian Indigenous Knowledge and Libraries*, eds. Martin Nakata and Marcia Langton (Canberra, Australia: Australian Academic and Research Libraries, 2005), 73–84.

22. Michel De Certeau, *The Practice of Everyday Life*, trans. Steven Randall (Oakland, CA: University of California Press, 1984), xiii.

23. Similar approaches can be seen in, for example, Ernesto Laclau, "Power and Representation," in *Politics, Theory, and Contemporary Culture*, ed. Mark Poster (New York: Columbia University Press, 1993); Costas Douzinas, Peter Goodrich and Yifat Hachamovitich, eds., *Politics, Postmodernity and Critical Legal Studies: The Legality of the Contingent* (London: Routledge, 1994); Aryeh Bostwinick, *Postmodernism and Democratic Theory* (Philadelphia: Temple University Press, 1993).

24. Edward J. Ingebretsen, *At Stake: Monsters and the Rhetoric of Fear in Public Culture* (Chicago: Chicago University Press, 2001), 43.

25. For an example of the use of antiterrorism laws against the Mapuche, see Gale Courey Toensing, "Inter-American Court Hears Mapuche Human Rights Case Against Chile," *Indian Country Today*, June 3, 2013, last accessed May 14, 2015, indiancountrytodaymedianetwork.com/2013/06/03/inter-american-court-hears-mapuche-human-rights-case-against-chile-149677. See also Luis Carcamo-Huechante, "Mapuche Political Prisoners Hearing at the Inter-American Court of

Human Rights," *Cultural Survival,* May 29–30, 2013, accessed May 14, 2015, www.culturalsurvival.org/news/mapuche-political-prisoners-hearing-inter-american-court-human-rights-may-29-30-2013; Ryan Seelau, "Mapuche Testify Against Chile Before Inter-American Court of Human Rights," *Indigenous News,* May 31, 2013, last accessed May 14, 2015, indigenousnews.org/2013/05/31/mapuche-testify-against-chile-before-inter-american-court-of-human-rights-oas/.

26. See generally, June Starr and Mark Goodale, *Practicing Ethnography.*

27. See generally, Caroline Joan "Kay" S. Picart, *Critical Race Theory and Copyright in American Dance: Whiteness as Status Property* (New York: Palgrave Macmillan, 2013) (stating that copyrighting choreography has not been gender or sexual neutral. The section on copyright and choreography has been adapted from this book).

28. Jacques Derrida, "Interview with Julia Kristeva," in *Positions,* trans. Alan Bass (Chicago: University of Chicago Press, 1981), 42. See generally Jacques Derrida, *Writing and Difference,* trans. Alan Bass (Chicago: University of Chicago Press, 1978).

29. For an autobiography of Fuller, see generally Loïe Fuller, *Fifteen Years of a Dancer's Life, with some account of her distinguished friends* (Boston: Small Maynard Publications, 1913); for a biography, see generally Ann Cooper Albright, *Traces of Light: Absence and Presence in the Work of Loïe Fuller* (Middletown, CT: Wesleyan University Press, 2007).

30. See *Fuller v. Bemis,* 50 F. 926 (C.C.S.D.N.Y. 1892) (showing the importance of this trial to choreography and copyright).

31. For biographies of Josephine Baker, *see generally* Bennetta Jules-Rosette, *Josephine Baker in Art and Life: The Icon and the Image* (Champaign, IL: University of Illinois Press, 2007); and T. Denean Sharpley-Whiting, *Black Venus: Sexualized Savages, Primal Fears, and Primitive Narratives in French* (Durham, NC: Duke University Press, 1999). For an edited autobiography, see generally Josephine Baker and Jo Bouillon, *Josephine,* trans. Mariana Fitzpatrick (New York: Harper & Row, 1977).

32. For an autobiography of Katherine Dunham, see generally Joyce Aschenbrenner, *Katherine Dunham: Dancing a Life* (Chicago: University of Illinois Press, 2002); for writings by and about Katherine Dunham, see generally, Vévé A. Clark and Sara E. Johnson, eds., *Kaiso!: Writings by and about Katherine Dunham* (Madison, WI: University of Wisconsin Press, 2005).

33. Dunham had a master's degree in anthropology from the University of Chicago; among her mentors were Robert Redfield, Melville Herkovits, Edward Sapir, A. R. Radcliffe-Brown, Bronislaw Malinowski, and Lloyd Warner. Aschenbrenner, *Dancing a Life,* 29. Dunham's master's thesis, *The Dances of Haiti,* was eventually published by Northwestern University in 1947. Nancy Reynolds and Malcolm McCormick, *No Fixed Points: Dance in the Twentieth Century* (New Haven, CT: Yale University Press, 2003), 341.

34. See Constance Valis Hall, "Collaborating with Balanchine on *Cabin in the Sky*: Interviews with Katherine Dunham," in *Kaiso!,* ed. Clark and Johnson, 235–47 (where Dunham was evasive regarding the extent of Balanchine's actual contributions to the choreography).

35. For the invisibility of black choreographers, see generally, Danielle Robinson, "'Oh, You Black Bottom!' Appropriation, Authenticity and Opportunity in

the Jazz Dance Teaching of 1920s New York," *Dance Research Journal* 38, no. 1/2 (2006): 19–42.

36. This thesis is argued more extensively in Picart, *Critical Race Theory*, 105–11.

37. For cases that establish Balanchine's ownership of his copyright, and the scope of that copyright, see *Horgan v. MacMillan, Inc.*, 621 F. Supp. 1169 (S.D.N.Y. 1985); *Horgan v. MacMillan, Inc.*, 789 F.2d 157 (2d Cir. 1986). For biographical accounts of Balanchine's choreography and its eventual copyrighting, see generally Bernard Taper, *Balanchine: A Biography with a New Epilogue* (Berkley, CA: University of California Press, 1984) and Robert Gottlieb, *George Balanchine: The Ballet Maker* (New York: Harper Perennial, 2004).

38. Ibid. See also *Fuller v. Bemis*, 50 F. 926 (where Fuller attempted to raise a copyright claim over her choreography of the skirt dance but failed).

39. "Skirt dancing" was a popular dance that hung, uneasily, as a compromise between "the overly academic ballet of the time and the more outrageous step-kick dancing such as the can-can (le chahut) or its English derivative, the "la-ra-ra-boom-de-ay." J. E. Crawford Flitch, *Modern Dancing and Dancers* (Binsted, U.K.: The Noverre Press, 1912), 72. The "skirt dance" was then associated with the burlesque, or "low" art; Fuller's conversion of the "skirt" dance into the "serpentine" dance lay largely in her restaging of it, through the incorporation of a carefully designed staged and lighting effects, for which she successfully established patents. For a biographical account, *see* Albright, *Traces of Light*, 185.

40. *See* generally *Fuller v. Bemis*.

41. Ibid.

42. For a proliferation of these metaphors in relation to Josephine Baker, see generally Wendy Martin, "'Remembering the Jungle:' Josephine Taylor and the Modernist Parody," *Prehistories of the Future: The Primitivist Project and the Culture of Modernism*, ed. Elazar Barkan and Ronald Bush (Redwood City, CA: Stanford University Press, 1996), 310.

43. Samir Dayal, "Blackness as Symptom: Josephine Baker and European Identity," *Blackening Europe: The African American Presence*, ed. Heike Raphaeil-Hernandez (New York: Routledge, 2004), 50.

44. For a biographical account of Josephine Baker's self-transformations, see generally Jean-Claude Baker and Christ Chase, *Josephine Baker: The Hungry Heart* (New York: Cooper Square Press, 2001).

45. Julia Foulkes locates Baker's rise to stardom as part of the flowering of the Harlem Renaissance in the 1920s. Julia L. Foulkes, *Modern Bodies: Dance and American Modernism From Martha Graham to Alvin Ailey* (Chapel Hill, NC: University of North Carolina Press, 2002), 23. For an account of Josephine Baker and the star system of France during the time of her ascent in popularity, see generally Terri Francis, "The Audacious Josephine Baker: Stardom, Cinema, Paris," in *Black Europe and the African Diaspora* eds. Darlene Clark Hine, Trica Danielle Keaton, and Stephen Small (Champaign, IL: University of Illinois Press, 2009).

46. This "authentic" Africanist style was characterized as "primitivist," "animal," "sensual," and "uninhibited." For example, see description of Baker's sensationalized entrance at the Théâtre des Champs-Élysées during the opening of La Revue Nègre on October 2, 1925 in Baker and Chase, *Josephine Baker: The Hungry Heart*, 5–6.

47. U.S. Constitution, Article 1, Section 8, Clause 8.

48. At the federal level, copyrights do not protect ideas, procedures, processes, systems, methods of operation, concepts, principles, or discoveries; copyright protection extends to physical representations because these fulfill the "fixation" requirement. 17 U.S.C. § 102(b). Anything unrecorded is not copyrightable, in as much as it is not "fixed"; for example, dances and improvisations themselves are not copyrightable: only visual recordings or written descriptions of them are. Baker was seen more as a spontaneous performer, than a choreographer who planned, and recorded, his choreography. The Constitution provides: "The Congress shall have Power . . . [t]o promote the Progress of Science and useful Arts, by securing for limited Times to Authors and Inventors the exclusive Right to their respective Writings and Discoveries." US Const, Art I, § 8, cl 8. The Supreme Court has interpreted the term "Writings" expansively "to include any physical rendering of the fruits of creative intellectual or aesthetic labor." *Goldstein v. California*, 412 U.S. 546, 561 (1973).

49. Martha Woodmansee, "The Genius and the Copyright," *Eighteenth Century Studies* 17, no. 4 (1984): 44. See also Caroline Joan "Kay" S. Picart and Marlowe Fox, "Beyond Unbridled Optimism and Fear: Indigenous Peoples, Intellectual Property, Human Rights and the Globalization of Traditional Knowledge and Expressions of Folklore (Part I)," *International Community Law Review* 15, no. 3 (2013): 3, 319–39 (explaining how the Eurocentric origins of intellectual property law make it difficult to protect the intellectual property rights of indigenous peoples).

50. Ibid., 50.

51. For biographical accounts of the rivalry between Dunham and Baker in relation to their celebrity and beauty, see Aschenbrenner, *Dancing a Life*, 143, and Baker and Chase, *Josephine Baker: The Hungry Heart*, 285.

52. Foulkes, *Modern Bodies*, 72.

53. For an analysis of the ethnographic origins of Dunham's choreography, based on her field studies in the West Indies (Jamaica, Trinidad, Cuba, Haiti, Martinique), see generally Halifu Osumare, "Dancing the Black Atlantic: Katherine Dunham's Research-to-Performance Method in Migration of Movement: Dance Across Americas," *Ameriquest* 7, no. 2 (2010), available at ejournals.library.vanderbilt.edu/index.php/ameriquests/article/view/165.

54. Ann Barzel, Mark Turbyfill and Ruth Page, "The Lost Ten Years: The Untold Story of the Dunham-Turbyfill Alliance," in *Kaiso!*, ed. Clark and Johnson, 179.

55. Ibid., 179.

56. Katherine Dunham, quoted in Harriet Jackson, "American Dancer, Negro," *Dance Magazine* 40 (September 1966). This same information is stated in Dunham's autobiography, *A Touch of Innocence: Memoirs of Childhood* (Chicago: University of Chicago Press, 1994).

57. Aschenbrenner, *Dancing a Life*, 29.

58. See generally Ramsay Burt, "Katherine Dunham's Rite de Passage: Censorship and Sexuality," in *Embodying Liberation: The Black Body in American Dance*, ed. Dorothea Fischer-Hornung and Alison D. Goeller (Hamburg: LIT Verlag, 2001) (detailing American critics' struggles to reconcile Dunham's status as an intellectual and a dancer who celebrated the sexualized elements that characterized her choreography).

59. Vévé A. Clark, "Designing Dunham: John Pratt's Method in Costume and Décor: An Interview with John Pratt," in *Kaiso!*, ed. Clark and Johnson, 208.

60. Phyllis Rose, *Jazz Cleopatra: Josephine Baker in her Time* (New York: Doubleday, 1989); 67 (describing how Baker drew from American popular street dances, which included the element of comedically eye-rolling).

61. Joyce Aschenbrenner, "Katherine Dunham: Reflections on the Social and Political Contexts of Afro-American Dance," *Dance Research Journal Annual* XI (1980): 45, quoting "Katherine Dunham, The Future of Negro Dance," *Dance Herald* 5 (1938).

62. Among the African American dances Dunham used in her choreography were the juba, cakewalk, ballin' the jack, and strut. Reynolds and McCormick, *No Fixed Points*, 341. See also Dunham's quoted remarks regarding her project of conducting "an intensive study of the Negro under less absorbing cultural contacts [than the white system of slavery in the United States]; in the West Indies, the French, Spanish, and English influence have been of far less importance than that of the American in preserving the dance forms which are truly Negro." Aschenbrenner, "Katherine Dunham," 45, quoting Katherine Dunham, "The Future of the Negro Dance," *Dance Herald* 5 (1938).

63. *See* Aschenbrenner, *Dancing a Life*, 125–26.

64. Valis Hall, "Collaborating with Blanchine" in *Kaiso!*, 235.

65. Aschenbrenner, *Dancing a Life*, 125.

66. Reynolds and McCormick, *No Fixed Points*, 344.

67. *Feist Publications, Inc. v Rural Telephone Service Co.*, 499 U.S. 340, 346 (1991) ("Originality is a constitutional requirement."); *Burrow-Giles Lithographic Co. v. Sarony*, 111 U.S. 53, 58 (1879); The Trademark Cases, 100 U.S. 82 (1879). See generally Howard B. Abrams, *The Law of Copyright* § 1.02[C][4] (Clark Boardman, 1991). Graham, unlike Dunham, who did extensive ethnographic fieldwork, created choreographic works that drew from what she perceived as elements of Native American, Egyptian, Cambodian, Indian, and Japanese dances. See generally Deborah Jowitt, "Monumental Martha," *What is Dance?*, ed. Roger Copeland and Marshall Cohen (Oxford: Oxford University Press, 1983), 456–58. Balanchine, in his "collaboration" with Dunham in *Cabin in the Sky*, received credit for her choreography while she was not named as a choreographer in the program. Aschenbrenner, *Dancing a Life*, 125.

68. *See* Valis Hall, "Collaborating with Balanchine," in *Kaiso!*, 238 (showing Dunham stressing her credentials as a ballerina trained by Ludmilla Speranzeva, who was just as "Russian" and classically trained as Balanchine).

69. Jane Anderson, "The Making of Indigenous Knowledge in Intellectual Property Law in Australia," *International Journal of Cultural Property* 12 (2005): 347–73, 353.

70. Ibid., 352–53.

71. Ibid., 353.

72. Ibid.

73. Baker and Bouillon, *Josephine*, 51–52.

74. "Josephine Baker" *Biography.com*, accessed June 3, 2015, www.biography.com/people/josephine-baker-9195959.

75. Dorothea Fischer-Hornung, "'Jungle in the Spotlight?': Primitivism and Esteem: Katherine Dunham's 1954 German Tour," *Blackening Europe: The African American Presence*, ed. Heike Raphael-Hernandez (London and New York: Routledge, 2004), 53–72.

76. Library of Congress, "Katherine Dunham Timeline," Selections from the Katherine Dunham Collection at the Library of Congress, accessed June 3, 2015, lcweb2.loc.gov/diglib/ihas/html/dunham/dunham-timeline.html.

77. Aschenbrenner, "Katherine Dunham," 45, quoting from Katherine Dunham, "The Future of the Negro Dance," *Dance Herald* (1938): 5.

78. Vévé A. Clark, "Performing the Memory of Difference in Afro-Caribbean Dance: Katherine Dunham's Choreography, 1938–1987," in *Kaiso!*, ed. Vévé A. Clark and Sara E. Johnson (Madison, WI: University of Wisconsin Press, 2005), 324.

79. Anderson, "The Making of Indigenous Knowledge," citing Wright, Shelley. "Intellectual Property and the 'Imaginary Aboriginal,'" *Majah: Indigenous Peoples and the Law*, ed. Great Bird, Gary Martin and Jennifer Neilson (Sydney, Australia: The Federation Press, 1996).

80. 17 USC § 102(a), amended by 104 Stat 5133. For a general survey of American case law on the issue of originality in relation to copyright, see, Howard B. Abrams, "Originality and Creativity in Copyright Law," *Law and Contemporary Problems* 55, no. 2 (Spring 1992): 3–44.

81. "Copyright Act 1968 - SECT 32," *Commonwealth Consolidated Acts*, accessed June 3, 2015, www.austlii.edu.au/au/legis/cth/consol_act/ca1968133/s32.html. For a brief survey of relevant American and Australian copyright case law in relation to the issue of originality, see, Noric Dilanchian and Samantha Waldon, "Copyright requirements for originality and authorship," *Lightbulb Blog on Business, IT and IP Law*, July 2010, 27, accessed June 3, 2014, www.dilanchian.com.au/index.php/lightbulb-blog/23-ip-technology-e-business/618-copyright-requirements-for-originality-and-authorship.

82. See generally Colin Perrin, "Approaching Anxiety: The Insistence of the Postcolonial in the Declaration of the Rights of Indigenous People," *Laws of the Postcolonial*, ed. Eve Darian-Smith and Peter Fitzpatrick (Ann Arbor: University of Michigan Press, 1999).

83. See, for example, Martha M. Traylor, "Choreography, Pantomime and the Copyright Revision Act of 1976," *New England Law Review* 16 (1980–1981): 227; Barbara Singer, "In Search of Adequate Protection for Choreographic Works: Legislative and Judicial Alternatives vs. The Custom of the Dance Community," *University of Miami Law Review* 38 (1984): 288; Leslie Wallis, "The Different Art: Copyright and Choreography," *UCLA Law Review* 33 (1985–1986): 1442; Anne Weinhardt, "Copyright Infringement of Choreography: The Legal Aspects of Fixation," *Journal of Corporate Law* 13 (1987–1988): 839; Adaline Hilgard, "Can Choreography and the Copyright Waltz Together in the Wake of Horgan v Macmillan Inc.?" *U.C. Davis Law Review* 27 (1994): 757; Julie Van Camp, "Copyright of Choreographic Works," *Entertainment, Publishing and Arts Handbook 1994–1995*, ed. Stephen F. Breimer, Robert Thoerne and John David Viera (New York: Clark Boardman Callaghan, 1994), 59–92.

84. Anthea Kraut, "'Stealing Steps' and Signature Moves: Embodied Theories of Dance as Intellectual Property," *Theatre Journal* 62, no. 2 (May 2010): 173–89;

Constance Valis Hill, "Stepping, Stealing, Sharing and Daring," *Taken By Surprise: A Dance Improvisation Reader*, ed. Ann Cooper Albright and David Gere (Middletown, CT: Wesleyan University Press, 2003), 93.

85. Carys Craig challenges copyright's conception of a clearly identifiable author as a "bearer of rights and an owner of property;" its emphasis on original expression as requiring a stable, fixed object; and its automatic relegation of users of copyrighted material as potential or actual "pirates." Instead, she proposes locating a "relational author as a participant in a process of cultural dialogue and exchange;" the copyrighted work as "a text, utterance or communicative act; and of users of copyrighted materials as "active and equal participants in the very process of meaning-making and exchange that underpins copyright norms." Carys J. Craig, *Copyright, Communication and Culture Towards a Relational Theory of Copyright Law* (Northampton, MA and Cheltenham, Glos., UK: Edgar Elgar Publishing Limited, 2011), 3.

86. Anderson, "The Making of Indigenous Knowledge," 347–73.

87. Rosemary Coombe has been very prolific in exploring various ways in which legal forums have functioned as sites of construction and contestation in relation to intellectual property issues. See, for example: Rosemary J. Coombe, "Tactics of Appropriation and the Politics of Recognition in Late Modern Democracies," *Political Theory: An International Journal of Political Philosophy* 21 (1993): 411; Rosemary J. Coombe, "The Properties of Culture and the Politics of Possessing Identity: Native Claims in the Cultural Appropriation Controversy," *Canadian Journal of Law and Jurisprudence* 6 (1993): 249; Rosemary J. Coombe, "Embodied Trademarks: Mimesis and Alterity on American Commercial Frontiers," *Cultural Anthropology* 11 (1996).

5

Attempting to Balance First Generation Human Rights and Third Generation Human Rights[1]

This concluding chapter sketches a coherent flow across the current chapters and proposes various ways in which law can be negotiated and lived in and as culture. Rooted empirically on current and ongoing attempts at collaboration between majoritarian groups and indigenous peoples, some core principles have been identified as a way of balancing the rights of indigenous peoples to protect their cultural identities, traditional resources, and ancestral lands (technically, "first generation" human rights)[2] alongside the right, of developing countries, for example, to pursue development and scientific progress (technically, a "third generation" human right).[3] Among these are: prior informed consent, mutually agreed terms, and benefit-sharing.[4]

There is some evidence that using these principles, the use of a rights versus rights approach, allows more leeway for a judicial review. For example, in the *Narmada Bachao Andolan* case, the Supreme Court of India drew attention to the fact that "[a] natural river is not only meant for the people close by but it should be for the benefit of those who can make use of it, being away from it or nearby."[5] In that case, the court weighed the developmental dimension of the Sardar Sarovar Dam as a form of general interest that could justify the impact of this project on displaced persons along with the idea that the project was fundamental to fulfilling the right to water. Hence, the court argued that "[w]ater is [a] basic need for the survival of . . . human beings."[6] The court also pointed out that the right to access water was protected both nationally "as part of right [to] life and human rights as enshrined in Article 21 of the Constitution of India,"[7] and internationally by specific international instruments, such as the 1977 Mar del Plata action plan, which declared access to safe drinking water a human right.[8] Thus, the court reasoned: "availability of drinking water will benefit about 1.91 lakh [i.e., 191,000] people residing in 124 villages in arid and drought-prone border areas of Jalore and Barmer districts of Rajasthan who have no other source of water and are suffering grave hardship."[9]

When using a rights versus rights type of analysis, judges appear to weigh at least two elements: the nature of the rights (whether these rights are affected or fulfilled) and the number of persons (positively or negatively impacted). In the *Narmada Bachao Andolan* case, it is likely that the numerical comparison between the population benefiting from the project (i.e., the majority) and the relatively few to be adversely impacted by it played a significant role in the decision and justification of the court to uphold the project. Nevertheless, the analysis of the court revealed not a reductionist utilitarian calculation but a nuanced calculus. In spite of a general reluctance of the human rights community to recognize a clear hierarchy ranking fundamental rights,[10] courts implicitly tend to take into account the nature of the rights affected (whether they are first generation, second generation, or third generation human rights) as they weigh human rights costs and benefits in their analyses and justifications for their decisions.

Generally, as we have seen in case studies studied in prior chapters, the rights versus rights approach results in opposing first generation rights, such as the right to property[11] and the right to equality before the law[12] of those persons resettled or otherwise negatively impacted as a result of the construction of the hydroelectric project, to second or third generation rights, such as the right to water,[13] or to development, usually of the majority. Nevertheless, generations of rights have no clear hierarchy. Regional cultural priorities may play a role. Thus, developing Asian countries that have a more communitarian culture are generally more likely to authorize limitations on first generation rights in order to promote second and third generation rights, while Western liberal democracies, which have long-established cultures of individualism, generally may be less willing to concede to any limitation of first generation rights.[14]

In the *Narmada Bachao Andolan* case, the Indian Supreme Court explicitly recognized that "[c]onflicting rights had to be considered."[15] Nevertheless, the court considered that the relatively few who were displaced by the project could start a new life while "for the people of Gujarat [the majority, who lack access to drinking water], there was no other solution but to provide them with water from" the dam. Therefore, the court concluded that "the hardships of oustees from Madhya Pradesh could be mitigated by providing them with alternative lands, sites and compensation."[16] Although critics could point out that there might have been other solutions that could have been explored, such as relocating the displaced closer to the river, and that the court's use of a thoroughgoing rhetoric that appeared to make its decision the only solution, rather than simply a pragmatically and comparatively better solution, nevertheless, the jurisprudence illustrated in this decision "shows that the rights v[ersus] rights approach allows jurisdiction to review not only the legality, but also the decision to build a hydroelectric project."[17]

As an illustration of the effectiveness of these principles as a pragmatic heuristic to working across cultural differences, this chapter examines the case of the production of a commercially viable form of Jeevani, an anti-fatigue agent established in consultation and cooperation with the Kani tribe in India. Referring back to chapter 3, this case illustrates Rodolfo Stavenhagen's first description of culture: as "capital," and is one example of how the principles outlined above happened to work effectively, to produce an effective and materially lucrative outcome for both the indigenous tribe and a multinational corporation. Nevertheless, without idealizing this case, this chapter proposes that the Jeevani example is only one, among many ways, in which law in and as culture, can operate.

CHALLENGES IN RELATION TO ATTEMPTS TO USE IP LAW TO PROTECT THE EOF OF INDIGENOUS PEOPLES: LOOKING BACK, LOOKING FORWARD

As we have seen in prior chapters several hurdles hinder or effectively block various attempts to use intellectual property law to protect the expressions of folklore (EoF) of indigenous peoples, which are compounded by stereotypes of primitivism and racism.[18] As described in chapter 1, unbridled Optimism, one of the master narratives this book problematizes, has generated a myopic conception of folklore that implicitly privileges Western societies' consequential ethos and empirical epistemology. The resulting impasse, between indigenous and majoritarian cultures, is hardly surprising because majoritarian cultures, influenced by Western standards, fail to see value where consequences of act or invention are not readily quantifiable. In contrast, oral traditions of folklore, for example, have invaluable, nonquantifiable uses to indigenous communities; thus, these EoF are accepted as ends in and of themselves rather than as instrumental means of generating economic profit. Hence, the collective nature of generation of indigenous peoples' EoF or their "nonobviousness" should not preclude granting them intellectual property (IP) protection because the exploitation of this folklore, without adequate compensation, would most likely result in disastrous social and economic costs to an indigenous community.

As one example of the clash in viewpoints regarding what deserves intellectual property protection as opposed to what does not, the Western notion of "folklore" often implies clichés of the (merely) "collected" and (already) "dead" or "dying."[19] In sharp contrast, for the communities whose identities are bound up with traditional cultural expressions (TCEs), folklore is nothing short of a living heritage, which is inextricably intertwined with daily realities and as such, necessarily evolves.[20] Nevertheless, as we have seen in prior chapters, two principal characteristics of EoF make it immediately evident why IP law makes it difficult to use copyright, for example, to protect EoF as tribal property.

For example, two characteristic features of EoF, which make the effective use of copyright protection difficult, are EoF's anonymity and its traditional character as orally transmitted.[21] In consonance with this general description, the World Intellectual Property Organization (WIPO) characterization of EoF or TEC includes the following features:

(i) being handed down from one generation to another, either orally or by imitation;
(ii) reflecting a community's cultural and social identity;
(iii) consisting of characteristic elements of a community's heritage;
(iv) being made by "authors unknown" or by communities or by individuals communally recognized as having rights, responsibility, or permission to do so;
(v) being constantly evolving, developing, and being created within the community.[22]

However, it is precisely these characteristics that render the task of demarcating EoF as "private property" separate from the public domain challenging. As illustrated earlier, copyright law, resembling patent law in some ways, creates a binary between private property (usually individually owned and exploited) and the notion of the "commons" (generally not owned by any individual and free for use by all in the community). "Copyright law matured in the classical era of liberalism, which formally enshrined the ideal of the abstract individual freely exercising his or her creative capacity protected by a neutral system of natural rights, the most important of which was the right of property."[23] Thus, the counterpart to these clearly outlined individual rights is the undifferentiated "public domain," which is "usually equated with the non[-]propertied general welfare of the common people of a particular nation-state or, more generously, with the larger welfare of the undifferentiated global community as a whole."[24]

Yet, as explained earlier, what that binary obscures are precisely the epistemological foundations behind copyright law and its historical origins. Just as patent law insists upon an identifiable inventor, copyright law necessitates a cognizable author; furthermore, both invention and the authorship of literary texts (because copyright's historical genesis is rooted in the attempt to protect the ownership of the production and reproduction of books) became regarded as incontrovertible proof of the creativity and "genius" of a particular individual. As argued in prior chapters, within the historical context of eighteenth-century England, a book evolved to embody "the intellection of a unique [typically male/ masculine] individual,"[25] rather than a result of proficiency in learning the rules of craftsmanship. Thus, since a book is conceived as a specific embodied or "fixed" articulation of the author's unique mind, originally given voice, it is private intellectual property; hence, it follows that the right to harness this particular property belongs purely to this unique individual, its originator. Yet, as James Boyle argues, such an idealized view of authorship "blinds us to the importance of the commons—to the importance of the raw material from which information products are to be constructed."[26] Hardly surprisingly given this binary, EoF, like traditional knowledge (TK), becomes discredited as the opposite of what is "original"; to adopt a monstrous metaphor, EoF or TK become analogous to the "unfixed" body parts that the genius, Dr. Frankenstein, stitches together to breathe life into his creature. Read within this context, as exemplified in various ways in earlier chapters, "[i]ndigenous knowledge and generations of indigenous labour—mental and physical—are discredited. All that is credited is the 'chop-shop' labour of individual corporate and academic scientists who interject 'novelty' into what they have taken."[27] Hardly unexpectedly, the justificatory rhetoric for rendering invisible the contributions of TK and EoF to the development of highly profitable pharmaceutical inventions or musical innovations partakes of the patterns of colonialist reasoning.

> [A]ppeals to common property, private property, and usually both in succession constitute the legitimating rationale of cultural imperialism. It enables the dominant culture to secure political and social control as well as to profit economically from the cultural and genetic resources of indigenous cultures. Just as the concept of *terra nullius* once provided legal and moral cover for the imperial powers' treatment of indigenous peoples, the concept of public domain plays a comparable role within late capitalism.[28]

Thus, retrospectively, the early sections of this book arrived at the conclusion that the value of establishing a working description of indigenous peoples (as well as their traditional knowledge and expressions of folklore) as a pragmatic heuristic outweighed concerns that such a description may limit the rights of certain classes of individuals claiming indigenous personhood. Additionally, the earlier chapters have illustrated, using different case studies, that the differences between the definitions of TK and EoF or TCE are porous. Nevertheless, the position of this book, from the start, was that the pragmatic value of providing general descriptions, as schematic heuristics (not all-encompassing definitions), lies in posing multiple potential legal avenues to protect indigenous peoples' intellectual property interests. Furthermore, prior chapters have attempted concretely to illustrate why TK and EoF are challenging to protect using standard intellectual property legal strategies. Part of this difficulty, as prior chapters have illustrated, lies in that there is an inherent difference in various assumptions underlying Western and indigenous conceptions of invention, leading to a systematic imbalance in the protections of these two, weighed in favor of majoritarian cultures. For example, the Agreement on Trade Related Aspects of Intellectual Property (TRIPS Agreement) assumes that protecting the inventor's right to sole exploitation is the most effective method of promoting the utilitarian goal of continued innovation. In contrast, some indigenous peoples' innovations are communally derived, or otherwise without a clear individual author, which makes these works difficult to protect under the TRIPS Agreement.

This concluding chapter continues the task, started in earlier chapters, of exploring possible solutions to this issue, that is, how various legal strategies can be used to protect indigenous peoples' TK and EoF.

BEYOND FEAR AND UNBRIDLED OPTIMISM: PRAGMATIC SOLUTIONS, CORE PRINCIPLES, AND NEW DIRECTIONS

Pragmatic Solutions: Promises and Perils

This section starts by illustrating a long-standing debate regarding how best to protect against the uncompensated piracy of TK or EoF: choosing between either a *sui generis* approach or an amendment of existing property or intellectual property laws. The former may present a paradigm shift that would change our assumptions regarding authorized rights owners, that is, communitarian instead of individual entities, and, perhaps, promote the concomitant protection of the cultural and other human rights of indigenous peoples. The other approach merely modifies existing intellectual property law (e.g., allowing patents for collective knowledge and requiring "informed consent"). This section explores pragmatic ways of defining "informed consent"; attempts to synchronize existing treaties' intellectual property arrangements; and proposes a means of forging a consensus between developed countries and the developing nations. Lastly, this chapter analyzes proposed solutions, including: better regional policing by citizen groups and nongovernment organizations (NGOs); developing countries enforcing their bargaining power with multinational pharmaceutical companies; and denying patents that pose an environmental threat.

A *Sui Generis* Approach

Despite the numerous challenges surrounding attempts to protect the intellectual property rights of indigenous peoples, recent literature documents the multiplicity of venues in which discussions regarding these issues proliferate. To name only a few, as illustrated in the prior chapters, these venues or forums include the Food and Agriculture Organization of the United Nations (where in 2001 a treaty on plant genetic sources was negotiated), the Rio biodiversity regime, WIPO and also the World Trade Organization (WTO).[29] The principal theoretical issue seems to hinge on whether or not a radically novel *sui generis* approach is required in order to prevent the unauthorized or uncompensated piracy of biogenetic resources, TK or EoF, especially as grounded within the economic and cultural contexts that foreground these issues, or whether existing mainstream laws, especially property and intellectual property law, are adaptable enough to be reworked and applied to these evolving issues.[30] The *sui generis* approach is intimately imbricated with the issue of the degree of autonomy indigenous peoples can have, in relation to control of their ancestral lands, property, TK, and EoF. For example, the World Wildlife Fund, in a position paper at a WIPO-UNEP Program, advocated the establishment of *sui generis* models of intellectual property for countries to whom the preservation of indigenous patrimony is an important priority.[31] "By adopting this focus, [such] countries [concerned about preserving indigenous patrimony] can still comply with their obligations according to the international instruments as the CBD and the Agreement on TRIPS," while steering clear of the compulsory institutional requirements that veer more toward transnational monopolist control, such as the system of plant breeders' rights, such as the International Union for the Protection of New Varieties of Plants (UPOV).[32]

Certainly, there is the view that any truly novel approach should constitute a radical break from traditional forms of intellectual property law; such a radical break should expressly recognize the contributions of the communities that have protected and transmitted these sources of knowledge and financially reward these communities directly for these contributions.[33] For Hernandez-Truyol and Powell, the value of a *sui generis* approach is that it would span the gap separating traditional knowledge and the reigning intellectual property rights system.[34] More specifically, in addition to creation of a global database, such a system could re-envisage the different criteria used to legitimize what is protectable, thus overcoming existing obstacles presented by the requirements of novelty, non-obviousness, and usefulness.

Two examples of a national attempt to create databases and libraries that attempt to create better integration between its indigenous populations and the majority culture are the Indigenous Knowledge [Centers] (IKC) in Queensland, Australia, and the Indigenous Knowledge [Center] Millennium Library Project (IKC@MLP).[35] The IKC model involves a two-way learning process between the State Library and indigenous communities throughout Queensland's Cape York and Torres Strait regions; the State Library has established such IKCs New Mapoon, Lockhart River, Wujal Wujal, Pormpuraaw, Aurukun, Injinoo, Damley Island, Mabuiag Island, and Poruma Island.[36] Additionally, the IKC model attempts to design each particular center with maximum adaptability to suit the needs of the local indigenous population. During the initial stages, local staff are recruited, so as to ensure their involvement, ideally, in both planning and establishment; additionally, IKCs offer free community wide access to the resources of a traditional library, supplemented with materials to support the oral and visual traditions of indigenous peoples, thus generally aiming both to preserve the tribe's TK and EoF, and increase the literacy and numeracy of the members of the indigenous community.[37] Simply described, the IKC@MLP functions as a central hub for the physical and virtual network of Indigenous Knowledge [Centers] throughout the rest of Queensland, offering services and support in an analogous way that the State Library acts as a central spoke for the Queensland public library network.[38]

Despite the partial success and further potential in these initiatives for possibly designing and implementing *sui generis* approaches to ownership of TK and Eof, it is clear that practical hurdles remain. Among these are: problems in retaining trained staff; difficulties in sustaining access to and support for quality technology and communications; and equity in ownership of much of the material, which legally remains property of the State Library, not the indigenous peoples.[39] As Jacob Pilot describes the situation of intellectual property rights of the harvested and archived items of TK and EoF:

> In many cases the State Library is the owner of copyright, in others copyright is owned by the individuals or entities [that] created the particular work or material. However, the cultural and intellectual ownership rights of Indigenous peoples are not enshrined in legislation, whereas copyright is well covered. The State Library recogni[z]es the lack of a legal underpinning for Indigenous cultural and intellectual rights but acknowledges the importance of these rights for [i]ndigenous peoples.[40]

Nevertheless, potentially, a *sui generis* approach could also re-orient intellectual property law toward new directions or new purposes (such as exploring how to concomitantly protect the cultural and other human rights of indigenous peoples) and reconceptualize the notion of who are authorized rights owners (such as the community instead of the individual). Certainly, Paul Kuruk, for instance, has argued for community, rather than individual rights, over TK; even more aggressively, he has also argued that TK owners have rights to products developed from their TK regardless of whether IP rights have been gained over these products by third parties in other countries.[41]

Sui Generis Examples: Limited Common Property, Biodemocracy, the "Checklist Approach," and the Galiwin'ku Indigenous Knowledge Center

Various theoretical models have been proposed on how to accomplish a *sui generis* approach, which partakes of a general precautionary framework, rather than a corrective one. For example, there have been suggestions of using the notion of "limited common property" (LCP) that possesses characteristics to protect traditional knowledge holders while simultaneously encouraging TK use; such LCP would be "communal" for the "insiders" (e.g., the tribe) but would allow private exploitation outside of the community, under controlled conditions.[42]

Correlatively, Vandana Shiva proposes the notion of a "biodemocracy": a *sui generis* system that maintains the exchange of knowledge in developing countries' farming communities and recognizes their knowledge (the realm of TK) and production systems (the realm of bio-engineering) of biological organisms have equal validity.[43] Yet as Lorna Dwyer points out, many such promising proposals lack a discussion regarding how to identify the proper level of TK co-ownership, and what entity would be authorized to represent co-owners.[44] Furthermore, J. H. Reichmann has argued that there is a crucial difference between *sui generis* systems patterned after a copyright model versus *sui generis* systems derived from a patent model: while those generated by a copyright model result in relatively weak protection, those generated from a patent model appear to provide stronger protection against derivative users by preventing the production of derivative products.[45] Critical of the cycles of under- and over-protection that accompany failed *sui generis* systems, along with their anticompetitive ripples, Reichmann instead proposes a *sui generis* system that requires developers of TK to provide equitable compensation for borrowed improvements for a short term.[46] Nevertheless, Kaiser points out that a crucial issue in relation to *sui generis* systems is their enforceability beyond a national or regional structure; for example, in the case of computer and biogenetics innovations, the problems caused by "the lack of any credible *sui generis* alternative to correct the manifest defects of stretching the patent and copyright paradigms beyond their traditional boundaries" have effectively weakened their protection.[47]

Thus, while these *sui generis* approaches may present an opportunity to break from unbounded optimism, they may unwittingly be stunted by fear; that is, they fail to address practical concerns, the unintended consequence of which may be a cure worse than the disease. Nevertheless, more concretely, particularly in terms of TK and biogenetic resources, there have been attempts to explore new legal intellectual property systems. For example, at the national level Peru, Panama, New Zealand, and the Philippines have adopted *sui generis* systems to protect their TK.[48]

Indeed, there is some international momentum toward exploring the *sui generis* idea. For instance, the International Treaty on Plant Genetic Resources envisages a *sui generis* compensation mechanism using material transfer agreements, which would involve financial compensation as payment for commercially exploiting plant genetic resources, in order to benefit farmers and indigenous peoples in the countries where these resources can be found.[49] The treaty has a section that states that "recipients [of the genetic resources] shall not claim any intellectual property or other rights that limit the facilitated access to the plant genetic resources for food and agriculture, or their genetic parts and components, in the form received from the Multilateral System (Article 12.3(d))."[50]

For example, both WIPO and the Convention on Biological Diversity (CBD) suggest a "checklist approach" built upon the principles of prior disclosure of information, prior consent, and benefit sharing. Much like the Plant Genetic Resources Treaty, the emphasis is on the CBD provisions connected to the "disclosure of information on the human source, country of origin, detailed nature of [TK] used in an invention."[51] Additionally, this checklist approach entails the use of relevant national rules concerning the presentation of evidence of obtaining informed consent as well as proof of compliance with benefit sharing.[52] Ultimately, such a prevention-centered approach requires developing countries actively to collect and publish their intellectual property.[53] For example, India and South Africa have experimented with such an approach.[54]

The checklist procedure may provide a happy medium between fear and optimism, parts of which focus on the disclosure of information, prior informed consent and benefit sharing. In the short-term, perhaps the financial benefits would incentivize developing countries to share their traditional knowledge, rather than fearfully hoard it. Ideally, as well, such financial benefits would serve as compensation and recognition for prior uncompensated exploitation. In the long term, perhaps a universal database system cataloguing all these sources of TK and EoF could be developed.[55] As Dwyer observes, there would be numerous advantages to the development of a universal database: it "would serve as a filter to unjust patents (evidence as prior art); would strengthen current patents and reduce litigation; enable the preservation and documentation of [TK]."[56]

Additionally, Hernandez-Truyol and Powell, drawing on lessons from the history of colonialism, propose an additional precautionary measure: publish the catalogue in the language of the tribe, so that use of the material would require translation, thus ensuring better control of the material by the tribe. (Again, this assumes that the traditional language would remain alive and viable among the younger members of the tribe, which can be a problematic assumption.) Nevertheless, cataloguing the different medicinal plants used by indigenous peoples in their own languages would simultaneously fulfil Western intellectual property requirements and could "result in pharmaceutical companies asking permission to use the handbook and paying royalties."[57] Certainly, such a careful market-accepting approach would perhaps mediate effectively between a cautionary framework and a view that all trade automatically yields wealth and all that is "Good." Of course, the disadvantage approach is that for this approach to work, it requires the cooperation of the developed world; unfortunately, the American and Japanese posture in relation to this approach has been that disclosure is irrelevant to patentability and would be ineffective in preventing patent abuses. Indeed, Dwyer acknowledges that, given the interests concerned, there is probably no consensus and, therefore, no cooperation possible.[58]

Finally, Jane Anderson also documents her own ethnographic experiences at collaborating with the Galiwin'ku Indigenous Knowledge Centre (GIKC) (under the aegis of the Australian Institute of Aboriginal and Torres Strait Islander Studies (AIATSIS)), in the Northern Territory of Australia, where she has worked with various individuals, such as Joe Neparrŋa Gumbula, Richard Gandhuwuy Gurrawurra, Matthew Baltha Gaykamanuguy, Ruth Almakarra, Garrawurra, and Jessica De Largy Healy.[59] Facing squarely the issues of the power differentials embedded in the institutional and legal frameworks of archives, Anderson remarks: "[L]egal authority becomes consolidated in the archive through categories of authorship and ownership—categories that are not only socially produced but are authori[z]ed by legal narratives that, in turn, strategically deploy such narratives for the purposes of identifying rights of property."[60]

Given that in Australia, a majority of material that documents indigenous people's lives and traditions is owned legally by non-indigenous people, certain tensions over authorship, ownership, and access, are inevitable. Specifically in relation to her own work, Anderson comments on the complex problems associated with "returning," for example, photographs of the tribe taken by researchers, for tribal use (e.g., if they wish to create Web sites of their own, using these photographs), while acknowledging that these materials are technically and legally not tribal property.[61] The result, in Anderson's words, is an intellectual property protocol[62] that "emanate[s] from Galiwin'ku"[63] rather than external organizations; the resultant document itself is "quite distinctly a Galiwin'ku document and it incorporates both Yolŋu understandings of knowledge management as well as the intellectual property issues."[64] Aspirationally, Anderson's vision of the protocol's pragmatic and localized reworking of intellectual property law is reminiscent of a Nietzschean metaphor of "dancing across different worlds":

> We are looking at material that is produced, for example, when researchers come in and take photos of the community. We want to develop something so that researchers have some responsibility and obligation to leave some of those photographs with the GIKC so that the community knows that they have them and they can show their children—the purpose is not complex. In developing the protocol, *we are seeking to bridge a gap between Yolŋu needs and systems and these quite rational systems of law and ownership and authorship and to re-jig them—dance around copyright, if you will—so that the community does have ownership, does have rights that are recogni[z]ed* [italics added]. When people do come into the community they are under an obligation to respect those rights.[65]

Additionally, the result of the protocol, ideally, does not remain limited to the protected sphere of the GIKC. Thus, when a member of the particular indigenous community interacts with external institutions, because of the protocol, these institutions are encouraged to form new types of relationships with the GIKC, the tribe, and a particular member of the tribe because of the protocol's highlighting of the issue of intellectual property ownership.

> Similarly when Joe Gumbula goes down to deal with different libraries and archives, for example, the Donald Thomson collection at Museum Victoria, or the University of Melbourne, he has something that confirms to them that the GIKC has ideas about intellectual property issues, as well. This is a significant development, as there is reluctance on the part of organi[z]ations to hand back materials because of copyright questions. However, if the GIKC is being proactive in how its dealing with these issues, then the institutions can see that there is room for a new and different relationship to be built between institutions and [indigenous] communities.[66]

Anderson is quick to acknowledge that the site-specific protocol is not without flaws, and that the arrangement is a process undergoing transition; nevertheless, the process does empower the particular indigenous population and encourage new relationships with external institutions, while "dancing around copyright."[67]

Modifying Existing Intellectual Property Law

The second precautionary approach involves not so much creating a new system as simply modifying current intellectual property law. Instead of a *sui generis* approach that breaks away completely from any of the standard criteria, this approach has novel elements (e.g., allowing patents for collective knowledge as well as tribal practices that indigenous peoples have not reduced to precise laboratory terms) while keeping the same general criteria for standard patent applications. Yet again, even this approach has challenges because it entails "informed consent" from the tribe. Yet what does "informed consent" really entail? Additionally, even if an objective standard can be established for "informed consent," as Hernandez-Truyol and Powell point out, "indigenous populations may not want western forms of compensation, such as royalty payments and profit sharing but nonmonetary compensation, including infrastructure development and training."[68] In other words, the very act of "translating" what indigenous populations want or need, as "compensation" for the commercial exploitation of their TK or EoF is already in Western terms; as such, how "informed" that "consent" is, is already problematic and must be treated with the greatest of care.

Notwithstanding these difficulties, there are pragmatic ways in which one could access "informed consent." As Dwyer points out, to the greatest extent possible, governments, especially of developing countries, should try to ensure the participation of indigenous tribes in the formulation of international intellectual property policies. Ideally, in keeping with the principles of prior consultation, informed consent, and benefit sharing, the inclusion of these communities should emphasize: "capacity-building; consultation; and the promotion of regional, national and local dialogue to be managed and directed in close collaboration with indigenous peoples and local communities."[69] Of course, Dwyer acknowledges that even this solution remains haunted by stumbling blocks, such as the difficulty in achieving regional representational balance and sufficient diversity in sampling what communities' needs and interests are, as well as the need for criteria to help ensure that the results of negotiations are reasonably reflective of all indigenous community interests.[70]

Perhaps part of this endeavor to preserve but tailor existing intellectual property law would be an attempt to harmonize and coordinate treaties and different forums. As a concrete, regional example, Arowolo argues for a "bottom up" approach to harmonizing protection mechanisms enabled by the two functional regional organizations, the Organisation Africaine de la Propriete Intellectuelle (OAPI) and African Regional Industrial Property Organisation (ARIPO), which are currently at odds, or at least uncoordinated, with each other.[71] Given the complex and multipronged nature of biopiracy, it is important to generate "synergy between the different forums and processes that are dealing with the biopiracy problem."[72] An associated issue, of course, is that there is no easy and obvious mechanism or forum in which to attempt to forge consensus. TRIPS Article 27(2)[73] governs intellectual property drawn from living sources.[74] Although the TRIPS Agreement has effective enforcement mechanisms, its rules and structure, as we have seen, tend to privilege developed countries over developing countries. On the other hand, WIPO is a "good forum to reach consensus but is plagued by bureaucratic processes."[75] But as earlier chapters have shown, there is an increasing consensus that these are issues that need to be discussed and, if possible, negotiated. Perhaps achieving consensus at the regional level might be an effective way of forging effective alliances, as this middle-tier approach ideally avoids the weaknesses of a top-down or a bottom-up approach,[76] while dialectically preserving the dialogical and enforcement strengths of both.

Aggressive Alternatives Aimed at Protecting Traditional Knowledge

Nevertheless, there are other more aggressive precautionary ways to protect TK, which could be effective, in tandem with the less forceful approach proposed earlier. Dwyer points out that both citizen watchdog groups and NGOs, in collaboration with governments, could be mobilized as part of an extensive network to help police biopiracy. "Cooperative notification efforts between watchdog groups and developing countries' governments may be very effective in the fight against biopiracy."[77] Finally, regional organizations could also play a role in policing biopiracy, as we have seen, for example, in the case of the ayahuasca vine controversy. As another example, the Andean Genetic Resources Commission (AGRC) "was created to define a comprehensive regional strategy for dealing with the international community's use of genetic resources and ensure equitable benefit-sharing for their communities."[78]

Yet this business of policing the borders of intellectual property interests should not be delegated purely to citizen watchdog groups and NGOs, as governments ideally could also have a powerful role to play in this process. Self-defense should be proactive and not simply reactive; thus, local police and regulatory laws, such as domestic immigration, intellectual property, and criminal law, for example, can be used to prevent and control the misappropriation of TK.[79] "In addition to protective legislation, governments in developing countries should aim to generate revenue to contribute to technical and legal counselling for indigenous communities and to fund projects in defen[s]e of [TK]."[80] Thus, governments, especially in developing countries, should enhance communication and strive to improve their relationship with indigenous communities,[81] given the particular and local tensions globalization imposes on developing countries and their indigenous populations.

In order to assess current TK-protection weaknesses, Dwyer suggests that governments should engage in the kind of cataloguing multi-national pharmaceuticals are extremely interested in, in order to establish prior ownership of these resources. This entails certain practical steps: (1) "acknowledge the content, extension and potential economic uses of [TK]"; (2) effectively "address the protection of plant genetic resources [PGRS] and prevent their extinction"; and (3) "document [TK] and establish it as a 'prior art' developed by indigenous communities."[82] As a more militant spoke of this strategy, developing countries should also focus on improving their negotiation skills with multinational pharmaceutical companies,[83] much as Brazil did, in its development of its HIV-containment program.[84]

The Kani Peoples of Southwest India: An Example of Successful Benefit Sharing (and Culture as "Capital")

A successful example of a benefit-sharing strategy is the case of the development of an antifatigue agent established in consultation and cooperation with the Kani indigenous population in India (see figure 5.1). This case also illustrates Stavenhagen's first description of culture as "currency," and is one example of how the principles outlined above, and in prior chapters, can, given a confluence of certain factors, work to produce an effective and materially lucrative outcome for both an indigenous tribe and an MNC. This is not to idealize this case, but to illustrate how the pragmatic deployment of a benefit-sharing strategy, together with other principles, can help to overcome what seem like incommensurable differences.

The product Jeevani (which helps stave off fatigue) was developed based on the TK of the Kani, an ethnic group who live in southwest India. Working alongside three Kani consultants, the Tropical Botanical Garden and Research Institute (TGBRI) heard of the antifatigue properties of a wild plant cultivated by the Kani. TGBRI scientists successfully purified and isolated the active ingredient to invent the drug, Jeevani.[85] When the TGBRI transferred manufacturing rights to Aryavaidya Pharmacy Coimbatore Ltd., they agreed to share half the license and royalty income with the Kani. It took some time for the Kani clans to speak with one voice, but eventually they established the Kerala Kani Samudaya Kshema Trust to manage the resultant income.[86] The outcome is one of the most successful narratives illustrating the principles of prior consultation, informed consent, and benefit sharing between a pharmaceutical and a tribe. "Through 2001, the Trust Society-fully managed by the Kani—has received 1,350,000

Figure 5.1. The Kani tribe is a nomadic tribe from Tamil Nadu. They live in parts of Western Ghats (Tirunelveli and Kanyakumari Districts) of India. In this photo, an elder tribe performs the Lamp Dance during Kumari Sangamam. January 18, 2011.

Photography by K. I. Aron Joshva Rusewelt.

Indian rupees (about $30,000) of royalties and fees. This income has been invested in an interest-bearing account, and only the interest from the account is expended."[87] The success story continues today. As sales of Jeevani have increased, so has, in turn, the demand for the raw material, leading the Forestry Department to allow the Kani to cultivate the plant and sell the raw materials in semi-processed form to the manufacturer in order to respond effectively to the spike in demand.[88]

As J. Michael Finger and Philip Schuler note, the Kanis' TK would not have qualified for a patent,[89] given the usual obstacles of requiring an inventor, novelty, and fixation, among others. In keeping with the usual patterns, it was the TGBRI research team who had the resources and technical knowledge to purify and isolate the active ingredient in the plant, invent a herbal formulation that readily lent itself to medicinal application and went through the arduous process of patenting this discovery. Because India, at that time, didn't have the legislation to protect TK, the Kanis would not have been able to benefit financially without this partnership.[90]

Nevertheless, one must not idealize the Jeevani example. The problems that plague the issue of what constitutes "informed consent" plague the Kani case. For example, the Kanis do not constitute a clearly delineated cohesive tribe; rather, they are a loose, scattered group entity and only one subgroup was represented and consulted.[91] Within that subgroup, only three younger members of the tribe served as consultants.[92] In contrast, nine medicine men, elders of the tribe, wrote to the chief minister of the district, vigorously protesting the sale of their TK to a pharmaceutical.[93] Furthermore, as Gerard Bodeker points out, challenging conditions remain in place, even in this successful model emphasizing benefit sharing:

> First, the Kani Trust has to negotiate with state government for transfer of funds. Second, the Kerala Forest Department is seeking a share of royalties and licen[s]e fees. Third, the Kani does not hold title to their customary land and the Forest Department has been reported to be preventing them from harvesting Jeevani. Fourth, a high return on Jeevani plants has resulted in over-harvesting by immigrant workers drawn to this source of income.[94]

In addition, generally, the problem is that pharmaceutical technology has evolved since then. The most recent scientific technologies "synthetically generate numbers of first-stage compounds, computerization provides faster ways to screen out the ones that merit further development, and new techniques provide better ways to transform the new compounds into effective products."[95] In addition, in contemporary healthcare, research focuses more on human material and then utilizes drug design to reverse-engineer from the human material.[96] Thus, in this research environment, which is heavily dependent on artificial simulation and chemical reverse-engineering, "natural products are often too slow, costly and problematic."[97] It is therefore unlikely that many indigenous communities would normally have as much bargaining power as the Kani did. Finally, much TK has already lapsed into the public domain and hence, can be accessed through publications. Consequently, TK nowadays is seldom derived from interviews with local and indigenous communities in a way that requires prior consent that enables benefit-sharing negotiations.[98]

Nevertheless, the Kani example shows how in cases where intellectual property law is functioning to demarcate a sphere in which culture is functioning as "capital" (Stavenhagen's first description), it is potentially possible, enacting the principles of prior informed consent and benefit sharing, to form collaborations that address the issue of economic justice for indigenous populations, in relation to the commercial exploitation of their TK. The example is particularly powerful because the active ingredient in Jeevani had no religious or spiritual significance to the Kani tribe, and therefore, could be relatively cleanly excised from the problematic issue of the cultural identity or integrity of the tribe. The issue becomes more difficult to resolve when what is at issue is a TCE whose expression is bound up with the cultural lifeblood of a tribe (Stavenhagen's third description of culture in copyright law as a "total way of life"), as we have seen in the case of the Australian Aboriginal visual artists.

The Correctional Approach

Other than the precautionary approach, it is also possible to deploy a correctional approach and re-examination process. Although a correctional approach is cumbersome, compared with a precautionary approach, and is expensive, India, for example, has explored this path by examining the entries in the U.S. Patent and Trademark Office (USPTO), the United Kingdom Intellectual Property Office (UKIPO) and the European Patent Office (EPO), and has reported some patents that appear to be based on its TK.[99] Following this more militant approach, developing countries could emphasize the detection of misappropriations and apply pressure for "expedited review and liability for illegally gained profits."[100] Along a similar track, Hernandez-Truyol and Powell suggest deploying TRIPS' Article 27.2,[101] which permits WTO members to deny patents to inventions when prevention of commercial exploitation within their territory "is necessary to protect *ordre public* or morality, including to protect human, animal, or plant life or health or to avoid serious prejudice to the environment.[102] Hernandez-Truyol and Powell also suggest creatively using the TRIPS' morality clause, which protects the environment, to try to extend this protection to TK, given "[CBD]'s strong linkage of protection of [TK] with preservation of biodiversity."[103] Such a move actually reveals how prevention and correction cannot be thoroughly separated from each other, as approaches. Finally, Hernandez-Truyol and Powell show how the appeal to the "morals" clause also inheres in the patent-busting threats of the United States and Canada in the aftermath of the September

11, 2001, terrorist attacks on the United States, when access to an anthrax vaccine seemed restricted because of an existing patent.[104]

In terms of protecting EoF more specifically, fair trade importers or (alternative trading organizations, "northern ATOs") have been operating for years. These commercial entities are designed to operate at sufficient profit levels to be self-sustaining, "while sharing with poor producers the rents implicit in the differential between market prices in rich and poor countries."[105] Two American examples of northern ATOs, Ten Thousand Villages and SERVV International, began in the 1940s and remain financially stable. The idea behind fair trade organizations is that northern ATOs partner with southern ATOs, which typically are organizations of growers or artisans. Northern ATOs have to be strategic in partnering with developing country ATOs, which are required to meet criteria such as "transparency in financial operations, efficient management for reasonable profits, fair returns for individual producers and fair working conditions."[106] However, an idealistic element of fair trade is the aim to forge respectful, long-term relationships with marginalized producers. The long-term goal is thus to create opportunities for "contracts for annual supply, fair prices, advances against future production, training for producer skill development, and fair working conditions."[107] Thus, fair trade organizations emphasize the importance of good intentions; they illustrate the balance this book aspires to approach, between caution and optimism: "they are market-accepting organizations and accept that over the longer term, commercial viability is necessary."[108] Ultimately, fair trade organizations aim to redirect profits beyond their operating costs to developing country suppliers, "even when these suppliers don't have the market power or market knowledge to command these returns in the marketplace."[109]

A Precautionary Approach to Protect EoF: U.S. Native Americans

Contrary to the TRIPS assumption that developing countries would remain essentially intellectual property consumers rather than producers or owners of intellectual property, artisan handicrafts represent an estimated $30 billion worldwide market.[110] With globalization, ironically, industrial counterfeiting is common and often displaces the livelihood of artisans from indigenous tribes or developing nations. For example, counterfeit southwestern Native American basketry are manufactured in Pakistan, and in a bizarre postmodern twist, companies in Romania manufacture and sell knockoffs of Taiwanese knockoffs of Native American jewelry.[111] Given the comparative costs of production, artisans cannot compete with the prices and volume at which machine-made articles are created and marketed. Thus, there is a compelling need to deploy a precautionary approach to protect these EoF.

For example, in the United States, the Native American community has played an active role in establishing both state and federal legislation[112] to protect their arts and crafts. "U.S. law [in specific the Omnibus Trade and Competitiveness Act] requires Indian-style imported products to be indelibly labelled with the country of origin and imposes penalties for marketing non-Indian goods as Indian made."[113] This helps the discerning buyer to establish authenticity. In addition, the USPTO advises tribes to create detailed lists of tribal symbols and to register these lists. The registration helps prevent misuse by outsiders, and, integrating a corrective approach, can be used as a tool to push for the cancellation of existing trademarks that exploit Native American symbols.[114] Finally, much as with the protection of TK, NGOs, often in cooperation with tribal or artisans' associations, have been at the foreground in combating confusing or deceptive representations of Native American art in both the United States and Canada. Such groups have lobbied extensively and have been an active force in assisting Native American tribes in developing certificates of authenticity.[115]

Despite the promise of this approach, there is a caveat. The effectiveness of such certification as both precautionary and corrective depends on purchasers being both educated about the use of trademark to protect Native American art from counterfeit versions and on the consumers' dedication to buying only authentic items. Unfortunately, investigative surveys by NGOs have found "widespread lack of awareness of both the laws and certification systems to protect Indian-made articles, among buyers and Indian artists."[116]

In summary, theoretical models of a *sui generis* approach intersect with conceptualizations of a "limited common property" and "biodemocracy." Despite its promise, a *sui generis* approach lacks pragmatic discussion on how to delineate TK co-ownership and representation of authorized co-owners. There appears to be a broad-based international push to a *sui generis* approach while WIPO and the CBD advocate a checklist approach based on disclosure, prior informed consent, and benefit sharing. Advocates hope a checklist approach will incentivize developing countries to share their TK rather than hoard it, and, in the long term, help cooperatively generate a universal database. Such a database would catalogue all the sources of TK and EoF that may contribute to a more efficient system of regulation and lessen litigation. On the other hand, as argued earlier, merely modifying existing intellectual property law does not sufficiently define "informed consent," and Western conceptions of "compensation" may not adequately address indigenous peoples' wants or needs. The CBD inextricably links the conservation of biodiversity (i.e., a therapeutic/

preventive measure) with the protection of TK (a policing/corrective mechanism). One cannot have effective prevention without some policing, and vice versa. Thus, the protection of TK and EoF inevitably must be both partially proactive and partially reactive.

Suggested Core Principles and New Directions

This section begins by outlining specific core principles to protect TK and EoF. Next, the section recommends strategies for implementing these principles, first generally, then more specifically. These specific recommendations are divided among patents, copyright and neighboring rights, and trademarks and associated geographic indicators.

Outline of Core Principles to Protect TK and EoF

Based on concrete practices in protecting TK and EoF described through case studies in the prior sections, using a principle of induction, this section arrives at the following core principles:

- Prior informed consent
- Mutually agreed terms
- Benefit sharing
- Valuation of what is "authentic" to TK and EoF
- Respect for collective, as well as individual authorship

The use of induction is important in this study because it begins first with an examination of concrete instances of practice, rather than theoretical generalizations (which is not to decry a more theoretically oriented approach as one without value). Furthermore, the analysis throughout the book has also emphasized not simply the strengths of these concrete practices (the optimistic lens) but also the weaknesses of these approaches (the cautionary lens). These principles can then be used, deductively, to animate and guide other concrete instances of praxis that can be explored and related back to prior instances of praxis, in an organic feedback loop, emphasizing a holistic approach that always remains sensitive to changing contexts.

General Recommendations for Strategies Protecting TK and EoF

In terms of general recommended strategies for protecting TK and EoF, which flow from the principles listed above, there are several courses of action listed below:

1. Clarifying and reframing intellectual property discourse;
2. Promoting the voices of TK and EoF holders;
3. Capacity-building and awareness-raising, particularly among indigenous and local communities;
4. Practical initiatives, such as the prevention of unauthorized acquisition of TK and EoF;
5. Longer-term structural developments—for example, the development of a *sui generis* system.

Specific Recommendations for Strategies Protecting TK and EoF

Finally, in terms of strategies to be potentially deployed in the realm of specific forms of intellectual property protection (patents, copyright, trademarks), this chapter also itemizes the following more specific recommendations.[117]

To begin, here are some recommendations for patents. First, governments could deploy the (optional) morality requirement in the TRIPS Agreement[118] to turn down the registration application of a patent in some cases. Examples include cases where the application is connected to an invention that has a particular cultural or spiritual significance for indigenous and local communities, and where the application is likely to be considered culturally insensitive to such communities. Another case might be where the application displaces or robs indigenous communities of access to and control of their traditionally owned land and resources.

Second, ideally, patent statutes could provide some precautionary steps where it is highly likely that the acquisition or exploitation of indigenous peoples' TK have been acquired without prior informed consent. Perhaps, for example, in cases where an applicant for the revocation of a patent based on the lack of prior informed consent can show proof that the invention exploits or is derived from a genetic resource found within its territory, or from the TK of an indigenous or local community, one could presume that the patentee has taken such resource or knowledge without prior informed consent of the affected indigenous or local community. Such a presumption tips the balance in favor of protecting indigenous peoples' intellectual property rights, and places the burden of proving the acquisition of prior informed consent on the patent applicant.

Additionally, instead of simple revocation (which has limited punitive effects), patent statutes could perhaps authorize the transfer of the offending patent to the successful applicant, effective from the filing date of the patent application. Such a measure could be both corrective in the short run and potentially precautionary in the long run, as precedent becomes binding. Finally, third, ideally, patent statutes could explicitly state that prior use by a local or indigenous community of an invention that utilizes that community's TK does not anticipate (or destroy the novelty of) such a communally derived invention.

In terms of copyright and neighboring rights, here are some recommendations. First, countries could adopt the WIPO World Copyright Treaty (WCT)[119] and WIPO Performances and Phonograms Treaty (WPPT)[120] as these recognize moral rights (the rights of attribution and integrity), compared with the TRIPS Agreement, which refuses to acknowledge these rights.

Second, governments could abolish the fixation requirement for EoF, much as the Berne Convention[121] does, as many EoF are rooted in oral traditions or at least exist in forms that resist the traditional characterization of "fixation" as existing in a material, nontransitory state.

Third, countries could adopt a *sui generis* system of protection for EoF similar to the UNESCO WIPO Model Provisions;[122] such a system would radically veer away from the requirements of the prevailing system that tends to reinscribe colonial structures of power.

Fourth, nevertheless, on a cautionary note, although the *sui generis* protection of "non-original" databases (i.e., collections that don't meet the Western-derived "originality" requirement) is important for the potential protection and exploitation of TK, developing countries could carefully try to map the possible negative effects, however unintended, of instituting a strong exclusive rights regime on science, technology and education in their countries. Notwithstanding any innovations, the balance between demarcating exclusive property and leaving a rich public domain should be kept.

Finally, in terms of trademarks and associated geographic indicators, here are a few recommendations. First, as a precaution, governments could decline to register trademarks (or correctively cancel the registration) of marks that are likely to offend or disenfranchise a significant section of indigenous or local communities. Similarly, governments could refuse the registration application of, or correctively revoke, trademarks that falsely suggest a connection with such communities, or bring these indigenous communities to contempt or disrepute because of this false and often stereotypically racist depiction.

Second, ideally, countries could strengthen the protection of geographical indications to include, using a proactively preventative strategy, not just wines, but also, for instance, handicrafts and agrofood products distinctively associated with indigenous or local communities.

Third, ideally, governments could, as a safety measure, register designations of authenticity in the form of certification marks, which guarantee that these products not only meet a certain standard of quality but indicate a genuinely indigenous or local source.

In summary, using case studies, this chapter has distilled out core principles based upon empirical observations regarding the protection of TK and EoF. From these core principles, the chapter has also deduced general recommendations, thus essentially employing a hypothetico-deductive approach generally true of scientific methods. The chapter has further specified these recommendations by itemizing recommendations according to various specialized areas of intellectual property law, such as patent, copyright, and trademark. In terms of recommendations, these may be summarized in the following ways. Ideally, patent law could: (1) include a morality requirement; (2) presume a lack of prior informed consent in patent revocations, thus shifting the burden of proof to the patent-seeking party; and (3) not preclude the novelty of an invention that utilizes TK because of prior use by indigenous peoples. Similarly, *ceteris paribus*, copyright protection ideally could: (1) adopt the WIPO WCT and WIPO WPPT; (2) abolish the fixation requirements for EoF; and (3) implement a *sui generis* system for protecting EoF. In a like manner, ideally, trademark protection could: (1) deny trademarks that offend significant sections of indigenous communities; (2) strengthen the protection of geographical indicators, and (3) as a precautionary measure, register designations of authenticity associated with indigenous communities in the form of certification marks.

In conclusion, in terms of practice, existing intellectual property law is too narrowly construed to address adequately the complex issue of the intellectual property rights of indigenous peoples. As this book has shown through case studies, there is a gulf between current intellectual property law's provisions and their ability adequately to protect indigenous tribes from commercial exploitation. Accordingly, there is a need to arrive at new core principles as guiding heuristics; perhaps then, we can arrive at an interpretation of intellectual property law that can balance the "utilitarian" values of trade with the "deontological" values of indigenous peoples (understanding that these terms, and discussions that use them, are themselves Western). Future discourse should focus on core principles as general guides rather than strict programs or procedures. Such general schemas may be better suited to address the constant state of flux, and the generation of new pressures that will result from ever-increasing globalization.

Beyond Unbridled Optimism and Fear

Aspirationally and broadly, the discussions explored earlier could potentially open the door to further dialogue regarding indigenous peoples, human rights, and international trade law, among others, being conducted in a more pragmatic, solution-oriented manner, while being simultaneously sensitive to cultural differences. Even more importantly, developing countries and indigenous peoples could begin questioning assumptions behind the structural systems in place, such as the view that they are, and will remain, intellectual property consumers, rather than intellectual property producers or owners. Hence as Raj Bhala points out:

> [I]t is important to realize that [intellectual property] can be produced anywhere—wherever there is creative human capital. That means poor countries ought to see themselves not only as consumers of [intellectual property] products from overseas, but also—sooner or later as actual or potential producers of [intellectual property] exports for the rest of the world.[123]

And as we have seen earlier, in the area of EoF, and especially in the case of artisan handicrafts and fair trade practices, there are signs that some balance between market-accepting mechanisms and the preservation of EoF is not only possible but even, under certain closely monitored conditions, desirable.

Indeed, this book attempts to get at the chiaroscuro that characterizes the emerging landscape framing the interplay between law and culture. For every "advance," it is difficult not to see either a reaction or some unforeseen repercussion that nuances what seems clear "progress." For example, several countries, such as Australia,[124] Peru, the Philippines, and Canada[125] have theoretically added indigenous-rights protections to their constitutions or have enacted special indigenous-rights laws. Theoretically, these provisions require the enactment of the principles of prior informed consent, mutually agreed terms, benefit sharing and compensation, and the protection of health and the environment.[126] Nevertheless, as we have seen in prior chapters, governments could engage in willful blindness[127] in relation to, or even active cooperation with,[128] multinational corporations' violations of indigenous peoples' property and intellectual property rights because of either not having the infrastructure or institutional capacity to enforce these legal provisions,[129] or because of the government itself having a financial stake in the project.[130] Additionally, there are persistent problems of prejudice,[131] marginalization, and corruption,[132] and as we have seen in the case of Mapuche tribe, the subordination of indigenous peoples' property and intellectual property rights in favor of development goals for the nation.[133]

This book begins, and ends, naturally, with the premise that there are no "perfect" solutions. Every solution always has a potential pitfall, danger, or weakness; and there are always variables one cannot control. I return to the point at which I began: how to strike accord between fear and optimism. Perhaps the dynamic between trade and human rights, especially in relation to the possible protection of the intellectual property of indigenous peoples and the globalized drive toward development, is an essential tension, much like Nietzsche's characterization of the *agon* between the Apollinian force (reason) and the Dionysian drive (passion) in "The Birth of Tragedy."[134]

Indeed, Nietzsche's use of the verb *"reizen"*[135]—meaning to "stimulate" or even "irritate"—in his description of how the Apollonian and the Dionysian cause each other to generate new iterations of themselves, could perhaps be useful as a schema to adopt. One can argue that there are indeed affinities between trade and human rights in relation to indigenous peoples' intellectual property and property rights, such as their emphases on nondiscrimination; however, there are also significant differences in the way they apply what "nondiscrimination" means. For instance, trade relies on a utilitarian framework; human rights relies more on a natural law and deontological framework. There are senses in which they can and do converge; but they also retain their differences.

Nevertheless, rather than seeing these two terms as radical oppositions that must be viewed in "splendid isolation," it is important to plot their convergences as well as their differences in a holistic and balanced manner. Rather than collapsing trade into human rights or human rights into trade in relation to attempting to protect indigenous peoples' intellectual property and property rights, it is important to deploy these new similarity-differences into new conversations geared toward pragmatic ends. This project roots itself in the conviction it is that essential similarity-difference that generates new ways of re-examining potential paradigmatic shifts—of reframing timeless questions concerning what justice is within evolving contexts involving power differentials and institutional moorings. That tension, stealing from Thomas Kuhn's characterization of the relationship between different and thus, to some extent, "incommensurable,"[136] paradigms as an analogy, is an "essential"[137] tension—one both inevitable and potentially fruitful. It is that fundamental dynamic in which this book attempts to partake, in its analysis of the interactions between trade and human rights as applied to the dilemmas presented by the attempts to protect indigenous peoples' TK and EoF in the face of rapid globalization.

QUO VADIS?: LOOKING BACK, LOOKING FORWARD

Summarized briefly, chapter 1 contextualized the general coverage of the book and the various methodologies it uses. Acknowledging that definitional issues raise a host of complex problems, the first chapter attempted to avoid overreaching by describing pragmatic working descriptions for key terms such as "indigenous peoples," "traditional knowledge" (TK) and "expressions of folklore" (EoF). Additionally, chapter 1 located this book against the backdrop of evolving legal instruments that have attempted various levels of protection for indigenous peoples' intellectual property rights, and their ambiguous gains. Briefly glossed, chapter 1 outlined the key questions and general direction of the project.

Chapter 2, "Law In and As Culture," described the book's general framework, which began with Kuhn's insight that culture is "paradigmatic." Simply described, a paradigm is a communally generated way of interpreting "data" that focuses on certain questions and relegates others to the background, and elevates certain exemplars, or intersubjective methods of attempting to solve these paradigm-specific problems, for a particular community at a particular point in time. Culture, as the "collective programming of the mind,"[138] is analogically equivalent to the cultural training that enables a child to see an ambiguous figure—such as a duck-rabbit illusion—as either a duck or a rabbit, alternately, but not simultaneously, through a gestalt shift. Hence, chapter 2 affirms the sociological insight that there is no omniscient perspective from which one can record cultural interactions from a clinical distance, even when one is trained to be objective, such as a lawyer or hard scientist, without falling into the trap of utter cultural relativism.

Chapter 3, aptly titled "Cultural Meanings of Intellectual Property," began with Stavenhagen's three underlying conceptions of culture, implied in the practice of international and intellectual property law. These three meanings are: (1) culture as "capital"; (2) culture as "creativity"; and (3) culture as a "total way of life." This chapter also analyzed the tensions that result between majoritarian cultures and minority groups or indigenous peoples as an aftermath of these three simultaneously operating descriptions of culture in intellectual property law. Such descriptions of culture also intersect with transnational cultural understandings of "property" and "ownership."

Chapter 3 made attempting to negotiate differences in cultural clashes between majoritarian cultures and indigenous peoples its focus. The chapter examined two particular case studies involving cultural differences along the axes of individualism versus communitarianism (in the case involving ownership of the performance of a fragment of a Taiwanese tribe's folk song) and hierarchy versus egalitarianism (in the case involving the Mapuche tribe's struggle to maintain control of its ancestral lands). The chapter relied upon Geert Hofstede, Gert Jan Hofstede, and Michael Minkov's framework of cultural programming; general pragmatic strategies and more specific recommendations; as well as an analysis of the dynamics that resulted from the reliance on Stavenhagen's descriptions of "culture" embedded in intellectual property laws. Ultimately, the chapter found that in the case involving culture as "creativity," where the axes of cultural difference were mapped along an individualism-versus-communitarian continuum, and the indigenous performers had acquired their own rivaling celebrity and commercial success as performers, a private settlement was harmoniously and spontaneously achieved, resulting in benefit sharing with the tribe. In contrast, the case involving culture as a total "way of life," where the axes of cultural difference were discernible along a hierarchy-versus-egalitarianism dichotomy, and the Mapuche tribe retained an "outsider" status, only an external intervention by the Inter-American Human Rights Commission produced an uneasy "friendly" settlement, producing reparation from the Chilean government to the tribe in exchange for the loss of its ancestral lands. Although celebrity and media coverage clearly played a role in the resolution of the case of the Duanas and the Taiwanese Ami tribe, the Chilean Mapuche tribe did not have any "star spokespersons" and the effect of media coverage on its resolution was more uncertain. Finally, chapter 3 also employed an intersectional approach, hybridizing an analysis of the individualism-versus-communitarian continuum and the hierarchy-versus-egalitarianism dichotomy in the case of Australian Aboriginal artists attempts to gain intellectual property rights, as individuals and as members of their tribes.

Chapter 4, titled "Colonial Appropriations of Marginalized Cultures and Possible Strategies of Resistance," focuses on possible avenues of resistance, given that, as the book has argued, intellectual property law promotes particular cultural interpretations of knowledge, ownership, authorship, and property that are not necessarily consonant with indigenous peoples' understandings about the role and function of knowledge and knowledge practices, materialized in the practices and artifacts of their TK and EoF.[139] One such avenue involves giving voice to those normally silenced; another avenue involves unmasking front-stage myths of neutrality to reveal back-stage realities of systematic inequity; a third option lies in adapting prevailing legal and cultural categories to create new avenues and possibilities. These different but intersecting strategies were deployed in relation to a critique of the evolution of American dance choreography mapped against a history of copyright protection, as illustrated briefly in the examples of Loïe Fuller, Josephine Baker, and Katherine Dunham. By comparing these women's struggles for ownership of their choreographic creations and improvisations, the chapter argued that the evolution of copyright protection in the United States is best contextualized by examining the complex intersections and interactions of gender, race, and class that generated the jurisprudence regarding whose choreographic creations, and which choreographic creations, deserved demarcation from the public domain as private property. The chapter also drew out some similarities between the challenges Baker and

Dunham faced and the obstacles Australian Aboriginal artists confronted, while keeping in mind significant differences in their situations.

Finally, chapter 5, the concluding chapter, attempted to track the streams that connected the prior chapters into a coherent flow, and suggested various ways in which law can be negotiated and lived in and as culture. Drawing from current and ongoing attempts at collaboration between majoritarian groups and indigenous peoples, this chapter identified some core principles as a possible heuristic, balancing the rights of indigenous peoples to protect their cultural identities, TK and EoF and ancestral lands (technically, "first generation" human rights),[140] alongside the right, of developing countries, for example, to pursue development and scientific progress (technically, a "third generation" human right).[141] Among these guiding principles were: prior informed consent, mutually agreed terms, and benefit sharing.[142] The effectiveness of these principles as pragmatic guidelines to working across cultural differences was instantiated in the case of the successful collaboration between an MNC and an indigenous Indian tribe to produce a commercially viable form of Jeevani. This third case, hinging on Stavenhagen's first description of culture, as "capital," serves as an example of how the principles outlined above can produce a successful rapprochement, which, while not being devoid of weakness, did result in a financially rewarding outcome for both the indigenous tribe and a multinational corporation. Nevertheless, the chapter acknowledged that the Jeevani example is only one, among many ways, in which law in and as culture, can operate, finding an uneasy compromise, however contingent, between protecting indigenous peoples' intellectual property rights and a developing country's right to progress.

Thus, this book has striven to describe why, generally speaking, intellectual property law is problematic as a means of protecting indigenous peoples' intellectual property rights because there are fundamental incongruities separating Western conceptions of innovation and invention from the communal values of many indigenous peoples. Clearly, the evolution of the intellectual property rights of indigenous peoples is anything but a linear process of "progression"; but then again, arguably, using Kuhn's model, neither is the history of science as unambiguously indicative of "progress" in the clash of paradigms. As this book has shown, even the history of the legal instruments designed to promote intellectual property protection, in relation to indigenous peoples' intellectual property rights, is a contested affair. For example, noted scholars have argued that the CBD was a progressive step from the TRIPS Agreement and similarly, that the protocol was an evolution from the CBD. In contrast, other scholars have argued that the protocol merely reiterates dominant intellectual property rights norms. A solution to the current rhetorical impasse is difficult, as the disagreement hinges upon two radically oppositional narratives. Thus, this project has aspired to go beyond this apparent impasse of incommensurable perspectives, akin to a Nietzschean refusal of absolute binaries. More pragmatically, the book, through its method, has argued that one concrete way to deconstruct these apparently insurmountable binaries lies in being open to patient and cooperative communication, fortified by empirical analysis and nuanced case studies. Other tools this book has employed are the judicious use of logic balanced by a moral imperative for fairness, as well as the use of a hypothetico-deductive model to generate core principles from which one could deduce recommendations, both general and specific, for strategies to protect TK and EoF. Finally, the book concludes with specific recommendations in addressing current issues in intellectual property law, and proposed core principles, based on already-existing practices, which may be used as starting points to address what is, admittedly, a continually and dynamically evolving set of issues.

NOTES

1. A portion of this chapter previously appeared as part of a two part-article: Caroline Joan "Kay" S. Picart and Marlowe Fox, "Beyond Unbridled Optimism and Fear: Indigenous Peoples, Intellectual Property, Human Rights and the Globalization of Traditional Knowledge and Expressions of Folklore (Part I)," *International Community Law Review* 15, no. 3 (2013): 319–39; and Caroline Joan "Kay" S. Picart and Marlowe Fox, "Beyond Unbridled Optimism and Fear: Indigenous Peoples, Intellectual Property, Human Rights and the Globalization of Traditional Knowledge and Expressions of Folklore (Part II)," *International Community Law Review* 16, no. 2 (March 2014): 3–37. I thank the *International Community Law Review* and Brill for permission to adapt the material for this book.

2. First Generation or "Civil and Political Rights" include the right to nondiscrimination based on race, gender, language, religion, culture, family, ethnicity, national origin, and social origin. See Berta Hernandez-Truyol and Stephen J. Powell, *Just Trade: A New Covenant Linking Trade and Human Rights* (New York: New York University Press, 2009), 59. Realistically, "first," "second," and "third" generation rights are inextricably intertwined but may be analytically parsed apart, to some extent.

3. Third Generation or "Solidarity Rights" include, ironically, the rights to both development as well as environment, peace, democracy, a common heritage, communication, and humanitarian assistance. Hernandez-Truyol and Powell, *Just Trade*, 61.

4. "About the Nagoya Protocol," *Convention on Biological Diversity*, last modified 2012, accessed May 9, 2015, www.cbd.int/abs/about/#objective. There

are other regionally based suggestions as well. For example, Latin American reforms, in relation to protecting the rights of indigenous peoples in general has led to the following recommendations: (1) support the U.N. indigenous programs that use the Human Rights model; (2) increase funding for legal education and human rights training for indigenous tribes; (3) advocate for increasing use of indigenous law for local use; (4) maintain and continue the attempts to develop even more effective international indigenous rights instruments. Justin Dargin, "Indian Question in Latin America: An Overview of the Legal and Social Position of Indigenous Peoples," *Guild Practitioner* 63 (2006): 149, 154–55. See also, *Right of Food of Indigenous People in Latin America* (Cologne, Germany: FIAN Inernational, 2012), PDF, accessed May 17, 2014, www.fian.org/fileadmin/media/publications/2012.04.29_-_Article_The_Right_to_Food_oF_indigenous_Peoples_in_Latin_America.pdf.

5. Supreme Court of India, *Narmada Bachao Andolan v. Union of India*, 18 October 2000, writ petition (civil) No.319 of 1994, AIR (2000) SC 3751, in particular at para. 267.

6. Ibid., para. 274.

7. Ibid.

8. Ibid. See also Action Plan adopted at the Mar del Plata international Water Conference, 1977.

9. Supreme Court of India, *Narmada Bachao Andolan v. Union of India*, at para. 276.

10. Eckart Klein, "Establishing a Hierarchy of Human Rights: Ideal Solution or Fallacy?" *Israel Law Review* 41 (2008): 477, accessed May 17, 2015, ssrn.com/abstract=1333295.

11. *Universal Declaration of Human Rights*, GA Res. 217(III), UN GAOR, 3d Sess., Supp. No. 13, UN Doc. A/810 (1948) 71 ["*Universal Declaration*,"] art. 17(1).

12. Ibid., art. 7; International Covenant on Civil and Political Rights, December 16, 1966, 999 U.N.T.S. 171, art. 26.

13. Supreme Court of India, *Narmada Bachao Andolan v. Union of India*, 274.

14. See, for example, Bilahari Kausikan, "Asia's Different Standard," *Foreign Policy* 92 (1993): 24, 37; Simon Tay, "Human rights, Culture, and the Singapore example," *McGill Law Journal* 41 (1995): 743, 746.

15. Supreme Court of India, *Narmada Bachao Andolan v. Union of India*, para. 264.

16. Ibid.

17. Benoît Mayer, "Judicial Review of Human Rights Impacts of Hydroelectric Projects," in *Legal Working Paper Series on Legal Empowerment for Sustainable Development*, Centre for International Sustainable Development Law, Faculty of Law (Montreal, Quebec, Canada: McGill University, 2012), 15, accessed May 17, 2015, cisdl.org/public/docs/Mayer_Judicial_Review.pdf.

18. See, for example, Rosemary J. Coombe, *The Cultural Life of Intellectual Properties: Authorship, Appropriation, and the Law* (Dunham, NC: Duke University Press, 1998), 199–204 (analysis of the controversy over a malt whiskey company's appropriation of Lakota statesman Crazy Horse's name as the trademark for its product).

19. Janice G. Weiner, "Protection of Folklore: A Political and Legal Challenge," *International Review of Industrial Property and Copyright Law* 18 (1987): 58.

20. Terri Janke, "UNESCO-WIPO World Forum on the Protection of Folklore: Lessons for Protecting Indigenous Australian Cultural and Intellectual Property," *Copyright Rep* 15 (1997): 109.

21. Agnés Lucas-Schloetter, "Folklore," in Silke von Lewinski (ed.), *Indigenous Heritage and Intellectual Property: Genetic Resources, Traditional Knowledge and Folklore*, 2nd ed., ed. Silke von Lewinski (The Netherlands: Kluwer Law International, 2008), 346.

22. WIPO, *Intergovernmental Committee on Intellectual Property and Genetic Resources, Traditional Knowledge and Folklore* no. 50, WIPO/GRTFK/IC/6/3 (1 December 2003), 17.

23. Thomas Streeter, "Broadcast Copyright and the Bureaucratization of Property," in *The Construction of Authorship: Textual Appropriation in Law and Literature*, ed. Martha Woodmansee and Perer Jaszi (Durham and London: Duke University Press, 1994), 306.

24. Marlon B. Ross, "The New Negro Displayed: Self-Ownership, Proprietary Sites/Sights, and the Bonds/Bounds of Race," in *Claiming the Stones, Naming the Bones: Cultural Property and the Negotiation of National and Ethnic Identity*, eds. Elazar Barkan and Ronald Bush (Oxford: Oxford University Press, 2002), 259.

25. Martha Woodmansee, "The Genius and the Copyright," *Eighteenth Century Studies* 17, no. 4 (1984): 447.

26. James Boyle, *Shahmans, Software and Spleens: Law and the Construction of the Information Society* (Cambridge, MA: Harvard University Press, 1996), xiv.

27. Laurelyn Whitt, *Science, Colonialism and Indigenous Peoples: The Cultural Politics of Law and Knowledge* (New York: Cambridge University Press, 2009), 162.

28. Ibid., 162.

29. See Kal Raustiala and David G. Victor, "The Regime Complex for Plant Genetic Resources," *International Organisation* 58 (2004): 277; R. Lettington and K. Nnadozie, "A Review of the Intergovernmental Committee on Genetic Resources, Traditional Knowledge and Folklore at WIPO," (December 2003), complied in *Trade-Related Agenda, Development and Equity*, no. 12 (2012) accessed January 1, 2014, www.ciel.org/Publications/Occassional_ SouthCentre_Dec03.pdf.

30. Michael J. Trebilcock and Robert Howse, *The Regulation of International Trade*, 3rd ed. (New York: Routledge, 2010), 436.

31. "World Intellectual Property Organization and United Nations Environment Programme," *WIPO-UNEP Study on the Role of Intellectual Property Tights in the Use of Biological Resources and Associated Traditional Knowledge*, 20–21, last accessed May 18, 2015, www.wipo.int/tk/en/publicationsn769e_unep tk.pdf.

32. "World Wildlife Fund Position Paper," Conference of the Parties to the Convention on Biological Diversity (Mar. 20–31, 2006), assets.panda.org/downloads/wwf position_cop 8_article_8j 10march_2006.doc (date downloaded unspecified), cited in: Mindahi Crescencio Bastida-Muñoz and Geraldine A. Patrick, "Traditional Knowledge and Intellectual Property Rights: Beyond TRIPS Agreements and Intellectual Property Chapters of FTAs," *Michigan State Journal of International Law* 14 (2006): 259, 278–79.

33. Lorna Dwyer, "Biopiracy, Trade, and Sustainable Development," *Colorado Journal of International Environmental Law and Policy* 19 (2008): 250.

34. Hernandez-Truyol and Powell, *Just Trade*, 228.

35. Jacob Pilot, "Developing Indigenous Knowledge Centres," in *Australian Indigenous Knowledge and Libraries*, ed. Martin Nakata and Marcia Langton (Sydney, Australia: UTsE Press, 2005), 40, accessed May 21, 2015, steve3067095.pbworks.com/f/Developing+indigenous+knowledge+Centres.pdf.

36. Ibid., 39.

37. Sandi Taylor, "State Library of Queensland Library Services: Overcoming Barriers and Building Bridges" *Australian Academic & Research Libraries* 34, no. 4 (December 2003): 280–81.

38. Pilot, "Developing Indigenous Knowledge," 43.

39. Ibid., 40, 44.

40. Ibid., 44.

41. Paul Kuruk, "Protecting Folklore Under Modern Intellectual Property Regimes: A Reappraisal of the Tensions Between Individual Rights and Communal Rights in Africa," *American Law Review* 49 (1999): 769.

42. Dwyer, "Biopiracy," 250.

43. Vandana Shiva, *Biopiracy: The Plunder of Nature and Knowledge* (New York: South End Press, 1997), 80–81. On a more pragmatic note, Luisa Maffi and Ellen Woodley advocate a "biocultural diversity approach" (envisages "the diversity of life in all of its manifestations—biological, cultural and linguistic—which are interrelated (and likely co-evolved) within a complex socioecological adaptive system"), and create a list of grassroots-level projects that embody this connectedness, often intersecting with proprietary issues concerning TK and EoF. Luisa Maffi, "Introduction: Why a Sourcebook on Biocultural Diversity?" in *Biocultural Diversity Conservation: A Global Sourcebook*, eds. Luisa Maffi and Ellen Woodley (London: Earthscan, 2010), 5.

44. Dwyer, "Biopiracy," 250.

45. J. H. Reichmann, "Of Green Tulips and Legal Kudzu: Repacking Rights in Sub-patentable Innovation," *Vanderbilt Law* 53 (2000): 1743.

46. Ibid., 1798.

47. Jocelyn Kaiser, "NIH to Limit Scope of Foreign Patents Science," *Science* 296, no. 5577 (2002): 2316.

48. Ibid., 249. See also Marcia Langton and Zane Ma Rhea, "Traditional Indigenous Biodiversity-related Knowledge," *Australian Indigenous Knowledge and Libraries* 36, no. 2, (2005): 45–69 (citing a number of incentive measures being implemented, in relation to the development of *sui generis* negotiations, alongside other strategies, also linked with *sui generis* initiatives, such as poverty reduction schemes, access to benefit sharing strategies, tax exemptions, and collaborative research projects, functioning as collaborative approaches to explore conservation and economic development on the basis of the use of traditional biodiversity-related knowledge).

49. Trebilcock and Howse, *The Regulation of International Trade*, 436.

50. Ibid.

51. Dwyer, "Biopiracy," 245.

52. Ibid.

53. Ibid.

54. Ibid.

55. Ibid., 246.

56. Ibid.
57. Hernandez-Truyol and Powell, *Just Trade*, 227.
58. Dwyer, "Biopiracy," 246.
59. Jane Anderson, "Indigenous Knowledge, Intellectual Property, Libraries and Archives: Crises of Access, Control and Future Utility," in *Australian Indigenous Knowledge and Libraries*, ed. Martin Nakata and Marcia Langton (Sydney, Australia: UTsE Press, 2005), 78–79, accessed May 21, 2015, opus.lib.uts.edu.au/research/bitstream/handle/2100/57/Libraries%20and%20Indige;jsessionid=F55E41A2518BFC5D539F8D715CD562A3?sequence=1.
60. Ibid., 78.
61. Ibid., 79.
62. Terri Janke differentiates between *sui generis* solutions and indigenous protocols—a differentiation that hinges on the issue of how locally and specifically tailored the attempted legal solution is; since *sui generis* solutions, generally characterized, attempt to use national/local law tailored to fit particular circumstances, for pragmatic and strategic reasons, this book does not parse these categories as strictly. Terri Janke, "Managing Indigenous Knowledge and Indigenous Cultural and Intellectual Property," in *Australian Indigenous Knowledge and Libraries*, ed. Martin Nakata and Marcia Langton (Sydney, Australia: UTsE Press, 2005), 87–88, accessed May 21, 2015, opus.lib.uts.edu.au/research/bitstream/handle/2100/57/Libraries%20and%20Indige;jsessionid=F55E41A2518BFC5D539F8D715CD562A3?sequence=1.
63. Anderson, "Indigenous Knowledge, Intellectual Property," 78.
64. Ibid., 79.
65. Ibid., 79–80.
66. Ibid., 80.
67. Ibid.
68. Hernandez-Truyol and Powell, *Just Trade*, 228.
69. Dwyer, "Biopiracy," 252.
70. Ibid.
71. Ayoyemi Arowolo, "A Continental Approach to Protecting Traditional Knowledge Systems and Related Resources in Africa," July 1, 2009, *Social Science Research Network (SSRN)*, available at: papers.ssrn.com/sol3/papers.cfm?abstract_id=1313582 (last visited June 4, 2015).
72. Dwyer, "Biopiracy," 251–52.
73. Agreement on Trade-Related Aspects of Intellectual Property Rights, Apr. 15, 1994, Marrakesh Agreement Establishing the World Trade Organization, Annex 1C, The Legal Texts: The Results of The Uruguay Round of Multilateral Trade Negotiations, 1869 U.N.T.S. 299, 22 I.L.M. 1197 (1994), Art. 27(2) (hereinafter TRIPS Agreement).
74. Dwyer, "Biopiracy," 252.
75. Ibid.
76. See Olufunmilayo B. Arewa, "Piracy, Biopiracy, and Borrowing: Culture, Cultural Heritage and the Globalization of Intellectual Property," *Case Legal Studies Research Paper No. 04–19* (March 2006), 76 (recommendation of a bottom-up approach); Paul Kuruk, "Protecting Folklore Under Modern Intellectual Property Regimes: A Reappraisal of the Tensions Between Individual and Com-

munal Rights in Africa and the United States," Part III, *The American University Law Review* 48 (1999): 769 (recommendation of a bottom-up approach). See also, generally, Olufunmilayo B. Arewa, "TRIPS and Traditional Knowledge: Local Communities, Local Knowledge, and Global Intellectual Property Frameworks," *Marquette International Property Law Review* 10 (2006): 155.

77. Dwyer, "Biopiracy," 248.

78. Ibid., 248–49.

79. Ibid., 253.

80. Ibid.

81. Ibid.

82. Ibid., 254.

83. Ibid.

84. See Senator José Serra, Minister of Health of Brazil, Lessons from the Brazilian aids Program, Keynote Address, *AIDS 20 Years Later: An International Health Conference* (2001); "Brazil Industrial Property Law," art. 86, in *International Trade Law: Problems, Cases and Materials*, eds. Daniel C. K. Chow and Thomas J. Schoenbaum (New York: Aspen Publishers, 2008), 215.

85. J. Michael Finger, "Introduction and Overview," in *Poor People's Knowledge: Promoting Intellectual Property in Developing Countries*, eds. J. Michael Finger and Philip Schuler (Washington, DC: World Bank Publications and Oxford University Press, 2004), 20; Caroline Joan "Kay" S. Picart, "Cross Cultural Negotiations and International Intellectual Property Law: Attempts to Work Across Cultural Clashes between Indigenous Peoples and Majoritarian Cultures," *Southern California Interdisciplinary Law Journal* 23, no. 1 (January 2014): 37–65.

86. Finger and Schuler, *Poor People's Knowledge*, 20; Picart, "Cross Cultural," 37–65.

87. Finger and Schuler, *Poor People's Knowledge*, 20; Picart, "Cross Cultural," 37–65.

88. Finger and Schuler, *Poor People's Knowledge*, 20; Picart, "Cross Cultural," 37–65.

89. Finger and Schuler, *Poor People's Knowledge*, 20; Picart, "Cross Cultural," 37–65.

90. Finger and Schuler, *Poor People's Knowledge*, 20; Picart, "Cross Cultural," 37–65.

91. Finger and Schuler, *Poor People's Knowledge*, 27; Picart, "Cross Cultural," 37–65.

92. Finger and Schuler, *Poor People's Knowledge*, 27; Picart, "Cross Cultural," 37–65.

93. Finger and Schuler, *Poor People's Knowledge*, 27; Picart, "Cross Cultural," 37–65.

94. Gerard Bodeker, "Traditional Medical Knowledge, Intellectual Property Rights and Benefit Sharing," *Cardozo Journal of International and Comparative* 11 (2003–2004): 785, 799.

95. Finger and Schuler, *Poor People's Knowledge*, 21; Picart, "Cross Cultural," 37–65.

96. Finger and Schuler, *Poor People's Knowledge*, 21; Picart, "Cross Cultural," 37–65.

97. Finger and Schuler, *Poor People's Knowledge,* 21; Picart, "Cross Cultural," 37–65.

98. Finger and Schuler, *Poor People's Knowledge,* 21; Picart, "Cross Cultural," 37–65.

99. Dwyer, "Biopiracy," 219.

100. Ibid.

101. TRIPS Agreement, Art. 27(2).

102. Hernandez-Truyol and Powell, *Just Trade,* 29.

103. Ibid., 230.

104. Ibid.

105. Finger and Schuler, *Poor People's Knowledge,* 10.

106. Ibid., 12.

107. Ibid.

108. Ibid.

109. Ibid.

110. Betsy J. Fowler, "Preventing Counterfeit Craft Designs," in *Poor People's Knowledge: Promoting Intellectual Property in Developing Countries,* eds. J. Michael Finger and Philip Schuler (Washington, DC: World Bank Publications and Oxford University Press, 2004), 114.

111. Ibid.

112. The Indian Arts and Crafts Act of 1990 is federal legislation proscribing passing off non-Indian made goods as Indian-made; it can impose fines of up to U.S. $250,000 and up to five years in prison for fraud. Fowler, "Preventing Counterfeit," 119.

113. Ibid.

114. Ibid., 121. See also Phil Patton, "Trademark Battle Over Pueblo Sign," *New York Times* January 13, 2000, New York Edition, Section F.

115. Fowler, "Preventing Counterfeit," 121.

116. Finger and Schuler, *Poor People's Knowledge,* 18.

117. For a convergent account of these strategies, see Coenraad J. Visser, "Making Intellectual Property Laws Work For Traditional Knowledge," in *Poor People's Knowledge: Promoting Intellectual Property in Developing Countries,* eds. J. Michael Finger and Philip Schuler (Washington, DC: World Bank Publications and Oxford University Press, 2004), 232–34.

118. TRIPS Agreement, Art. 27(2).

119. WIPO Copyright Treaty, Dec. 20, 1996, S. Treaty Doc. No. 105-17 (1997), 36 I.L.M. 65 (1997).

120. WIPO Performances and Phonograms Treaty, Dec. 20, 1996, S. Treaty Doc. No. 105-17 (1997), 36 I.L.M. 76 (1997).

121. Berne Convention of the Protection of Literary and Artistic Works, Sept. 9, 1886, (revised in Paris, 24 July 1971, and amended in 1979), S. Treaty Doc. No. 99-27 (1986); Paris Convention for the Protection of Industrial Property, as last revised at the Stockholm Revision Conference, July 14, 1967, 21 U.S.T. 1583; 828 U.N.T.S. 303; Treaty on Intellectual Property in Respect of Integrated Circuits, May 26, 1989, 28 I.L.M. 1477.

122. WIPO-UN Educ., Scientific and Cultural Org. (UNESCO), *Model Provisions for National Laws on the Protection of Expressions of Folklore Against Illicit Exploita-*

tion and other Forms of Prejudicial Action, 1982 (1985), www.wipo.int/wipolex/en/details.jsp?id=6714.

123. Raj Bhala, *International Trade Law: Interdisciplinary Theory and Practice*, 3rd ed. (Danvers, MA: LEXISNEXIS, 2008), 1623.

124. "Native Title Act 1993," *Commonwealth Consolidated Acts*, last modified July 6, 2015, accessed May 17, 2015, www.austlii.edu.au/au/legis/cth/consol_act/nta1993147/.

125. See, for example, Dwight G. Newman, *The Duty to Consult: New Relationships with Aboriginal Peoples* (Saskatoon, Canada: Purich Publishing Limited, 2009), 9–45; Karen E. Bravo, "Balancing Indigenous Rights to Land and the Demands of Economic Development: Lessons from the United States and Australia," *Columbia Journal of Law and Social Problems* 30 (Summer 1997): 559; Joji Cariño, "Indigenous Peoples' Right to Free, Prior Informed Consent: Reflections on Concepts and Practice," *Arizona Journal of International Law and Comparative Law* 22, no. 1 (2005): 19, 26–29; Allison M. Dussias, "Indians and Indios: Echoes of the Bhopal Disaster in the Achuar People of Peru's Struggle Against the Toxic Legacy of Occidental Petroleum," *New England Law Review* 42, no. 4 (2008): 809, 812–19; Janeth Warden-Fernandez, "Indigenous Communities' Rights and Mineral Development," *Journal of Energy and Natural Resources Law* 23 (2005): 395, 420–24; Siegfried Wiessner, "Rights and Status of Indigenous Peoples: A Global Comparative and International Legal Perspective," *Harvard Human Rights Journal* 12 (1999): 57, 60–92.

126. George K. Foster, "Foreign Investment and Indigenous Peoples: Options for Promoting Equilibrium between Economic Development and Indigenous Rights," *Michigan Journal of International Law* 33 (2012): 627, 654, accessed May 17, 2015, repository.law.umich.edu/mjil/vol33/iss4/1.

127. See, for example, Evaristus Oshionebo, "World Bank and Sustainable Development of Natural Resources in Developing Countries," *Journal of Energy and National Resources Law* 27, no. 2 (2009): 193, 219–20.

128. Andrew Nikiforuk, *Tar Sands: Dirty Oil and the Future of a Continent* (Vancouver: Greystone Books, 2010), 188.

129. See, for example, Oshionebo, "World Bank," 219–20; Nigel Sizer and Dominiek Plouvier, *Increased Investment and Trade by Transnational Logging Companies in Africa, the Caribbean and the Pacific: Implications for the Sustainable Management and Conservation of Tropical Forests* (Brussels, Belgium: European Commission, 2000), 30.

130. See, for example, Nikiforuk, *Tar Sands*, 29; Dussias, "Indians and Indios," 837.

131. See "Dirty Metals: Mining Communities and the Environment," *Earthworks and Oxfam America* (2004), 22, last accessed May 17, 2015, www.earthworksaction.org/files/publications/NDG_DirtyMetalsReport_HR.pdf; Rodolfo Stavenhagen, "Making the Declaration on the Rights of Indigenous Peoples Work: The Challenge Ahead," in *Reflections on the UN Declaration on the Rights of Indigenous Peoples*, eds. Stephen Allen and Alexandra Xanthaki (Oxford, UK: Hart Publishing, 2011), 147, 158–59.

132. Sizer and Plouvier, *Increased Investment*, 30; Oshionebo, "World Bank," 109, 220; Alan Khee-Jin Tan, "All That Glitters: Foreign Investment in Mining

Trumps the Environment in the Philippines," *Pace Environmental Law Review* 23 (2005): 183, 199–200.

133. Susan A. Crate and Natalia Yakovleva, "Indigenous People and Mineral Resource Extraction in Russia: The Case of Diamonds," in *Earth Matters: Indigenous Peoples, the Extractive Industries and Corporate Social Responsibility*, eds. Ciaran O'Faircheallaigh and Saleem Ali (Sheffield, UK: Greenleaf Publishing, 2008), 222, 239.

134. Friedrich Nietzsche, "The Birth of Tragedy," in *The Birth of Tragedy and the Case of Wagner*, trans. Walter Kaufmann (Toronto: Random House, 1967), 33.

135. Friedrich Nietzsche, "Sämtliche Werke: Die Geburt der Tragödie, Unzeitgemäβe Betrachtungen 1–4," in *Nachgelassene Schriften 1870–1873*, eds. Giorgio Colli and Mazzino Montinari (Munich: Deutscher Taschenbuch Verlag, 1988), 5 cited in Caroline Joan "Kay" S. Picart, *Resentment and the "Feminine," in Nietzsche's Politico-Aesthetics* (University Park: Pennsylvania State University Press, 1999), 43.

136. Thomas Kuhn, *The Structure of Scientific Revolutions* (Chicago: University of Chicago Press, 1970), 110.

137. Thomas Kuhn, "Preface" in *The Essential Tension*, ed. Thomas Kuhn, (Chicago and London: University of Chicago Press, 1977), xvii–xviii.

138. Lieh-Ching Chang, "An Examination of Cross-Cultural Negotiation: Using Hofstede Framework," *Journal of American Academy of Business, Cambridge* 2, no. 22 (March 2003): 567, two.nitbj.com.cn/nit/content/references/Chang,%20L..pdf.

139. See, for example, views of indigenous peoples expressed in Catherine E. Bell and Val Napolean, eds., *First Nations Cultural Heritage and Law: Case Studies, Voices and Perspectives* (Vancouver, B.C., Canada: University of British Columbia Press, 2008); Terri Janke, *Our Culture: Our Future: Report on Australian Indigenous Cultural and Intellectual Property Rights* (Sydney, Australia: Michael Frankel & Co, 1998).

140. See note 2.

141. See note 3.

142. See note 4.

Bibliography

"0817 #80 Difang Duana & Enigma Copyrights Issue." YouTube video. 2:46. Posted by TITV Weekly. August 19, 2008. www.youtube.com/watch?v=EaVnHFHj6MM.

"110301 Debate on Access to Medicine and Biodiversity at the WTO." *Africa Europe Faith and Justice Network*. Accessed May 9, 2015. www.aefjn.org/index.php/357/articles/id-110301-debate-on-access-to-medicines-and-biodiversity-at-the-wto.html.

17 USC § 101 (2010).

17 USC § 102(a), amended by 104 Stat 5133, 1990.

35 U.S.C. § 102(a) and (b) (2002).

"About the Nagoya Protocol." *Convention on Biological Diversity*. Accessed May 9, 2015. www.cbd.int/abs/about/.

Abrams, Howard B. *The Law of Copyright (Intellectual Property Library)* § 1.02[C][4]. New York: Clark Boardman, 1991.

———. "Originality and Creativity in Copyright Law," *Law and Contemporary Problems* 55. No. 2 (Spring 1992): 3–44.

Adewopo, Adebambo. "Developments in Intellectual Property in Africa." *International Association for the Advancement of Teaching and Research in Intellectual Property (ATRIP)*. Accessed April 22, 2015. www.atrip.org/Content/Activities/Adewopo%20Dev.%20of%20IP%20in%20Africa.doc.

Agrawal, Arun. *The Politics of Indigenous Knowledge,* in *Australian Indigenous Knowledge and Libraries*. Eds. Martin Nakata and Marcia Langton. Canberra, Australia: Australian Academic and Research Libraries, 2005.

"Agreement on Trade-Related Aspects of Intellectual Property Rights, April 15, 1994, Marrakesh Agreement Establishing the World Trade Organization." Annex 1C. *The Legal Texts: The Results of The Uruguay Round of Multilateral Trade Negotiations*. 1869 U.N.T.S. 299, 22 I.L.M. 1197 (1994) (TRIPS Agreement).

"Agreement Revising the Bangui Agreement of March 2, 1977, on the creation of an African Intellectual Property Organization, (Bangui [Central African Republic], February 24, 1999)." *World Intellectual Property Organization (WIPO)*. Accessed April 21, 2015. www.wipo.int/wipolex/en/details.jsp?id=644.

Albright, Ann Cooper. *Traces Of Light: Absence and Presence in the Work of Loïe Fuller*. Middleton, CT: Wesleyan University Press, 2007.

Anderson, Jane. "Indigenous Knowledge, Intellectual Property, Libraries and Archives: Crises of Access, Control and Future Utility." In *Australian Indigenous Knowledge and Libraries*, ed. Martin Nakata and Marcia Langton. NSW, Australia: UTSePress, 2006. Accessed May 21, 2015. opus.lib.uts.edu.au/research/bitstream/handle/2100/57/Libraries%20and%20Indige;jsessionid=F55E41A2518BFC5D539F8D715CD562A3?sequence=1.

———. *Law, Knowledge, Culture: The Production of Indigenous Knowledge in Intellectual Property Law*. Cheltenham, UK: Edward Elgar Publishing, 2009.

——— "The Making of Indigenous Knowledge in Intellectual Property Law in Australia." *International Journal of Cultural Property* 12. No. 3 (2005): 347–73.

———. "The Politics of Indigenous Knowledge: Australia's Proposed Communal Moral Rights Bill." *University of New South Wales Law Journal* 27. No. 3 (2004): 585–604.

Andrews, Lori, and Dorothy Nelkin. *Body Bazaar: The Market for Human Tissue in the Biotechnology Age*. New York: Crown Publishers, 2001.

"Annex to WIPO, The Protection of Traditional Knowledge: Revised Objectives and Principles," WIPO/GRTK/IC/11/5(c) (reproducing WIPO/GRTKF/IC/9/5) (26 April 2007) ("draft WIPO TK provisions," first circulated in this form as "WIPO, The Protection of Traditional Knowledge: Revised Objects and Principles," WIPO/GRTKF/IC/8/5 (8 April 2005), Art. 3.

Anzaldua, Gloria E. "Preface: (Un)natural bridges, (Un)safe spaces." In *This Bridge We Call Home: Radical Visions for Transformation*. Ed. Gloria Anzaldúa and AnaLouise Keating. New York: Routledge, 2002.

Appadurai, Arjun. (1986) "Introduction: Commodities and the Politics of Value." In *The Social Life of Things: Commodities in Cultural Perspective*. Ed. A. Appadurai. Cambridge: Cambridge University Press, 1986.

Arewa, Olufunmilayo B. "Piracy, Biopiracy, and Borrowing: Culture, Cultural Heritage and the Globalization of Intellectual Property." *Case Legal Studies Research Paper No. 04–19* (March 2006): 1–85.

———. "TRIPS and Traditional Knowledge: Local Communities, Local Knowledge, and Global Intellectual Property Frameworks." *Marquette Intellectual Property Law Review* 10. No. 2 (2006): 155–80.

Armour, Kenneth J. and Peter S. Harrison. "Indigenous Rights and IP Protection." *World Patent Information* 29 (2007): 255–61.

Arowolo, Ayoyemi Lawal. "A Continental Approach to Protecting Traditional Knowledge Systems and Related Resources in Africa" (July 1, 2009). Social Science Research Network (SSRN). Accessed April 22, 2015. papers.ssrn.com/sol3/papers.cfm?abstract_id=1313582.

Asante, S. K. B. "Fiduciary Principles in Anglo-American Law and The Customary Law of Ghana." *International and Comparative Law Quarterly* 14. No. 4 (1965): 1145. Cited in Blakeney, Michael. "Communal Intellectual Property Rights of

Indigenous Peoples in Cultural Expressions." *The Journal of World Intellectual Property* 1. No. 6 (November 1998): 985–1002.

Aschenbrenner, Joyce. *Katherine Dunham: Dancing a Life*. Chicago: University of Illinois Press, 2002.

———. "Katherine Dunham: Reflections on the Social and Political Contexts of Afro-American Dance." *Dance Research Journal* Annual XI (1980): 3–118.

Australian Institute of Professional Counsellors (AIPC) (1995), 91–116. Cited in Blakeney, Michael. "Communal Intellectual Property Rights of Indigenous Peoples in Cultural Expressions." *The Journal of World Intellectual Property* 1. No. 6 (November 1998): 985–1002.

Baker, Jean-Claude, and Chris Chase. *Josephine Baker: The Hungry Heart*. New York: Cooper Square Press, 2001 (1993).

Baker, Josephine, and Jo Bouillon. *Josephine*. Trans. Mariana Fitzpatrick. New York: Harper & Row, 1977 (1976).

Barkai, John. "Cultural Dimension Interests, the Dance of Negotiation, and Weather Forecasting: A Perspective on Cross-Cultural Negotiation and Dispute Resolution." *Pepperdine Dispute Resolution Law Journal* 8. No 3. (2008): 403–48.

Barrionuevo, Alexei. "Tribes of Amazon Find Ally Out of 'Avatar.'" *New York Times*, April 10, 2010: A1.

Barsh, Russell Lawrence. "Indigenous Peoples: An Emerging Object of International Law." *American Journal of International Law* 80. No. 2 (1986): 369–385.

———. "Pharmacogenomics and Indigenous Peoples: Real Issues and Actors." *Cardozo Journal of Comparative and International Law* 11. No. 2 (2003–2004): 365–392.

Barzel, Ann, Mark Turbyfill, and Ruth Page. "The Lost Ten Years: The Untold Story of the Dunham-Turbyfill Alliance." In *Kaiso!: Writings by and about Katherine Dunham*. Ed. Vévé A. Clark and Sara E. Johnson. Madison, WI: University of Wisconsin Press, 2005.

Bass, Randall, and Joy Young. "Introduction." *Beyond Borders: A Cultural Reader*. Ed. Randall Bass and Joy Young. New York: Houghton Mifflin, 2003.

Bastida-Muñoz, Mindahi Crescencio and Geraldine A. Patrick. "Traditional Knowledge and Intellectual Property Rights: Beyond TRIPS Agreements and Intellectual Property Chapters of FTAs." *Michigan State Journal of International Law* 14. No. 2/3 (2006): 259–89.

Bavikatte, Kabir and Daniel F. Robinson, "Towards a People's History of the Law: Biocultural Jurisprudence and the Nagoya Protocol on Access and Benefit Sharing." *Law, Environment and Development Journal* 7. No. 1 (2011): 37–51.

Beck, Angelica. "The Right to Food of Indigenous Peoples in Latin America: The Fight of the Sawhoyamaxa in Paraguay and the Guarani-Kaiowá in Brazil for Their Rights." *FIAN International*. Cologne, Germany: FIAN International and FIAN Germany, 2012. www.fian.org/fileadmin/media/publications/2012.04.29_-_Article_The_Right_to_Food_oF_indigenous_Peoples_in_Latin_America.pdf.

Beebe, Barton. "Intellectual Property Law and the Sumptuary Code." *Harvard Law Review* 123 (2010): 875–80.

Bell, Catherine E., and Val Napolean. Eds. *First Nations Cultural Heritage and Law: Case Studies, Voices, and Perspectives*. Vancouver, B.C., Canada: University of British Columbia Press, 2008.

Bentham, Jeremy, "Chapter VIII—Of Property." *Property: Mainstream and Critical Positions*. Ed. Crawford Brough Macpherson. Toronto: University of Toronto Press, 1978 (1789).

Berne Convention for the Protection of Literary and Artistic Works: Paris Act of July 24, 1971, as Amended on September 28, 1979. Geneva: World Intellectual Property Organization, 1992.

Beroiza. "Case No. 4617/02." *Comisión Interamericana de Derechos Humanos*. No. 30/04 (2004). Accessible at: www.cidh.oas.org/Indigenas/Chile.4617.htm.

Beyer, Steve, "The Ayahuasca Patent Case," Singing to the Plants, www.singingtotheplants.com/2008/01/ayahuasca-patent-case/.

Bhala, Raj. *International Trade Law: Interdisciplinary Theory and Practice*, 3rd ed. Danvers, MA: LexisNexis, 2008.

Blakeney, Michael. "Communal Intellectual Property Rights of Indigenous Peoples in Cultural Expressions." *The Journal of World Intellectual Property* 1. No. 6 (November 1998): 985–1002.

Bochner, Arthur P., and Carolyn Ellis, eds. *Ethnographically Speaking: Autoethnography, Literature, and Aesthetics*. Walnut Creek, CA: AltaMira Press, 2002.

Bode, Maarten. "Taking Traditional Knowledge to the Market: The Commoditization of Indian Medicine." *Anthropology- & Medicine* 13. No. 3 (2006): 225–236.

Bodeker, Gerard. "Traditional Medical Knowledge, Intellectual Property Rights and Benefit Sharing." *Cardozo Journal of International & Comparative Law* 11 (2003): 785–814.

Bostwinick, Aryeh. *Postmodernism and Democratic Theory*. Philadelphia: Temple University Press, 1993.

Bowrey, Kathy. *Law and Internet Cultures*. Cambridge: Cambridge University Press, 2005.

Boyle, James. *Shamans, Software, and Spleens: Law and the Construction of the Information Society*. Cambridge, MA: Harvard University Press, 1997.

Bravo, Karen E. "Balancing Indigenous Rights to Land and the Demands of Economic Development: Lessons from the United States and Australia" *Columbia Journal of Law and Social Problems* 30 (Summer 1997): 529–89.

"Brazil Industrial Property Law," Art. 86. In *International Trade Law: Problems, Cases and Materials*. Ed. Daniel C. K. Chow and Thomas J. Schoenbaum. New York: Aspen Publishers, 2008.

Brown, Michael. *Who Owns Native Culture?* Cambridge, MA: Harvard University Press, 2004.

Burke, Iris. "A Short Summary of Strategies for Working Across Cultural Differences." Lecture, University of Florida Levin College of Law, May 21, 2012.

———. Introduction to "Basic Cultural Worldviews: The Neuroscience of Culture." Lecture at the University of Florida Levin College of Law, Gainesville, FL, May 21, 2012.

Burrow-Giles Lithographic Co. v. Sarony (1879) 111 U.S. 53, 58 (1879).

Burt, Ramsay. "Katherine Dunham's Rite de Passage: Censorship and Sexuality." In *Embodying Liberation: The Black Body in American Dance*. Hamburg: LIT Verlag Münster, 2001.

Carcamo-Huechante, Luis. "Mapuche Political Prisoners Hearing at the Inter-American Court of Human Rights, May 29–30, 2013." *Cultural Survival*. May 15,

2013. www.culturalsurvival.org/news/mapuche-political-prisoners-hearing-inter-american-court-human-rights-may-29-30-2013.

Cariño, Joji. "Indigenous Peoples' Right to Free, Prior Informed Consent: Reflections on Concepts and Practice." *Arizona Journal of International and Comparative Law* 22. No. 19 (2005): 19–40.

Cariño, Jacqueline K. "Country Technical Notes on Indigenous Peoples' Issues, Republic of the Philippines." *International Fund for Agricultural Development (IFAD)*. November 2012. www.ifad.org/english/indigenous/pub/documents/tnotes/philippines.pdf.

Carpenter, Kristen A., Sonia Katyal, and Angela Riley. "In Defense of Property." *Yale Law Journal* 118 (2009): 1022–1125.

"The CBD Secretariat: Role." *Convention on Biological Diversity*. Accessed June 4, 2015. www.cbd.int/secretariat/role.shtml.

Chander, Anupam, and Madhavi Sunder. "Romance of the Public Domain." *California Law Review* 92 (2004): 1331–1374.

Chang, Chiung-Wen. "'Return to Innocence': In Search of Ethnic Identity in the Music of the Amis of Taiwan." *College Music Symposium: Exploring Diverse Perspectives* 49/50 (2009/2010): 327–32.

Chang, Lieh-Ching. "An Examination of Cross-Cultural Negotiation: Using Hofstede Framework." *Journal of American Academy of Business* 2. No. 22 (March 2003): 567–570.

Chavez, Leo Ralph. *The Latino Threat: Constructing Immigrants, Citizens, and the Nation*. Stanford, CA: Stanford University Press, 2008.

"Chile: Mapuche Increase Opposition to Bío Bío River Dam." *Toward Freedom*. December 1, 2008. www.towardfreedom.com/32-archives/environment/1408-chile-mapuche-increase-opposition-bbriver-dam.

"Chile Invokes Pinochet-Era Anti-Terrorism Law Against Mapuche Demonstrators." *Council on Hemispheric Affairs*. November 19, 2009. www.coha.org/chile-invokes-pinochet-era-anti-terrorism-law-against-mapuche-demonstrators/.

Chong, Hui-Yeung, "IPR draft law for Aborigines under attack." *Taipei Times*. August 23, 2000. www.taipeitimes.com/News/local/archives/2000/08/23/49186.

Clark, Vévé A. "Designing Dunham: John Pratt's Method in Costume and Décor: An Interview with John Pratt." In *Kaiso!: Writings by and about Katherine Dunham*. Ed. Vévé A. Clark and Sara E. Johnson. Madison, WI: The University of Wisconsin Press, 2005.

———. "Performing the Memory of Difference in Afro-Caribbean Dance: Katherine Dunham's Choreography, 1938–1987." In *Kaiso!: Writings by and about Katherine Dunham*. Ed. Vévé A. Clark and Sara E. Johnson. Madison, WI: The University of Wisconsin Press, 2005.

Clark, Vévé A., and Sara E. Johnson. *Kaiso!: Writings by and about Katherine Dunham*. Madison, WI: The University of Wisconsin Press, 2005.

The Coalition of Concerned NGOs on Bakun (Gabungan), Malaysia. "The Resettlement of Indigenous People affected by the Bakun Hydro-Electric Project, Sarawak, Malaysia (Final Report)." *World Commission on Dams*. December 1999. Accessed June 26, 2015. www.internationalrivers.org/files/attached-files/resettlement_of_indigenous_people_at_bakun.pdf.

Coe, Paul. "ATSIC: Self-Determination or Otherwise." *Race and Class* (April 1994): 35–39.

Colli, Giorgio and Mazzino Montinari, eds. *Nachgelassene Schriften 1870–1873*. Berlin and New York: de Gruyter, 1988.

Concerning the Protection and Integration of Indigenous and Other Tribal and Semi-Tribal Populations in Independent Countries. International Labour Organization ¶3 (2012). Accessed May 9, 2015. www.ilo.org/indigenous/Conventions/no107/lang--en/index.htm.

Convention No. 169. International Labour Organization. Accessed May 9, 2015. www.ilo.org/indigenous/Conventions/no169/lang--en/index.htm.

Convention on Biological Diversity (CBD), Art. 15 (5 June 1992): 1760 U.N.T.S. 79, 143; 31 I.L.M. 818 (1992).

Coombe, Rosemary J. "Contingent Articulations: A Critical Cultural Studies of Law." In *Law in the Domains of Culture*. Ed. Austin Sarat and Thomas R. Kearns. Ann Arbor, MI: University of Michigan Press, 2000.

———. *The Cultural Life of Intellectual Properties: Authorship, Appropriation, and the Law*. Durham, NC: Duke University Press, 1998.

———. "Embodied Trademarks: Mimesis and Alterity on American Commercial Frontiers." *Cultural Anthropology* 11 (1996): 202–224.

———. "Intellectual Property, Human Rights and Sovereignty: New Dilemmas in International Law Posed by the Recognition of Indigenous Knowledge and the Conservation of Biodiversity." *Indiana Journal of Global Legal Studies* 6 (1998). www.repository.law.indiana.edu/ijgls/vol6/iss1/3.

———. "The Properties of Culture and the Politics of Possessing Identity: Native Claims in the Cultural Appropriation Controversy." *Canadian Journal of Law and Jurisprudence* 6 (1993): 249–285.

———. "Tactics of Appropriation and the Politics of Recognition in Late Modern Democracies." *Political Theory: An International Journal of Political Philosophy* 21 (1993): 411–433.

Copyright Act 1968: Section 32, Commonwealth Consolidated Acts. Accessed June 3, 2015. www.austlii.edu.au/au/legis/cth/consol_act/ca1968133/s32.html.

Cour d'appel [CA][regional court of appeal]. Paris. April 10, 1995. RIDA 1995, 166 (Fr.).

Craig, Carys J. *Copyright, Communication and Culture Towards a Relational Theory of Copyright Law*. Northampton, MA and Cheltenham, Glos., UK: Edgar Elgar Publishing Limited, 2011.

Crate, Susan A. and Natalia Yakovleva. "Indigenous People and Mineral Resource Extraction in Russia: The Case of Diamonds." In *Earth Matters: Indigenous Peoples, the Extractive Industries and Corporate Social Responsibility*. Ed. Ciaran O'Faircheallaigh and Saleem Hassan Ali. Sheffield, UK: Greenleaf Publishing, 2008.

Crawford, Michael H. "Anthropological genetics in the 21st Century: An introduction." *Human Biology* 72. No. 1 (2000): 3–13.

Cunnean, Chris and Terry Libesman. *Indigenous People and the Law in Australia*. Sydney, Australia: Butterworths, 1995.

Cunningham, Anthony B. "Ethics, Biodiversity, and New Natural Products Development." *WWF—World Wide Fund For Nature*. Gland, Switzerland (September 1996).

Cunningham, Hilary. "Colonial Encounters in Postcolonial Contexts: Patenting Indigenous DNA and the Human Genome Diversity Project." *Critique of Anthropology* 18. No. 2 (1998): 205–33.

Dargin, Justin. "Indian Question in Latin America: An Overview of the Legal and Social Position of Indigenous Peoples." *Guild Practitioner* 63 (2006): 149–157.

Dayal, Samir. "Blackness as Symptom: Josephine Baker and European Identity." *Blackening Europe: The African American Presence*. Ed. Heike Raphael-Hernandez. New York: Routledge, 2004.

Deazley, Ronan. *On the Origin of the Right to Copy: Charting the Movement of Copyright Law in Eighteenth Century Britain (1695–1775)*. Portland, OR: Hart Publishing, 2004.

de Certeau, Michel. *The Practice of Everyday Life*. Trans. Steven Rendall. Berkeley, CA: University of California Press, 1984.

Denzin, Norman K., and Yvonna S. Lincoln. "The Discipline and Practice of Qualitative Research." In *The SAGE Handbook of Qualitative Research,* 3rd ed. Ed. Norman K. Denzin and Yvonna S. Lincoln. Thousand Oaks, CA: SAGE Publications, 2005.

Denzin, Norman K., and Yvonna S. Lincoln. *The SAGE Handbook of Qualitative Research,* 3rd ed. Thousand Oaks, CA: SAGE, 2005.

Derrida, Jacques. "Interview with Julia Kristeva." In *Positions*. Trans. Alan Bass. Chicago: University of Chicago Press, 1981.

Derrida, Jacques. *Writing and Difference*. Chicago: University of Chicago Press, 1978.

"Difang and Igay Duana." *Project Gutenberg Self-Publishing Press*. Accessed June 5, 2015. self.gutenberg.org/articles/difang_and_igay_duana#cite_note-2.

"Difang and Igay Duana." *Wikipedia*. Accessed May 31, 2013. en.wikipedia.org/wiki/Difang_and_Igay_Duana.

"Difang and Igay singing 'Weeding and Paddyfield Song No. 1.'" YouTube video. 1:00. Posted by "DebraShick." August 3, 2012. www.youtube.com/watch?v=ePKKeXNZnaY.

"Difang—Elders Drinking Song." YouTube video. 3:58. Posted by "bafagu2." September 19, 2008. www.youtube.com/watch?v=6oHGUr6HEow.

Dilanchian, Noric, and Samantha Waldon. "Copyright Requirements for Originality and Authorship." *Lightbulb blog on Business, IT and IP Law*. July 27, 2010. www.dilanchian.com.au/index.php/lightbulb-blog/23-ip-technology-e-business/618-copyright-requirements-for-originality-and-authorship.

Dodson, Mike. "Towards the Exercise of Indigenous Rights: Policy, Power and Self-Determination." *Race and Class* 35. No. 4 (April–June 1994): 65–66.

Dodson, M., and R. Williamson. "Indigenous Peoples and the Morality of the Human Genome Diversity Project." *Journal of Medical Ethics* 25 (1999): 204–8.

Douzinas, Costas, Peter Goodrich, and Yifat Hachamovitich, eds. *Politics, Postmodernity and Critical Legal Studies: The Legality of the Contingent*. London: Routledge, 1994.

Drahos, Peter. *A Philosophy of Intellectual Property*. Aldershot, UK: Ashgate, 1996.

Dunham, Katherine. "The Future of the Negro in the Dance." *Dance Herald (*March *1938): 5.* Cited in Joyce Aschenbrenner. "Katherine Dunham: Reflections on the Social and Political Contexts of Afro-American Dance." *Dance Research Annual* 12. New York: Congress on Research in Dance, 1981.

Dussias, Allison M. "Indians and Indios: Echoes of the Bhopal Disaster in the Achuar People of Peru's Struggle Against the Toxic Legacy of Occidental Petroleum." *New England Law Review* 42. No. 4 (2008): 809.

Dwyer, Lorna. "Biopiracy, Trade, and Sustainable Development." *Colorado Journal of Environmental Law and Policy* 19 (2008): 219–257.

Earthworks and Oxfam America. *Dirty Metals: Mining, Communities and the Environment* (2004). www.earthworksaction.org/files/publications/NDG_Dirty MetalsReport_HR.pdf.

"Elders Drinking Song by Difang." YouTube video. Posted by "tnfshbest." October 12, 2007. www.youtube.com/watch?v=uROdVAV1zQo.

Eliot, T. S. "The Love Song of J. Alfred Prufrock." In *Prufrock and Other Observations* (1920). *Bartleby.com*. www.bartleby.com/198/1.html/.

"Enigma (musical project)." Last updated January 9, 2013. en.wikipedia.org/wiki/Enigma_%28musical_project%29.

Esarey, Ashley. "An Ami Couple Seeks Recognition for Their Music." *Travel in Taiwan: Special*. Accessed May 12, 2015. www.sinica.edu.tw/tit/special/0996_Innocence.html.

Factsheet. "Indigenous Peoples, Indigenous Voices." In *United Nations Permanent Forum on Indigenous Issues*. Accessed June 5, 2012. www.un.org/esa/socdev/unpfii/documents/5session_factsheet1.pdf.

Farley, Christine H. "Protecting Folklore of Indigenous Peoples: Is Intellectual Property the Answer?" *Connecticut Law Review* 30 (1997): 1.

Fecteau, Leanne M. "The Ayahuasca Patent Revocation: Raising Questions about Current U.S. Patent Policy." *Boston College Third World Law Journal* 21 (2001): 69–104.

Feist Publications, Inc. v. Rural Telephone Service Co. (1991) 499 U.S. 340, 346.

Finger, J. Michael, and Philip Schuler. "Introduction and Overview." In *Poor People's Knowledge: Promoting Intellectual Property in Developing Countries*. Ed. J. Michael Finger and Philip Schuler. Washington, DC: World Bank Publications and Oxford University Press, 2004.

Fischer-Hornung, Dorothea. "'Jungle in the Spotlight?': Primitivism and Esteem: Katherine Dunham's 1954 German Tour." In *Blackening Europe: The African American Presence*. Ed. Heike Raphael-Hernandez. London and New York: Routledge, 2004.

Fitzpatrick, Peter. *Modernism and the Grounds of Law*. Cambridge: Cambridge University Press, 2001.

Fitzpatrick, Peter. *The Mythology of Modern Law*. London: Routledge, 1992.

Flitch, J. E. Crawford. *Modern Dancing and Dancers*. Binsted, UK: The Noverre Press, 1912.

Foster, George K. "Foreign Investment and Indigenous Peoples: Options for Promoting Equilibrium between Economic Development and Indigenous Rights." *Michigan Journal of International Law* 33 (2012): 627–691.

Foucault, Michel. *Discipline and Punish: The Birth of the Prison*, 2nd ed. New York: Vintage 1995.

Foulkes, Julia L. *Modern Bodies: Dance and American Modernism from Martha Graham to Alvin Ailey*. Chapel Hill, NC: University of North Caroline Press, 2002.

Fowler, Betsy J. "Preventing Counterfeit Craft Designs," in *Poor People's Knowledge: Promoting Intellectual Property in Developing Countries* Ed. J. Michael Finger and Philip Schuler. Washington, DC: World Bank Publications and Oxford University Press, 2004.

Franchise Council of Australia (FCA) (3 September 1998) 1082. Reported at Mvw.austlii.edu.au/au/cases/cth/federd-ct/1998q082.html. Cited in Michael Blakeney. "Communal Intellectual Property Rights of Indigenous Peoples in Cultural Expressions." *The Journal of World Intellectual Property* 1. No. 6 (November 1998): 985–1002.

Francis, Terri. "The Audacious Josephine Baker: Stardom, Cinema, Paris." In *Black Europe and the African Diaspora*. Ed. Darlene Clark Hine, Trica Danielle Keaton, and Stephen Small. Champaign, IL: University of Illinois Press, 2009.

Françon, André and Jane C. Ginsburg. "Authors' Rights in France: The Moral Right of the Creator of a Commissioned Work to Compel the Commissioning Party to Complete the Work." *Columbia VLA Journal of Law & the Arts* 9 (1985): 381–385.

Fuller, Loïe. *Fifteen Years of a Dancer's Life*. Boston: Small, Maynard, 1913.

Fuller v. Bemis (C.C.S.D.N.Y. 1892) 50 F. 926.

Garfinkle, A. M., J. Fries, D. Lopez, and L Possessky. "Art Conservation and the Legal Obligation to Preserve Artistic Intent." *Journal of the American Institute for Conservation* 36. No. 2 (1997): 165–179.

"General Agreement on Tariffs and Trade 1947." In *International Trade Law: Documents Supplement*, 2010–2011 ed. Ed. Daniel C. K. Chow and Thomas J. Schoenbaum. New York: Aspen Publishers, 2010.

Goicoechea, A. S., Carnese, F. R., Dejean, C., Avena, S. A., Weimer, T. A. et al. "Genetic Relationships Between Amerindian Populations of Argentina." *American Journal of Physical Anthropology* 115 (2001): 133–43.

Goldstein v. California (1973) 412 U.S. 546, 561.

Gottlieb, Robert. *George Balanchine: The Ballet Maker*. New York: HarperCollins, 2004.

Greely, H. T. "Legal, Ethical, and Social Issues in Human Genome Research." *Annual Review of Anthropology* 27 (1998): 473–502.

Greenhouse, Carol. "Constructive Approaches to Law, Culture and Identity." *Law and Society Review* 28 (1994): 1213–1241.

Guy, Nancy. "Regaining their Voices: Music, Cultural Ownership, and the Amis Copyright Struggle," *Copyright and Conceptions of Intellectual Property in Cross-Cultural Perspective*. Austin, TX: Popular Music Section of the Society for Ethnomusicology, 1999.

Hanks, P., and B. Keon-Cohen, eds. *Aborigines and the Law*. Sydney, Australia: George Allen and Unwin, 1984.

Hernandez-Truyol, Berta Esperanza. "Culture Clashes: Indigenous Populations and Globalization-The Case of Belo Monte." *Seattle Journal for Social Justice* 12. No. 3. Article 3 (2014). digitalcommons.law.seattleu.edu/sjsj/vol12/iss3/3/.

Hernandez-Truyol, Berta, and Stephen J. Powell. *Just Trade: A New Covenant Linking Trade and Human Rights*. New York: New York University Press, 2009.

Hilgard, Adaline. "Can Choreography and the Copyright Waltz Together in the Wake of Horgan v. Macmillan Inc.?" *U.C. Davis Law Review* 27 (1994): 757–787.

Hill, Constance Valis. "Stepping, Stealing, Sharing and Daring." In *Taken By Surprise: A Dance Improvisation Reader*. Ed. Ann Cooper Albright and David Gere. Middletown, CT: Wesleyan University Press, 2003.

Hirsch, Susan, and Mindie Lazarus-Black, eds. *Contested States: Law, Hegemony and Resistance*. New York: Routledge, 1994.

"History of the Clinics" *Levin College of Law, University of Florida*. Accessed May 12, 2015. www.law.ufl.edu/academics/clinics/about-the theclinics/history-of-the-clinics.

Hofstede, Geert, Gert Jan Hofstede, and Michael Minkov. *Cultures and Organizations: Software of the Mind*, 3d ed. New York: McGraw-Hill, 2010.

Horgan v. MacMillan, Inc. (2d Cir. 1986) 789 F.2d 157.

Horgan v. MacMillan, Inc. (S.D.N.Y. 1985) 621 F. Supp. 1169.

Hospital Products Ltd v. United States Surgical Corporation (1984) 156 CLR 41 (25 October 1984). Cited in Blakeney, Michael. "Communal Intellectual Property Rights of Indigenous Peoples in Cultural Expressions." *The Journal of World Intellectual Property* 1. no. 6 (November 1998): 985.

Huang, Shiu-Lan. "Aborigines Sue for Justice and Recognition: Justice for the Kuos." *Law News Network*. Accessed June 6, 2015. www.taiwanfirstnations.org/Difang.htm.

ILO Convention No. 169 Concerning Indigenous and Tribal Peoples in Independent Countries, Art. 1.1, June 27, 1989. Accessed May 12, 2015. www.zaoerv.de/59_1999/59_1999_2_s_543_592.pdf.

"Indigenous Peoples/Ethnic Minorities and Poverty Reduction, Philippines." *Asian Development Bank*. June 2002. adb.org/sites/default/files/pub/2002/indigenous_phi.pdf.

Indigenous People OP 4.10, Art. 4. *The World Bank*. July 2005. web.worldbank.org/WBSITE/EXTERNAL/PROJECTS/EXTPOLICIES/EXTOPMANUAL/0,,contentMDK:20553653~menuPK:4564185~pagePK:64709096~piPK:64709108~theSitePK:502184,00.html.

Indigenous Research Protection Act. *Indigenous Peoples Council on Biocolonialism*. Accessed April 20, 2015. www.ipcb.org/publications/policy/files/irpa.html.

Ingebretsen, Edward J. *At Stake: Monsters and the Rhetoric of Fear in Public Culture*. Chicago: University of Chicago Press, 2001.

International Covenant on Civil and Political Rights, Dec. 16, 1966, U.N.T.S. 3; S. Exec. Doc. D, 95-2 (1978); S. Treaty Doc. No. 95-19, 6 I.L.M. 360 (1967) (ICCPR).

International Covenant on Economic, Social and Cultural Rights, Dec. 16, 1966, 993 U.N.T.S. 3, S. Exec. Doc. D, 95-2 (1978); S. Treaty Doc. No. 95-19, 6 I.L.M. 360 (1967) (ICESR).

International Institute for Sustainable Development and ICTSD. "Intellectual Property Rights." *Doha Round Briefing Series* (February 2003): 4.

International Labour Organization, Indigenous and Tribal Peoples Convention, ILO Convention No. 169, Art. 1 (27 June 1989). www.ilo.org/dyn/normlex/en/f?p=NORMLEXPUB:12100:0::NO::P12100_ILO_CODE:C169.

Introduction to *Traditional Knowledge, Innovations and Practices. Convention on Biological Diversity*. Accessed June 4, 2015. www.cbd.int/traditional/intro.shtml.

"Iris A. Burke." *Levin College of Law, University of Florida*. Accessed May 12, 2015. www.law.ufl.edu/faculty/iris-a-burke.

Jackson, Harriet. "American Dancer, Negro." *Dance Magazine* (September 1966): 35–42.

Janke, Terri. "Managing Indigenous Knowledge and Indigenous Cultural and Intellectual Property." In *Australian Indigenous Knowledge and Libraries*. Ed. Martin Nakata and Marcia Langton. Sydney, Australia: UTSePress, 2006. opus.lib.uts.edu.au/research/bitstream/handle/2100/57/Libraries%20and%20Indige;jsessionid=F55E41A2518BFC5D539F8D715CD562A3?sequence=1.

———. *Our Culture: Our Future: The Report on Australian Indigenous Cultural and Intellectual Property Rights*. Sydney, Australia: Michael Frankel & Co., 1998.

———. "UNESCO-WIPO World Forum on the Protection of Folklore: Lessons for Protecting Indigenous Australian Cultural and Intellectual Property." *Copyright Reporter* 15 (1997): 104–107.

"John Bakai." *William S. Richardson School of Law, University Of Hawai'i at Manoa*. Accessed May 12, 2015. www.law.hawaii.edu/personnel/barkai/john.

Johnson, E., M. Hinton, and D. Rigney, eds. *Indigenous Australians and the Law*. Sydney, Australia: Cavendish Publishing, 1997.

"Josephine Baker." *The Biography.com*. Accessed July 3, 2015. www.biography.com/people/josephine-baker-9195959.

Jowitt, Deborah. "Monumental Martha." In *What is Dance?* Ed. Roger Copeland and Marshall Cohen. New York: Oxford University Press, 1983.

Jules-Rosette, Bennetta. *Josephine Baker in Art and Life: The Icon and the Image*. Champaign, IL: University of Illinois Press, 2007.

Kaiser, Jocelyn. "NIH to Limit Scope of Foreign Patents." *Science* 296. No. 5577 (June 28, 2002): 2316.

Kate, Kerry ten and Laird, Sarah A., eds. *The Commercial Use of Biodiversity: Access to Genetic Resources and Benefit Sharing* (London: Earthscan Publications Ltd. 1999).

Kausikan, Bilahari. "Asia's Different Standard." *Foreign Policy* 92 (1993): 24–41.

Kingsbury, Benedict. "Indigenous Peoples' in International Law: A Constructivist Approach to the Asian Controversy." *American Journal of International Law* 92. No. 3 (1998): 414–457.

Klein, Eckart. "Establishing a Hierarchy of Human Rights: Ideal Solution or Fallacy?" *Israel Law Review* 41 (2008): 477. ssrn.com/abstract=1333295.

Koester, Veit. "The Nagoya Protocol on ABS: ratification by the EU and its Member States and implementation challenges." *Studies No. 3/2012*. Paris, France: Institut du développement durable et des relations internationals, 2012.

Knight, Danielle. "An Enemy of Indigenous Peoples the Case of Loren Miller, COICA, the Inter-American Foundation and the Ayahuasca Plant." *Multinational Monitor* 19. No. 6 (1998): 1–37.

Koestler, Arthur. *Janus: A Summing Up*. London: Hutchinson, 1978.

Kraut, Anthea. "'Stealing Steps' and Signature Moves: Embodied Theories of Dance as Intellectual Property." *Theatre Journal* 62. No. 2 (May 2010): 173–89.

Kuhn, Thomas. Preface to *The Essential Tension*. Ed. Thomas Kuhn. Chicago: University of Chicago Press, 1977.

———. *The Structure of Scientific Revolutions*. Chicago: University of Chicago Press, 1970.

Kuruk, Paul. "Protecting Folklore Under Modern Intellectual Property Regimes: A Reappraisal of the Tensions Between Individual and Communal Rights in Africa and the United States." *The American University Law Review* 48 (1999): 769–843.

Laclau, Ernesto. "Power and Representation." In *Politics, Theory, and Contemporary Culture*. Ed. Mark Poster. New York: Columbia University Press, 1993.

Laird, Sarah A. *Biodiversity and Traditional Knowledge: Equitable Partnerships in Practice*. London: Earthscan Publications, 2002.

Laird, Sarah, A. B. Cunningham, and Estherine Lisginge. "Forests, Drugs, and Benefit Sharing: Putting the Formula to the Test—The Cameroon Case of Ansicstrocladus korupensis." In *People, Plants, and Justice*. Ed. Charles Zerner. New York: Columbia University Press, 2000.

Langman, James. "Company Vows More Chilean Dams on the Way." *Ecoamericas* (2013): 5. www.futaleufuriverkeeper.org/wp-content/uploads/2013/06/EcoAmericas-Futaleufu-DamsMay-2013.pdf.

———. "Indigenous Fight to Keep Land in Chile." *Washington Times*. February 11, 2003.

Langton, Marcia, and Zane Ma Rhea. "Traditional Indigenous Biodiversity-related Knowledge." *Australian Indigenous Knowledge and Libraries* 36. No. 2 (2005): 45–69.

LeJeune, Elisabetta. "Mu-Lan, the Chinese Woman Warrior." *Southeastern Louisiana University*. April 13, 2012. www2.selu.edu/Academics/Faculty/elejeune/mulan.htm.

Lettington, R., and K. Nnadozie, "A Review of the Intergovernmental Committee on Genetic Resources, Traditional Knowledge and Folklore at WIPO." *Occasional Papers* 12. South Centre, 2003. www.ciel.org/Publications/Occassional_SouthCentre_Dec03.pdf.

Liang, Bryan A. "Global Governance: Promoting biodiversity and protecting indigenous communities against biopiracy." *Journal Commercial Biotechnology* 17 (2011): 248.

Liu, Deming. "Can Copyright Lend Its Cinderellaic Magic to Chinese Folklore?" *The John Marshall Review of Intellectual Property Law* 5 (2006): 203–215.

Livermore, David. *Leading with Cultural Intelligence: The Real Secret to Success*, 2nd ed. New York: AMACOM Division of the American Management Association, 2015.

Locke, John. *Two Treatises of Government*. New York: Everyman Paperbacks, 1990.

Lone Dog, L. "Whose Genes are They? The Human Genome Diversity Project." *Journal of Health and Social Policy* 10. No. 4 (1999): 51–66.

"Lost in Music." *Far Eastern Economic Review* 158. No. 4 (1999): newint.org/features/1996/02/05/update/.

Lucas-Schloetter, Agnés. "Folklore." In *Indigenous Heritage and Intellectual Property: Genetic Resources, Knowledge and Folklore*. Ed. Silke von Lewinski. The Netherlands: Kluwer Law International BV, 2008.

Maffi, Luisa. "Introduction: Why a Sourcebook on Biocultural Diversity?" In *Biocultural Diversity Conservation: A Global Sourcebook*. Ed. Luisa Maffi and Ellen Woodley. London: Earthscan Publications, 2010.

"The Mapuche People of South America." *Human Rights Resource Center*. Accessed May 14, 2015. www.hrusa.org/indig/reports/mapuche.pdf.

Mar del Plata Action Plan (1977). Marsden, Susan. "Northwest Coast Adawx Study." In *First Nations Cultural Heritage and Law: Case Studies, Voices, and Perspectives*. Ed. Catherine Bell and Val Napoleon. Vancouver, British Columbia: The University of British Columbia Press, 2008.

Martin, Wendy. "'Remembering the Jungle': Josephine Taylor and the Modernist Parody." In *Prehistories of the Future: The Primitivist Project and the Culture of Modernism*. Ed. Elazar Barkan and Ronald Bush. Stanford, CA: Stanford University Press, 1996.

Matsushita, Mitsuo, Thomas J. Schoenbaum, and Petros C. Mavroidis, *The World Trade Organization: Law, Practice, and Policy*. Oxford, UK: Oxford University Press, 2003.

May, Christopher. "Why IPRs are a Global Political Issue." *European Intellectual Property Review* 25. No. 1 (2003): 1–6.

Mayer, Benoît. "Judicial Review of Human Rights Impacts of Hydroelectric Projects." *Legal Working Paper Series on Legal Empowerment for Sustainable Development*. Montreal, Quebec: Centre for International Sustainable Development Law, Faculty of Law, McGill University, 2012. cisdl.org/public/docs/Mayer_Judicial_Review.pdf.

Mei-Jung, Yvonne Lin. "Intellectual Property Rights of the Aboriginal Peoples of Taiwan." *Taiwan First Nations*. Accessed May 14, 2015. www.taiwanfirstnations.org/TFNIPR.html.

Menon, Narayana. "A Definition of Folklore." *INTERGU Yearbook* 4 (1979): 209.

Mertz, Elizabeth. "A New Social Construction for Sociolegal Studies." *Law and Society Review* 28 (1994): 1243–1265.

Mezey, Naomi. "The Paradox of Cultural Property." *Columbia Law Review* 107. No. 8 (2007): 2004–2046.

Moraga, M. L., Rocco, P., Miguel, J. F., Nervi, F., Llop, E. et al. "Mitochondrial DNA Polymorphisms in Chilean Aboriginal Populations: Implications for the Peopling of the Southern Cone of the Continent." *American Journal of Physical Anthropology* 113 (2000): 19–29.

Munzer, Stephen, and Kal Raustiala. "The Uneasy Case for Intellectual Property Rights in Traditional Knowledge." *Cardozo Arts & Entertainment Law Journal* 27 (2009): 37–97.

"Nagoya Gives New Context to Old Views in Intellectual Property Council." *World Trade Organisation* (March 1, 2011): ¶3, 5, 7–9, 12–14, 17. Accessed May 9, 2015. www.wto.org/english/news_e/news11_e/trip_01mar11_e.htm.

Native Title Act 1993 (Cth). *Commonwealth Consolidated Acts*. Accessed May 17, 2015. www.austlii.edu.au/au/legis/cth/consol_act/nta1993147/.

"Negotiations on CBD-TRIPS Relationship Still Deadlocked After Adoption of ABS Protocol." *International Institute for Sustainable Development (IISD) Reporting Services*. March 1, 2010). biodiversity-l.iisd.org/news/negotiations-on-cbd-trips-relationship-still-deadlocked-after-adoption-of-absprotocol/.

Newman, Dwight G. *The Duty to Consult: New Relationships with Aboriginal Peoples*. Saskatoon, Canada: Purich Publishing, 2009.

Newton, Lina. *Illegal, Alien, or Immigrant: The Politics of Immigration Reform*. New York: New York University Press, 2008.

Nietzsche, Friedrich. *Beyond Good and Evil: Prelude to a Philosophy of the Future.* Trans. Walter Kaufmann. New York: Vintage Books, 1989.

———. "The Birth of Tragedy." In *The Birth of Tragedy and the Case of Wagner*, trans. Walter Kaufmann. Toronto: Random House, 1967.

———. "Sämtliche Werke: Die Geburt der Tragödie, Unzeitgemäβe Betrachtungen 1–4." *Nachgelassene Schriften 1870–1873*. Ed. Giorgio Colli and Mazzino Montinari. Munich: Deutscher Taschenbuch Verlag, 1988.

Nikiforuk, Andrew. *Tar Sands: Dirty Oil and the Future of a Continent*. Vancouver: Greystone Books, 2010.

Nott, Emily. "Appropriation, Re-appropriation, and the Musical Fourth World: The Politics of 'Borrowing.'" *Emily Nott Presses Words*. April 2011. nottemil.wordpress.com/2011/04/18/appropriation-re-appropriation-and-the-musical-fourth-world-the-politics-of-%E2%80%9Cborrowing-%E2%80%9D/.

Novinger, Tracy. *Intercultural Communication: A Practical Guide*. Austin: University of Texas Press, 2001.

Orellana, Marcos O. "Indigenous Peoples, Energy and Environmental Justice: The *Pangue/Ralco* Hydroelectric Project in Chile's *Alto BíoBío*." *Center for International Environmental Law*. July 21, 2004. www.ciel.org/Publications/Ralco_Brief_22Jul04.pdf.

Oshionebo, Evaristus. "World Bank and Sustainable Development of Natural Resources in Developing Countries." *Journal of Energy & Natural Resources Law* 27. No. 2 (2009): 193–270.

Osumare, Halifu. "Dancing the Black Atlantic: Katherine Dunham's Research-to-Performance Method." *AmeriQuests* 7. No. 2 (2010). DOI: 10.15695/amqst.v7i2.165.

Pager, Sean A. "Folklore 2.0: Preservation Through Innovation." *Utah Law Review* (2012): 1835–1895.

Paris Convention for the Protection of Industrial Property, as last revised at the Stockholm Revision Conference, July 14, 1967. 21 U.S.T. 1583, 828 U.N.T.S. 303. Geneva: World Intellectual Property Organization, 2004.

Patel, Surendra J. "Can the Intellectual Property Rights System Serve the Interests of Indigenous Knowledge." *Valuing Local Knowledge Indigenous People and Intellectual Property Rights*. Ed. Stephen B. Brush and Noreen Stabinsky. Washington, DC: Island Press, 1996.

Paternostre, Rodolphe. "The Nagoya Protocol: A Legally Sound Framework for an Effective Regime?" Master's thesis, Utrecht University, 2011.

Patton, Phil. "Trademark Battle Over Pueblo Sign." *New York Times*, January 2000.

Perrin, Colin. "Approaching Anxiety: The Insistence of the Postcolonial in the Declaration of the Rights of Indigenous People." In *Laws of the Postcolonial*. Ed. Eve Darian-Smith, and Peter Fitzpatrick. Ann Arbor, MI: University of Michigan Press, 1999.

Picart, Caroline Joan "Kay" S. *Critical Race Theory and Copyright in American Dance: Whiteness as Status Property*. New York: Palgrave Macmillan, 2013.

———. "Cross Cultural Negotiations and International Intellectual Property Law: Attempts to Work Across Cultural Clashes Between Indigenous Peoples and Majoritarian Cultures." *Southern California Interdisciplinary Law Journal* 23. No. 1 (January 2014): 37–65.

———. *Resentment and the 'Feminine in Nietzsche's Politico-Aesthetics*. University Park: Pennsylvania State University Press, 1999.

———. "Rethinking Resistance: Reflections on the Cultural Lives of Property, Collective Identity, and Intellectual Property." *John Marshall Law Review* 47 (November 2014): 1349–69.

Picart, Caroline Joan "Kay" S., and Marlowe Fox. "Beyond Unbridled Optimism and Fear: Indigenous Peoples, Intellectual Property, Human Rights and the Globalization of Traditional Knowledge and Expressions of Folklore (Part I)." *International Community Law Review* 15. No. 3 (2013): 319–39.

———. "Beyond Unbridled Optimism and Fear: Indigenous Peoples, Intellectual Property, Human Rights and the Globalization of Traditional Knowledge and Expressions of Folklore (Part II)." *International Community Law Review* 16. No. 2 (March 2014): 3–37.

Pilot, Jacob. "Developing Indigenous Knowledge Centres," *Australian Indigenous Knowledge and Libraries*, ed. Martin Nakata and Marcia Langton (Sydney, Australia: UTsE Press, 2005), p. 40 available at: steve3067095.pbworks.com/f/Developing+indigenous+knowledge+Centres.pdf (downloaded May 21, 2015).

"Policy Brief: Indigenous Peoples." *The World Bank*. Accessed May 8, 2015. siteresources.worldbank.org/EXTINDPEOPLE/Resources/407801-1271860301656/HDNEN_ indigenous_clean_0421.pdf.

Posey, Darrell Addison. "Selling Grandma: Commodification of the Sacred through Intellectual Property Rights." *Claiming the Stones; Naming the Bones: Cultural Property and the Negotiation of National and Ethnic Identity*. Ed. Elazar Barkan and Ronald Bush. Oxford, UK: Oxford University Press, 2002.

Posey, Darryl A., and Graham Dutfield. *Beyond Intellectual Property: Toward Traditional Resource Rights for Indigenous Peoples and Local Communities*. Ottawa: International Development Research Centre, 1996.

"Positions unchanged on biodiversity issues, 'Para 6' system." *TWN: Third World Network*. March 10, 2011. www.twn.my/title2/health.info/2011/health20110303.htm.

Povinelli, Elizabeth. "Consuming Geist: Popontology and the Spirit of Capital in Indigenous Australia." In *Millennial Capitalism and the Culture of Neoliberalism*. Ed. Jean Comaroff and John Comaroff. Durham, NC: Duke University Press, 2001.

———. *The Cunning of Recognition: Indigenous Alterities and the Making of Australian Multiculturalism*. Durham, NC: Duke University Press, 2002.

———. "The State of Shame: Australian Multiculturalism and the Crisis of Indigenous Citizenship." *Critical Inquiry* 24 (1998): 575–610.

Putnam, Robert D. *Bowling Alone: The Collapse and Revival of American Community*. New York: Simon & Schuster, 2000.

Raustiala, Kal, and David G. Victor, "The Regime Complex for Plant Genetic Resources." *International Organisation* 58 (2004): 277–309.

Reichmann, J. H. "Of Green Tulips and Legal Kudzu: Repacking Rights in Subpatentable Innovation." *Vanderbilt Law Review* 53 (2000): 1743–1798.

Reynolds, Nancy, and Malcolm McCormick. *No Fixed Points: Dance in the Twentieth Century*. New Haven, CT: Yale University Press, 2003.

Riley, Angela R. "'Straight Stealing': Towards an Indigenous System of Cultural Property Protection." *Washington Law Review* 80 (2005): 69–164.

Robinson, Danielle. "'Oh, You Black Bottom!' Appropriation, Authenticity and Opportunity in the Jazz Dance Teaching of 1920s New York." *Dance Research Journal* 38. No. 1.2 (2006): 19–42.

Roper, Richard F. "Taiwanese Settle Lawsuit Claiming Their Original Composition Was Stolen; They Will Now Set Up Foundation." *Business Wire*, June 23, 1999. www.geocities.ws/enigmalair/rtiarticle4.html.

Rose, Mark. *Authors and Owners: The Invention of Copyright*. Cambridge, MA: Harvard University Press, 1993.

Rose, Phyllis. Jazz Cleopatra: Josephine Baker in Her Time. New York: Doubleday, 1989.

Ross, Marlon B. "The New Negro Displayed: Self-Ownership, Proprietary Sites/Sights, and the Bonds/Bounds of Race." In *Claiming the Stones, Naming the Bones: Cultural Property and the Negotiation of National and Ethnic Identity*. Ed. Elazar Barkan and Ronald Bush. Los Angeles, CA: Getty Publications, 2002.

Santa Clara Pueblo v. Martinez (1978) 436 US 49.

Schwandt, Thomas A. "Three Epistemological Stances for Qualitative Inquiry: Interpretivism, Hermeneutics, and Social Construction." In *Handbook of Qualitative Research*, 2nd ed. Ed. Norman K. Denzin and Yvonna S. Lincoln. Thousand Oaks, CA: Sage Publications, 2000.

Seelau, Ryan. "Mapuche Testify Against Chile Before Inter-American Court of Human Rights (OAS)." *Indigenousnews.org*. May 31, 2013. indigenousnews.org/2013/05/31/mapuche-testify-against-chile-before-inter-american-court-of-human-rights-oas/.

"Selections from the Katherine Dunham Collection at the Library of Congress: Katherine Dunham Timeline." *The Library of Congress*. Accessed June 3, 2015. lcweb2.loc.gov/diglib/ihas/html/dunham/dunham-timeline.html.

Serra, Senator José. "Minister of Health of Brazil, Lessons from the Brazilian aids Program." Keynote address, AIDS 20 Years Later: An International Health Conference, 2001.

Sharpley-Whiting, T. Denean. *Black Venus: Sexualized Savages, Primal Fears, and Primitive Narratives in French*. Durham, NC: Duke University Press 1999.

Sherman, Brad, and Lionel Bently. *The Making of Modern Intellectual Property Law: The British Experience, 1760–1911*. Cambridge: Cambridge University Press, 1999.

Shiva, Vandana. *Biopiracy: The Plunder of Nature and Knowledge*. New York: South End Press 1997.

Singer, Barbara. "In Search of Adequate Protection for Choreographic Works: Legislative and Judicial Alternatives vs. The Custom of the Dance Community." *University of Miami Law Review* 38 (1984): 287–319.

Singer, Joseph William. *Property Law: Rules, Policies and Practices*, 2nd ed. New York: Aspen Law and Business, 1997.

Sizer, Nigel, and Dominiek Plouvier. *Increased Investment and Trade by Transnational Logging Companies in Africa, the Caribbean and the Pacific: Implications for the Sustainable Management and Conservation of Tropical Forests*. Brussels, Belgium: European Commission, 2000.

Spain, Tian, and Mike Gatehouse. "Chile Accused of Racist Use of Anti-Terrorism Laws Against Mapuches." *Latin America Bureau (LAB) Council on Hemispheric*

Affairs. December 9, 2011. lab.org.uk/chile-accused-of-racist-use-of-anti-terror ism-laws-against-mapuches.

Starr, June, and Mark Goodale, eds. *Practicing Ethnography in Law: New Dialogues, Enduring Methods*. New York: Palgrave Macmillan, 2002.

Stavenhagen, Rodolfo. "Cultural Rights: A Social Science Perspective." In *Economic, Social and Cultural Rights: A Textbook*, 2nd ed. Ed. Ashbjørn Eide, Catrina Krause, and Allan Rosas. Dordrecht: Martinus Nijhoff Publishers, 2001.

———. "Making the Declaration on the Rights of Indigenous Peoples Work: The Challenge Ahead." In *Reflections on the UN Declaration on the Rights of Indigenous Peoples*. Eds. Stephen Allen and Alexandra Xanthaki. Oxford, UK: Hart Publishing Ltd., 2011.

Streeter, Thomas. "Broadcast Copyright and the Bureaucratization of Property." In *The Construction of Authorship: Textual Appropriation in Law and Literature*. Ed. Martha Woodmansee and Peter Jaszi. Durham, NC: Duke University Press, 1994.

Supreme Court of India, Narmada Bachao Andolan v. Union of India (2000) writ petition (civil) No. 319 of 1994, AIR (2000) SC 3751.

Tan, Alan Khee-Jin. "All That Glitters: Foreign Investment in Mining Trumps the Environment in the Philippines." *Pace Environmental Law Review* 23 (2005): 183–208.

Taper, Bernard. *Balanchine: A Biography, with a New Epilogue*. Berkeley, CA: University of California Press, 1996.

Taubman, Antony. "Genetic Resources." In *Indigenous Heritage and Intellectual Property: Genetic Resources, Knowledge and Folklore*. Ed. Silke von Lewinski. The Netherlands: Kluwer Law International BV, 2008.

Taubman, Antony, and Matthias Leistner. "Analysis of Different Areas of Indigenous Resources: Section 1: Traditional Knowledge." In *Indigenous Heritage and Intellectual Property: Genetic Resources, Knowledge and Folklore*. Ed. Silke von Lewinski. The Netherlands: Kluwer Law International BV, 2008.

Tay, Simon. "Human Rights, Culture, and the Singapore Example." *McGill Law Journal* 41 (1995): 743–780.

Taylor, Sandi. "State Library of Queensland Library Services: Overcoming Barriers and Building Bridges." *Australian Academic & Research Libraries* 34. No. 4 (December 2003): 280–81.

Taylor, Timothy D. "A Riddle Wrapped in a Mystery: Transitional Music Sampling and Enigma's 'Return to Innocence.'" In *Music and Technoculture*. Ed. René T. A. Lysloff and Leslie C. Gay, Jr. Middletown, CT: Wesleyan University Press, 2003.

Toensing, Gale Courey. "Inter-American Court Hears Mapuche Human Rights Case Against Chile." *Indian Country Today*. June 3, 2013. indiancountrytodaymedianetwork.com/2013/06/03/inter-american-courthears-mapuche-human-rights-case-against-chile-149677.

Tolkien, J. R. R. *Tree and Leaf; Smith of Wotton Major; The Homecoming of Beorhtnoth ' Beorthelm's Son*. London: Unwin Paperbacks, 1975.

The Trademark Cases, 100 U.S. 82 (1879).

Trade Related Aspects of Intellectual Property Rights, art. 27(1), Annex 1C, 1995. In *International Trade Law: Documents Supplement*. Ed. Daniel C.K. Chow and Thomas J. Schoenbaum. Charlottesville, MI: Wolters Kluwer Law & Business, 2008.

Traylor, Martha M. "Choreography, Pantomime and the Copyright Revision Act of 1976." *New England Law Review* 16 (1980–1981): 227–255.

Treaty on Intellectual Property in Respect of Integrated Circuits: Adopted at Washington on May 26, 1989. 28 I.L.M. 1477. World Intellectual Property Organization, 1989.

Trebilcock, Michael J., and Robert Howse. *The Regulation of International Trade*, 3rd ed. New York: Psychology Press, 2010.

Trompenaars, Fons, and Hampden-Turner, Charles. *Riding the Waves of Culture: Understanding Cultural Diversity in Business*, 2nd ed. New York: McGraw-Hill, 1998.

Tsosie, Rebecca, "Reclaiming Native Stories: An Essay on Cultural Appropriation and Cultural Rights." *Arizona State Law Journal* 34 (2002): 299–359.

UNCTAD-ICTSD Project on IPRs and Sustainable Development. *Intellectual Property Rights: Implications for Development*. Geneva, Switzerland: ICTSD and UNCTAD, 2003.

United Nations Committee on the Elimination of Racial Discrimination (UN CERD). "Reports Submitted by States Parties Under Article 9 of the Convention." International Convention on the Elimination of all Forms of Racial Discrimination (July 8, 2008).

"United Nations Convention on Biological Diversity, 1992." *Convention on Biological Diversity*. www.cbd.int/convention/text/.

"United Nations Declaration of Indigenous People," GA Res 61/925, UN Doc A/RES/61/295 (13 September 2007), Art. 33. *International Legal Materials* 46 (2007): 1013.

"United Nations Declaration on the Rights of Indigenous Peoples," G.A. Res. 61/925, U.N. Doc. A/RES/61/925 (September 13, 2007), Art. 4, 46 I.L.M. 1013 (2007) (UNDRIP).

United Nations Department of Economic and Social Affairs, Division for Social Policy and Development, Secretariat of the Permanent Forum on Indigenous Issues, Workshop on Data Collection and Disaggregation for Indigenous Peoples. "The Concept of Indigenous Peoples: Background Paper Prepared by the Secretariat of the permanent Forum on Indigenous Issues." PFII/2004/WS.1/3. New York: United Nations Publication, 2004.

United Nations Department of Economic and Social Affairs, Division for Social Policy and Development, Secretariat of the Permanent Forum on Indigenous Issues. "State of the World's Indigenous Peoples." ST/ESA/328. New York: United Nations Publication, 2009.

United Nations Department of Economic and Social Affairs (UN-DESA), "State of the World's Indigenous Peoples," 2nd volume, no date. www.un.org/esa/socdev/unpfii/documents/sowip2volume-ac.pdf, p. 3.

"Universal Declaration of Human Rights," GA Res. 217A (III), U.N. Doc. A/RES/217(III) (10 December 1948).

"Universal Declaration of Human Rights," GA Res. 217(III), UN GAOR, 3d Sess., Supp. No. 13, UN Doc. A/810 (1948) 71 ["*Universal Declaration*"], Art. 17(1).

U.S. Constitution, Article 1, Section 8, Clause 8.

USPTO. The Enablement Requirement, sec. 2164, 35 U.S.C. 112. In *Manual Patent Examining Procedure (MPEP)*, 8th ed. August 2011. www.uspto.gov/web/offices/pac/mpep/documents/2100_2164.htm.

Valis Hall, Constance. "Collaborating with Balanchine on *Cabin in the Sky*: Interviews with Katherine Dunham." *Kaiso!: Writings by and about Katherine Dunham*. Ed. Vévé A. Clark and Sara E. Johnson. Madison, WI: The University of Wisconsin Press, 2005.

van Camp, Julie. "Copyright of Choreographic Works." *Entertainment, Publishing and Arts Handbook 1994–1995*. Ed. Stephen F. Breimer, Robert Thoerne and John David Viera. New York: Clark Boardman Company, Ltd., 1994.

van der Geest, Sjaak, Susan Reynolds Whyte, and Anita Hardon. "The Anthropology of Pharmaceuticals: A Biographical Approach." *Annual Review of Anthropology* 25. No. 1 (1996): 153–78.

van Hofstede, Gert Jan, Paul Pedersen, and Geert Hofstede. *Exploring Culture: Exercises, Stories and Synthetic Cultures*. Yarmouth, Maine: Intercultural Press, 2002.

Visser, Coenraad J. "Making Intellectual Property Laws Work For Traditional Knowledge." In *Poor People's Knowledge: Promoting Intellectual Property in Developing Countries*. Ed. J. Michael Finger and Philip Schuler. Oxford, UK: Oxford University Press, 2004.

Visual Artists Rights Act, 17 U.S.C. § 106A (1990).

von Lewinski, Silke, ed. *Indigenous Heritage and Intellectual Property: Genetic Resources, Knowledge and Folklore*. The Netherlands: Kluwer Law International BV, 2008.

von Lewinski, Silke. Introduction to *Indigenous Heritage and Intellectual Property: Genetic Resources, Knowledge and Folklore*. Ed. Silke von Lewinski. The Netherlands: Kluwer Law International BV, 2008.

Wallis, Leslie. "The Different Art: Copyright and Choreography." *UCLA Law Review* 33 (1985–1986): 1442–1471.

Walters, Cristina. "Cross-Cultural Negotiations: A Role Evaluation of Four Cultural Dimensions and Two Cultural Components." *Michigan Business Law Journal* 27 (2007): 39–48.

Warden-Fernandez, Janeth. "Indigenous Communities' Rights and Mineral Development." *Journal of Energy & National Resources Law* 23 (2005): 395–426.

Weekly Law Reports (WLR) 1 (1960): 1087–87.

Weiner, Janice G. "Protection of Folklore: A Political and Legal Challenge." *International Review of Industrial Property and Copyright Law* 18 (1987): 56–92.

Weinhardt, Anne. "Copyright Infringement of Choreography: The Legal Aspects of Fixation," *Journal of Corporate Law* 13 (1987–1988): 839–860.

West, Simon. "Institutionalized Exclusion: The Political Economy of Benefit Sharing and Intellectual Property," 8(1) *Law, Environment and Development Journal* (2012): 21–42.

"What Comes After Nagoya? Addressing Developing Country Needs in Intellectual Property Rights and Biodiversity." United Nations Conference on Trade and Development (Geneva, Switzerland). March 3, 2011. http://ictsd.org/downloads/2011/05/ictsd-unctad-what-comes-after-nagoya-report.pdf.

"What is the Convention?," Convention on Biological Diversity (2012), accessed May 9, 2015, http:// www.cbd.int/convention/.

Whitt, Laurelyn. *Science, Colonialism and Indigineous Peoples: The Cultural Politics of Law and* Knowledge. New York: Cambridge University Press, 2009.

Whyte, Sandra Reynolds, Sjaak van der Geest, and Anita Hardon. (2002) *Social Lives of Medicines*. Cambridge, UK: Cambridge University Press, 2002.

Wiessner, Siegfried. "Rights and Status of Indigenous Peoples: A Global Comparative and International Legal Perspective." *Harvard Human Rights Journal* 12 (1999): 57–128.

Williams, Owain. "Life Patents, TRIPS and the International Political Economy of Biotechnology." In *The International Politics of Biotechnology: Investigating Global Futures*. Ed. Alan Russell and John Volger. Manchester, UK: Manchester University Press, 2000.

WIPO Copyright Treaty, Dec. 20, 1996, S. Treaty Doc. No. 105–17 (1997), 36 I.L.M. 65 (1997).

WIPO. "Intellectual Property and Traditional Cultural Expressions/Folklore." *World Intellectual Property Organization (WIPO)*. Booklet no. 1. WIPO Publication No. 913.

———. "Intellectual Property Needs and Expectations of Traditional Knowledge Holders" (2001), June 5, 2015. www.wipo.int/tk/en/tk/ffm/report.

———. "Intergovernmental Committee on Intellectual Property and Genetic Resources, Traditional Knowledge and Folklore." WIPO/GRTFK/IC/6/3. No. 50 (December 1, 2003: 17.

———. Performances and Phonograms Treaty, December 20, 1996, S. Treaty Doc. No. 105–17 (1997), 36 I.L.M. 76 (1997).

———. "Roundtables in Intellectual Property and Traditional Knowledge." Cited in Agnés Lucas-Schloetter, "Folklore." In *Indigenous Heritage and Intellectual Property: Genetic Resources, Knowledge and Folklore*. Ed. Silke von Lewinski. The Netherlands: Kluwer Law International BV, 2008.

WIPO-UN Educ., Scientific and Cultural Org. (UNESCO). "Model Provisions for National Laws on the Protection of Expressions of Folklore Against Illicit Exploitation and other Forms of Prejudicial Action, 1982." *World Intellectual Property Organization (WIPO)*. 1985. www.wipo.int/wipolex/en/details.jsp?id=6714.

Wong, Victor. "Taiwanese Aboriginal Singers Settle Copyright Lawsuit." *Billboard*. July 31, 1999.

Woodmansee, Martha. "The Genius and the Copyright." *Eighteenth Century Studies* 17, no. 4 (1984): 425–448.

Working Group on Indigenous Populations. "Working Paper by the Chairperson-Rapporteur, Mrs. Erica-Irene A. Daes, on the concept of 'indigenous peoples.'" U.N. Doc E/CN.4/Sub.2/AC.4/1996/2. Accessed May 9, 2015. www.unhchr.ch/Huridocda/Huridoca.nsf/TestFrame/2b6e0fb1e9d7db0fc1256b3a003eb999?Opendocument.

World Bank Operational Directive 4.20, 2001, which was replaced by the revised policy OP/BP 4.10,2005. *World Bank Operation Manual* 4.10. July 2005. Accessed May 9, 2015. web.worldbank.org/WBSITE/EXTERNAL/PROJECTS/EXTPOLICIES/EXTOPMANUAL/0,,contentMDK:20553664~menuPK:64701637~pagePK:64709096~piPK:64709108~theSitePK:502184~isCURL:Y,00.html.

World Intellectual Property Organization & United Nations Environment Programme. "Wipo-Unep Study on the Role of Intellectual Property Rights in the Sharing of Benefits Arising from the Use of Biological Resources and Associated

Traditional Knowledge." *World Intellectual Property Organization (WIPO)*. www.wipo.int/tk/en/publicationsn769e_unep tk.pdf.

World Trade Organization. "Council for Trade-Related Aspects of Intellectual Property Rights. February 8, 2006. *World Trade Organization*. www.wto.org/english/tratop_e/trips_e/ta_docs_e/4_ipcw368rev1_e.pdf.

———. "Trade Related Aspects of Intellectual Property Systems (TRIPS)." *World Trade Organization*. 2002. www.wto.org/english/thewto_e/minist_e/min01_e/mindecl_e.htm.

"World Wildlife Fund Position Paper." Conference of the Parties to the Convention on Biological Diversity (March 20–31, 2006). Cited in Mindahi Crescencio Bastida-Muñoz and Geraldine A. Patrick, "Traditional Knowledge and Intellectual Property Rights: Beyond TRIPS Agreements and Intellectual Property Chapters of FTAs." *Michigan St. James International Law Journal* 14 (2006): 259–287.

Wright, Shelley. "Intellectual Property and the 'Imaginary Aboriginal.'" In *Indigenous Peoples and the Law*. Ed. Greta Bird, Gary Martin, and Jennifer Neilson. Sydney, Australia: The Federation Press, 1996.

Wüger, Daniel. "Prevention of Misappropriation of Intangible Cultural Heritage through Intellectual Property Laws." In *Poor People's Knowledge: Promoting Intellectual Property in Developing Countries*. Ed. J. Michael Finger and Philip Schuler. Washington, DC: World Bank Publications, 2004.

Index

Page References for Figures or Tables are italicized.

About the Author

Caroline Joan "Kay" S. Picart is a scholar-attorney practicing in federal criminal law (Of Counsel/Attorney at Law at Tim Bower Rodriguez, PA, a private federal criminal defense firm), and a Special Assistant Public Defender at the Second District Court of Appeal of Florida, who publishes peer-reviewed journal articles and books principally on law, criminology, sociology, and film. A first generation naturalized U.S. citizen, she was born in the Philippines and has travelled extensively on international scholarships and academic appointments. Kay not only has a J.D. from the University of Florida Levin College of Law (*cum laude*; editor-in-chief, *Florida Journal of International Law*; research editor, *Journal of Technology Law and Policy*; Tybel Spivack Fellow; Florida Bar Foundation Fellow), but also a Ph.D. in political philosophy (doctoral minors in aesthetics and criticism and comparative literature) from the Pennsylvania State University; a postdoctoral fellowship on jurisprudence with the Cornell School of Criticism and Theory; and an M.Phil. from the University of Cambridge–Christ's College, United Kingdom (Sir Run Run Shaw Scholar and Wolfson Prize Winner in History and Philosophy of Science), and a B.S. in biology/pre-medical studies (*magna cum laude*) from the Ateneo de Manila University, Philippines. Prior to pursuing a law degree, she was a tenured associate professor of English and humanities, with a courtesy appointment at the Florida State University School of Law. After graduating from law school with a joint degree in law and women's studies, she was a postdoctoral fellow at the 8th Judicial Circuit, specializing in post-conviction relief. She has authored or edited sixteen peer-reviewed books with university and scholarly presses and numerous peer-reviewed scholarly articles both nationally and internationally, inclusive of *Critical Race Theory and Copyright in American Dance* (2013); (with Marlowe Fox) "Assumptions and Unintended Consequences of Florida's HB 87 and the Foreclosure Crisis" 119 *Penn State Law Review* 1, 93–130 (November 2014); and (edited with Michael Hviid Jacobsen and Cecil Greek, with two solo authored chapters), *Framing Law and Crime* (Rowman & Littlefield, forthcoming, 2016). She serves as editor of the Fairleigh Dickinson University Press (FDUP) Series on Law, Culture and Humanities, and is a member of the FDUP advisory board.

www.ingramcontent.com/pod-product-compliance
Lightning Source LLC
LaVergne TN
LVHW101447200926
848483LV00001B/81